# Growing Pains

# Growing Pains

## Billie Piper

HODDER

First published in Great Britain in 2006 by Hodder & Stoughton

An Hachette Livre UK company

First published in paperback in 2007

1

A CIP catalogue record for this title is available from the British Library

ISBN 978 0 340 93280 3

Typeset in Sabon by Hewer Text UK Ltd, Edinburgh
Printed and bound in Great Britain by Clays Ltd, St Ives plc

Hodder Headline's policy is to use papers that are natural, renewable and recyclable products and made from wood grown in sustainable forests. The logging and manufacturing processes are expected to conform to the environmental regulations of the country of origin.

Hodder & Stoughton Ltd
A division of Hodder Headline
338 Euston Road
London NW1 3BH

www.hodder.co.uk

# Contents

v

## Act Three: Living a Lie

## Act Four: Being a Wife

# Contents

# Prologue

**ROSE V/O**

Planet Earth. This is where I was born. And
this is where I died.

**ROSE V/O**

For the first nineteen years of my life,
nothing happened. Nothing at all. Not ever.
And then I met a man called the Doctor –

**ROSE V/O**

– a man who could change his face. And he took
me away from home, in his magical machine, he
showed me the whole of time and space –

**ROSE V/O**

I thought it would never end.

# Act One

*Living a Dream*

SCENE ONE:

# The Signing

INT:

## A Law Firm Office

One of the most vivid memories of my entire pop career is kicking Dad under the huge mahogany table in the board-room of the London-based law firm Harbot and Lewis. It was 19 December 1997, I had three months earlier turned fifteen years old and the Teletubbies were at number one with 'Say Eh-Oh'! The leather Chesterfield chair I was sitting in was so huge my trainers couldn't quite reach the floor. Wearing combat trousers and a T-shirt, I was mesmerized by the men in sharp suits who surrounded us. There were so many, and each one who came in seemed to have a fatter pen in his hand than the one before. I was itching to sign the papers piled up in front of us, but Dad kept on and on asking these annoying questions. Virgin Records, the brains behind Spice Girls and the man who rescued Take That had plucked me out of drama school and were offering me one million pounds and the chance to become a pop star. What was there to ask?

How was I going to continue my education? Who cared – lessons had never interested me that much anyway. Where would I live? Hotels. My knowledge of hotels was through films like *Pretty Woman* and *Home Alone 2*. I'd be very happy in the Regency Beverly Wiltshire, thank you very much. Who would make sure I did my homework? Tutors – well, I'd soon get round them. Just sign the paper. I knew Mum was nervous because she kept scratching her face, and Dad has always been over-protective. So he went on asking questions about a contract that we had no chance of under-standing, completely ignoring the death stares that I kept shooting him from under my fringe. Just sign the bloody page, I yelled silently in my head. Sign it, now, before they change their minds and take this golden ticket away.

And what a golden ticket! After the success of the Spice Girls, Virgin had a fair amount of excess cash in the coffers and wanted to start a new pop label. But Virgin weren't known for their mainstream sound and didn't have anyone in house who had a background in pop – or would admit to it, anyway. So they started looking for outside help. Hugh Goldsmith had been at RCA for a number of years and was handed Take That after a massive regime change. The boys were just about to be dropped and, whatever Hugh may say himself, he saw potential in them and worked very hard to turn their situation around. It was Hugh who was mainly responsible for making them into what they subsequently became. As with most of the A'n'R lot, Hugh's background was in guitar and alternative music, but he would be the first to admit that in his youth he was the one at parties who took off the punk record and put on George McCray – 'Rock Your Baby'. I can see him happily dancing around his handbag. But by now he had young kids and had to make a living, so, having seized the opportunity with Take That, he decided he'd take ownership of 'pop'. It was a wise business decision. When Virgin were looking for someone associated with mainstream music to start a new label, they came to Hugh. And Innocent was born.

One of their first aims for the label was to find a new British Madonna. There hadn't been a big British female solo since Gabrielle, and Hugh recognized a hole in the market. They had seen me in an advert for the relaunch of the magazine *Smash Hits* on the cover of *Music Week* on 23 August 1997, and he had come to Sylvia Young's Stage School to seek me out. Hugh had huge ideas for the label, and his enthusiasm and vision were infectious. I liked him the moment I met him, and I was so unbelievably excited about being given a chance not only to work, but to work with him and his brilliant team, that I was prepared to do anything. There was Cheryl Robson, Hugh's A'n'R person, the blinding Justine Bell (then Cavanagh), her then assistant and now top dog, Sara Freeman and others whose names I cannot recall and for which I apologize. Everyone was really excited about the concept, about me, about what we could achieve together. They thought I was exactly what they were looking for. And though this was a new label and I was their first big signing, Hugh wasn't a novice. I trusted him implicitly.

I absolutely worshipped Madonna – I'd been dancing around the living room to her songs for years. *Immaculate Collection* was my most treasured possession and she was my idol. The fact that my name and hers were being bandied around in the same sentence was heady stuff. If they were going to make me the New Madonna, then frankly they could have my head on a plate. So I made the demo tape they asked me for, expecting at any minute that one of them would turn around and tell me that regrettably my voice wasn't strong enough and they were going to have to find someone else. But it hadn't happened, and now I was only a signature away from making my dreams come true.

I was on such a high that I didn't listen to a word being said in that meeting. They talked a lot about 'longevity' – I had no idea what that meant but I liked the sound of it. There were other words I didn't understand, like 'recoupable', or words I thought I understood but in the context of a record deal knew nothing about. I'm sure it was all explained to me, but as I said, I wasn't listening. And what were 'balance' and 'advance' to me when I had a million quid sitting on the table? I liked Hugh, I trusted him, he had taken me out of school and was going to make me into a star – that was enough.

There was a connection between the two of us from the

moment we met – but not in any way sexual, nothing like that. Hugh was another kind of dad to me – a cool dad, a dad I could talk music with. And because he had found me I looked up to him. But it was a two-way thing – we made each other laugh. I think he saw something in me that no one else had ever seen, which pushed his pedestal that little bit higher. Hugh wasn't in on the signing that day – it was his wedding anniversary, so he was away with his wife. Would I have listened more if he'd been there? Maybe.

Stuck there in that boardroom I had to do everything in my power just to stop myself bouncing off the chair. I wanted to see the ink on the page and that's all I was thinking about. The wait was agony – I couldn't breathe as I heard Dad fire off yet another round of questions. I don't know whether he really wanted to ask so much or whether he just felt he should even though he actually wanted to sign the contract as much as I did. He wasn't going to roll over and give up his rights over me that easily, but he's always had a taste for adventure and we were being offered one hell of an adventure. At last the moment arrived: everyone was so excited, and the record company had made it all sound so great that thankfully Mum and Dad had put their whispering doubts aside and relented. At the end of the day I had been offered an incredible opportunity and they didn't want to hold me back. They were never pushy parents – I was the one pushing myself. There was such a fine-looking carrot being dangled that at the end of the day they couldn't say no. Anyway, I wouldn't have let them.

And so we all signed, as I think everyone in the room, apart from me, knew we always would. It was the first time I'd ever had to sign my name on anything – the endless loopy signatures that I'd scrawled all over my school books didn't count. They read 'Billie Price' – my boyfriend's surname. Well, it was goodbye to that little fantasy for one. After the signing I was taken to my first-ever press conference. I'd never laid eyes on a group of journalists before, but I wasn't even nervous. Whatever they may have thought about a fifteen-year-old signing a record contract they couldn't deny the smile on my face. I was confident, enthusiastic and ready, and that sort of wide-eyed wonder is infectious. The deal had been signed and I didn't have anything else to worry about. The questions bounced off me. Was I happy? How did I feel being the youngest artist to sign a record deal since Helen Shapiro? How had I been discovered? The record company executives talked about my 'soulful tone', my 'black sound', my early Madonna 'pitch', and before long they were all smiling with me, cracking jokes, giving me tips. I recognized some of the journalists' names. Dominic Monihan was there, for heaven's sakes, and others like him who were stars in their own fields. We had a laugh. They seemed to like me.

When the last question had been asked and the last photo taken Mum, Dad and I went out to celebrate. We sat in Café Rouge and I was treated to chocolate milkshake. Eight of them. My parents had no idea what I'd been getting up to in Swindon and in Bournemouth during the holidays. In front of them it was chocolate milkshake, but behind their backs it hadn't been quite so squeaky clean. It soon became so, however. Bucket bongs, skipping school and shop-lifting would be things of the past. I was a working girl now. I had to act like one.

We were all in a state of shock. As the milkshakes went down we talked about how crazy it was that I had just signed a million-pound record deal. We couldn't believe it. The endless, interminable performances I'd put my parents through while growing up in Swindon had always been about acting. Mum was the singer. Mum was the one who sang into her hairbrush. Not me. Should we have said no? Refused the money? No. It was left very much unsaid, but I knew that even if my voice wasn't my best asset it would open a door. And that door would open others, and who knew where it would all end? Beyond my wildest dreams, I hoped. The small voice of self-doubt was drowned out by milkshakes and excitement. Innocent were going to make me in to a star and I was prepared to do everything – anything – to make them pleased that they had picked me.

# The Recording

## A Stately Home

The first Christmas that I went home after I signed the deal someone said to me, 'My mum read you're getting a million quid.' Which of course I hadn't, because it doesn't work like that. *They* control the finances – and even if they didn't, who was going to hand over a million quid to a fifteen-year-old? So I'd bluff it a bit. In fact the only thing I bought was a Gucci wallet – I've still got it. I didn't tell Dad I'd bought it. At long last, no more justifying my spends. This was *my* cash now. Wow! But I wasn't as brave as I pretended to myself, and had a back-up explanation just in case Dad sprang a round of post-purchase questions on me. Even so, I knew something had changed. I might not have a million in my pocket, but I could buy a Gucci wallet if I wanted to, whatever Dad said.

I had left home at twelve to go to drama school, but came back every weekend to hang out with my old school friends and my boyfriend. But now that all stopped because the record industry doesn't have termtimes. Those guys work flat out – no six-week holidays for them. We were trying to create something from nothing, which meant we had a lot of work to do. In January 1998 we went into a recording studio, after which we started the endless rounds of school tours and press junkets, then shot a video and finally released our first single on 22 June of that year. It was eighteen-hour days, day in, day out. I distinctly remember saying to Hugh that I wanted to work and work and work until the songs got to number one. Hugh had put his faith in me and I didn't want to let him down – I truly wanted to be a success. I'd had teasers – flashes of what was to come if I worked hard enough: having a car sent to pick me up, recording, signing deals, meeting the fabulous people, meeting and befriending the company staff, being shown around the company, being shown off. But then it was back home for beans on toast and time to think about getting back out there. My burning ambition to act had to be replaced, because I wasn't acting. So I propelled myself into the mindset of being a pop success. I wanted to know everything about the music business, so everyone I met in the industry I would grill – gleaning, gleaning, gleaning, until I knew the role by heart. These were the people who had made the Spice Girls so unbelievably successful, so why shouldn't it happen to me?

In January we went away to a house in Surrey with a recording studio attached, called Jacobs. I thought I'd died and gone to princess heaven – here I was swanning about a stately home when I'd never even seen a place so big before. Recording the first album was an incredible experience. Just pulling up to the house was like something out of a James Bond movie. I remember the new-smelling car. You know the smell – is it new leather, new brakes or some queasy air-freshener? It seems to come through the air vents. I can recall the sound of tyres crunching on pea-shingle, the door being opened and then this kid stepping out who somehow appeared to be me.

Wendy and Jim, the lovely couple who'd made my demo tape, were brought on board to record the first album. There were other producers, an LA-based duo called Dion Rambo and Jacques Richmond, who could have freaked me out. But because I knew Wendy and Jim, and felt safe with them, I was really relaxed and happy and excited. Cheryl Robson had rooted out some US tracks for me to record, and Wendy and Jim had the ability to give them a British sound. The 'Billie' ethos was to produce an album of anthems: pop raps for the young, not too heavy on beat or soul. They were all very melodic, very catchy, with a really strong chorus and, most importantly, easy to listen to. Maybe I should have been called Solo Spice.

We stayed at Jacobs for about a month. We'd get up early every morning and sit round the table planning what we wanted to achieve that day. I was playing at being a grown-up: I had my own phone, my own bathroom, and really felt like I'd arrived. After a huge breakfast we'd go to the recording studio, which was in an outbuilding, and I'd do vocal warm-ups with Wendy. They knew and I knew that I didn't have the strongest voice in the world, but no one ever said anything. There was a lot of 'Great, Billie', and 'Sounding good, Billie' and 'Visualize the note, Billie.' Never 'That was flat.' Bless them, they were always very encouraging and I jumped at the chance to be encouraged. Though I doubted my ability to hit the notes all the time, mostly our sessions together felt brilliant. During the day when we were busy I could ignore the needle of doubt in my mind – and we were always busy. I might have been young, but I wasn't daft. I was very aware of people being dropped left, right and centre, so I wasn't going to tell the people who were backing me that standing in front of a mic with a pair of cans on my head made me feel like a fake. Anyway, I was working with producers who could make a voice sound as good as humanly possible. The equipment was incredible – the recording studio was like walking into the cockpit of a spaceship. It was a far cry from the tiny room in Wendy and Jim's attic in Clapham where we'd recorded my demo tape with a mic attached to the banisters. At Jacobs, once the recording was over and done with, the mixing – the actual making of the record – was great.

So in the daytime I was hanging out with adults, something I had always liked, feeling I was learning something new every day. We were all working towards the same goal. Wendy and Jim wanted the album to be good because it was their first big break as well as mine, and Cheryl and Hugh wanted it to be a first hit for a brand-new label. A lot of energy went into making that album, and I think we were a good team. Weekends were different, though. My best mate from Swindon, Sally Price (yes, sister to my boyfriend), would come and see me and often she'd sneak in a bottle of something. I remember one particular evening when the two of us were sitting in the jacuzzi drinking Malibu, Pernod or Southern Comfort – whatever she'd smuggled in. Her dad was a regular at the cash'n'carry – it was lucky for us that he bought in bulk. Yippee! We laughed our heads off at our good fortune, occasionally getting out of the jacuzzi to dive into the swimming pool. How we didn't drown in a drunken stupor I'll never know.

I called home and talked to Mum and Dad and my younger siblings every day to give them the latest news – there was always news. Andi Peters from *The Broom Cupboard* and *Going Live* wanted to do an EPK with me, a promotional documentary to take to Woolworth's. Andi Peters – to me it was like being invited on to the David Letterman show! It was an exciting time for everyone. Hugh came down from London and we nervously played the songs to him. He loved them. One thing that amused me about Hugh's enthusiasm for a tune was when he really got down and into the beat. He would close his eyes, purse his lips and tap his thigh along to the music. He said 'Because

We Want To' was sounding great, but I wasn't completely sure. I thought it sounded better on the demo tape than on my recording but Hugh had an incredible strike record, so what did I know? I was aware that the session singers on the demo tape had much deeper voices than mine – more R'n'B, more soul – and I thought the song sounded better when they sang it. The critics were right: there were shades of Madonna in the bridge that could have stood the test of time. But for my single the producers put lots of high hats on to it. That's the part of the drum kit that sounds like a synthetic brush, very trebly. With the bass gone and my higher pitch, the soul element to 'Because We Want To' went too. But after asking so many questions I was only too aware that the first album had to be commercial. I knew it had to hit the market hard and quickly and to have a massive impact. I reassured myself with the promise that on my second album – if I'd proved myself, if I'd worked hard enough and done everything they'd asked me to do – maybe I'd be able to write a bit, use my own style, take out the high hats.

And then, with the songs finally under our belts, it was time to take the record to the marketplace. A record company is down a million before a single record is sold, so naturally they want to make their money back. I had to get out and work it, and work it I did. I hit the promotional track and went on the road singing my songs. Actually I didn't sing. Singing meant too much technical stuff and we weren't appearing in big places. They explained to me that it was easier to mime over the tape – that way they didn't need to worry about sound checks on dodgy PA systems. And I was happy to do it. I sounded better on the CDs they were playing to me than I did in my head. As for talking the talk, maintaining enthusiasm, that was exciting. I'm a born talker, a born salesperson. In interviews I would come up with words to describe my single: fun, wild, celebration. Phrases that summed up the song: do what you want to do, don't listen to anyone else, be independent. It all came from a good place – no less than the rules I myself lived by.

For the moment I was still living in two worlds. When we weren't working I'd go home to Swindon and get stoned on an abandoned caravan site, downing the contents of Ma and Pa's mahogany drinks cabinet and then, inevitably, passing out. I'd always done household chores, but Mum was now so anxious for me to keep my feet on the ground that she'd have me unloading the dishwasher before I'd even put my bag down. While I was staying in stately homes, shooting promo movies with Andi Peters and attending press launches, she was left at home with the screaming kids that I used to help her with. I now had one life where I'd get picked up by a car and taken to London to get my hair and make-up done for a photo shoot, and another back home where I'd cook fish fingers for the kids and give them a bath. It was a strange existence, but you are so flexible when you are young that I soon got used to it.

When we started out on the road a car would come and get me at say seven in the evening to take me to Café de Paris to do a PA with other acts that the previous year I had watched on TV. I would stay until 2a.m. and then be driven back. I didn't think about being tired the next day. Did Mum stay up to talk to me about it? The first time, definitely. I gave her a detailed description of the wonderful Chris Moyles, whom I'd met that night. This was before he became thin and old. He was then just twenty-six and we were both embarking on exciting new careers, so we'd often compare notes in the wee small hours of the morning. But driving those distances every day was madness, so shortly after recording the album I moved into a hotel.

The hotel was in Maida Vale in West London. I may have had a chaperone during the day, but by night I was alone. I loved it. There was a little kitchen, so I could cook. I'd call mates up, or go and have a jacuzzi. Or, luxury of luxury, watch MTV without any kids trying to put *Barnie* on the video for the hundredth time. And I could smoke fags with impunity. As long as I had my mobile phone and an endless supply of baked beans I was quite happy. More than quite happy. I was working, doing something I enjoyed, earning hard cash. I had a Switch card, and my parents were giving me an allowance. To be honest, I didn't know how to write a cheque until I was eighteen. Occasionally I'd move rooms for the hell of it, and in each one set up my photos of my family, scented candles, a few throws and the essential sequinned cushions. Anything to make it feel like home. Don't get me wrong – I honestly didn't mind being on my own in a hotel in a city where I knew no one. It never scared me. Not then. I loved it – it made me feel like the luckiest Swindon mite there ever was.

SCENE THREE:

# Nappy Nights

INT:

## An Under–eighteens Club

The workload increased as that year progressed, so my visits home, already sporadic, decreased and I began a long relationship with my mobile phone. It was my way back to the people I'd left behind, but the few minutes I had to spare were not necessarily a good time at home. I had hurried, unsatisfactory conversations with people, then ended the call wishing I hadn't rung. None more so than with David, the boyfriend – once much loved but now grown out of – whom I had abandoned. By this point ours was nothing more than a phone relationship – I had simply lost more and more interest in him as I had started to meet people who were older and more intriguing – men who drank Chianti and ate hummous, which impressed me. I didn't even know what hummous was. It was hard for David: I was his famous girlfriend who was never there. I didn't go to birthday parties, or to his mum's house for tea – all the things I'd done a year before. I was not only the absent girlfriend – I was also the absent sister and daughter. I was absent from all of them, yet the only person anyone else would ask them about was me. 'How's Bill, then?' 'What's she up to?' Poor Mum and Dad and David. How could they admit that they didn't know what I was up to, that I hadn't called in a while? I didn't feel bad about it at the time because I was having a blast, loving the attention and meeting people I admired. I was living the dream and sod the consequences. I never cared that I was becoming famous – it wasn't about that. But I did love the access it gave me: access to creative, brilliant people.

Janet bloody Jackson for one. I met her – she was another Virgin artist – just before her show. My God, the beads of sweat that fell from my forehead that night! She's a super-star, right? Actually, she was incredibly shy. Her nervous-ness and rabbit-in-headlights behaviour made me wish I'd never met her. Was this an indication of what happens to people in this industry, I wondered. I never let on what I'd seen that day. When interviewed, I told the journalists what an inspiration she was – because she was. But what I realized was that so much of it was just bravado. On stage she was fiery and compelling, but backstage she was just a scared little girl. Would this happen to me? I didn't think so. And anyway, as long as I wasn't in Swindon doing the things I'd been fighting or trying to resist, then I was happy to take the risk. Whatever happened, I knew I was having a better time than I'd ever had before. So I allowed myself to move on, to slip away from the people who loved me, to put my head down and my nose to the grindstone and carry on.

All I did was work. When the album had come together we shot the videos, which was great fun. The video for 'Because We Want To' had a sort of fifties vibe to it, with a huge crowd dancing down a terraced street: *Coronation Street* meets *Thriller*. It was filmed in Greenwich. This hilarious early-edition CGI boy jumped out of a poster and started dancing with me, then all these people started jumping out of the houses and I had what felt like a vast crowd behind me, dancing and calling out the words of our teenage anthem. I loved doing videos because they meant one thing: dance routines. And dance routines were what I did best.

Everything really fell into place during this time, when I was out of the recording studio and in a dance studio to learn routines and be choreographed. I was back on firm ground, back where I knew I deserved the applause, back where it had all started. The Pineapple Studio, where at the age of seven I had auditioned for an American cereal ad and vowed to get back. Everything I'd dreamed of was coming true. I fell absolutely 100 per cent head over heels in love with my choreographer. The fact that I had a choreographer at all was out of this world. He was a beautiful person and I immediately thought we had a future together – it wasn't until afterwards that it dawned on me he was gay. I hadn't met any gay people in Swindon, not knowingly anyway.

As soon as the routines were rehearsed we were out on the road with five dancers, going up and down the country performing at schools and under-eighteen clubs to promote my first single. I was prepared to do as many as necessary for as long as it would take to start a fan base for the first single. I was loving it more and more, feeling increasingly in control of the process and better able to handle it. I absolutely adored the people I was working with. James, the tour manager, was a legend and the dancers were great – we were inseparable. We had a really good time together but my God, it was unhealthy! We lived on a diet of service station fast food: McDonald's, KFC and Little Chef's finest. Aside from the freedom to eat an abundance of Whoppers I was really enjoying the twenty-something conversations in the back of the Renault Espace. It was like being away filming would be for me later – the crew become your best mates.

These dancers were very physical people with big personalities, always coming up with banter and impersonations and always laughing. It didn't matter who you were – they embraced all walks of life as long as you were artistic and could keep up. I wanted to show them I could handle what was happening to me so that they would include me in everything. The last thing I wanted them thinking was that I was some silly little teenager who couldn't take the pace. I was convinced that I was no longer a kid – and they seemed to be convinced, too. I was existing in an adult world, so I would talk the talk, discuss the industry. I would ask the dancers about sex and drugs and all the other things that were taboo subjects with other adults. At this point it would have been inappropriate to discuss such things with my employers. The dancers knew all the answers to my long-winded questions, and never censored their responses or conversations, nor did they judge me and my ignorance. They truly enlightened me, and gave me an insight into a very exciting world that I was itching to be a part of.

My first PA was at a club in Kingston, just west of London. I was petrified. It wasn't so very long ago that I'd been at those sorts of events myself. They were called nappy nights – a disco for under-aged kids getting busy with their hormones. I knew what was going on in the crowd because I'd been there. When the bands came on, when you were happily snogging someone's face off to Cotton Eyed Joe, it was a nuisance, a distraction. You didn't care who was up on the platform – you didn't know the song, so you weren't looking forward to hearing it. Now that it was my turn I wasn't looking forward to going out there. I knew my appearance was likely to ruin their party – it would have ruined mine if some squeaky kid had come on stage and sung 'Because We Want To' at me. I just had to pray that the whole package – the dancers, the moves, the energy – would be enough.

If there was a problem, and I wasn't quite ready to admit that there was, it was this. I had grown up listening to soul, Motown, and R'n'B. I had inherited my love of music from my parents: Dad played the double bass, and Mum would sing her heart out at any given opportunity. I think my encyclopaedic knowledge of the top forty worked as much in my favour as against me. I could talk the talk, but to be absolutely honest I was making music I feared I wouldn't necessarily have listened to. I wished that 'Because We Want To' had kept more of its soul. I wanted a sound like the goddesses All Saints had, with more of an R'n'B lilt. I really liked that group and continued to do so throughout my musical career. I always thought of them as the cool girls in the music business, the ones who were going out with rock stars and getting off their faces and having public rows. They always seemed to exist in a more exciting world than mine and to sing better songs. I knew in my heart of hearts that 'Because We Want To' wasn't the right sound to come out with.

But that problem of wanting to go in a different direction from the one my records were going in was a secret frustration that I shared with no one. Who was I going to complain to? I didn't want to upset anyone – I didn't want this new-found reality to be pulled out from under my feet and find myself back in Swindon at school, or back at Sylvia Young's waiting, waiting, waiting like everyone else for the break you think you deserve. Rule number one: don't bite the hand that feeds. And so I always tried really hard to be what they wanted me to be. Slyly I'd try to introduce some of my own ideas and occasionally they'd go down well, but not in the beginning. In the beginning I kept stumm.

Hugh knew what sort of music I liked. When he first came to Sylvia Young's we spent a long time talking about it. He was interviewing me but without me knowing it, so I had no reason to be anything but honest. I suspected that 'Because We Want To' wasn't going to hold the test of time, wasn't going to be a song I'd still be proud of years later. It wasn't an anthem, like Madonna's 'Holiday' or Britney's 'Hit Me Baby'. To put it mildly, standing in the corridor waiting to go out and do my first PA I was absolutely shitting myself.

Thankfully, the first night was a success, and although I was miming I got all the dance routines right, so when I came off I felt amazing. I became obsessed with that post-performance feeling, which is like nothing else on earth. You are on such a high and all that adrenaline makes you feel mad, invincible, unstoppable. You wouldn't feel it if someone completely leathered you. It's a trance state, and when you're sitting on this natural high you're quite likely to do naughty things or make bad choices. It's totally addictive.

I'd been on stage before, of course, but it had never been like that. It had never been solely about me. At Sylvia Young's I'd been one of many chorus girls, and never got picked for the solo. That coveted place went to one of Sylvia's favourites, and I remember feeling massively cheated at the end of the school year. This was different. It wasn't just another league but another game altogether, and it was amazing! At that point I didn't know what to do with the feeling. I was ecstatic that I'd got all my dance steps right, but as I said I was only miming, so the applause and the congratulations from my touring partners were difficult to place. After all, they'd got their steps right too. I'd find myself returning to my empty hotel room, whether in Maida Vale or on the road, going to bed and waiting for the next day. Maybe the next day I would feel differently.

Sometimes I'd lie in bed for hours, unable to sleep, drinking tea and thinking all about the show: what I could improve, what I'd missed, how I could tighten the steps. I have always been a perfectionist – you just have to see the dolls lined up to within a millimetre of the shelf edge in my bedroom in Swindon to know that. Sometimes I'd call my friends back home, but of course they couldn't really under-stand what was happening to me – and maybe I didn't give them a chance to. I was aware that as soon as I signed that record deal people were going to tell me I'd changed, so I almost went the opposite way. Look, I'm so normal, get me . . . and, playing the whole thing down, I would steer the conversation back to what was going on in *their* lives.

That PA in Kingston was the first outing for the Billie suit. Burgundy, oversized, could belong to your über-trendy boyfriend. Choice. The Billie suit is not to be confused with the boiler suit, which I later became obsessed with. People always say, I bet they made you wear this and that, told you what to say, how to sound – but they didn't. I was speaking for my own generation. I was allowed a voice, an opinion, because in this instance I knew better than them. I'd studied MTV for years. So actually they did listen to me when I said I didn't want to be in a titty suit. They let me wear boys' skateboard trainers and a boy's suit. Of course that changed pretty quickly when I became more aware of being called sexy by the press, and being a sex symbol, and the power of *Loaded* and *FHM* hit home. I'd always been a bit of a tomboy, except when I was tottering about in gold lamé at the Rockley Park caravan site in Bournemouth. I had this big belt, my Billie Belt. It was leather with a Billie buckle in the style that my name was written on my records, with a star over one letter I and a crown over the other. There were pockets for a mobile phone, lipstick, pens. It was like a Bob the Builder belt for girls. I wore it everywhere and all the kids thought it was cool.

Life now was generally hectic. Promotional tours consisted of something like two school performances during the day and a club performance in the evening. In between we were travelling across the country, staying in a hotel and the following day setting up and doing it all over again. At night when we'd finished the dancers would naturally go to the bar and let off steam. I would go to my room because at my age I still wasn't legally allowed to drink.

On tour it felt like everyone was constantly hung over except for me. They could get pissed and have sex, but I couldn't. I was under constant scrutiny. Not by the press, though there was a lot of that, but by the ten or fifteen people who thought they stood *in loco parentis* to me. From my manager right down to the driver everyone felt, because I was so young, that they could tell me what to do. I'd escaped two parents and found myself with fifteen. I started to get envious of the people on the periphery, who could have so much fun and never have to be part of the shit. They could have boyfriends. I didn't have time.

But actually, for all the advice and friendly warning, I was not really being parented at all. And because my real parents thought that someone else was doing the job, I slightly fell between two stools with a lot of space to manoeuvre in. When I threw my books across the table and said I'd had enough of trying to do school work and keep ahead of my schedule, no one flinched. Hugh had managed me for a while after I left school but that was a conflict of interest, so he brought Steve Blackwell and his partner into the equation. I knew that Steve had managed Gabrielle and Dave Stewart, and Gabrielle had had that massive hit with 'Rise' which was frankly good enough for me. I never went into the details because I was too impatient. But actually if I'd read the small print I would have discovered that Gabrielle had left Steve prior to recording 'Rise'. He was then fifty-something, very, very nice, and very responsible, but probably not very suitable to be acting as my manager. He tried to be my friend, but what did he really know about fifteen-year-old girls, or the pop industry for that matter? Mum and Dad never knew what was going on – ironically, because I was away working every hour they thought I was safe. I wasn't hanging out on the Waterloo estate, or in the park after dark, missing my curfew. Actually when I think about it I never did miss a curfew – it wasn't worth it because I'd have been grounded. Then again, maybe it was only because I didn't get the chance. Mum and Dad thought I was tucked up in bed in a hotel. And in the beginning I was.

But as the touring progressed I realized I couldn't simply go and sit alone in my room on a high night after night. For a while I'd go and sit with the dancers and the tour manager in the bar just to get out of the room – even I couldn't watch MTV indefinitely. Gradually I started going to their rooms with them, because there I could get a drink and no eyebrows would be raised. It wasn't out of hand and certainly less than I'd been getting up to at home, because mostly I just wanted to work. I still had no real taste for alcohol. Talking to adults was fun, but I had no desire to party as such. And though in Swindon getting stoned was a major occupation, I had given it up because that was not what 'pop stars' did. It was what dossers did, and I had too much to do.

# Because We Want To

## Top of the Pops

On 22 June 1998, six months after signing my deal, 'Because We Want To' came out. I did thirty appearances on telly in the week leading up to the release. The ground work had paid off and it went straight in at number one. Everyone was absolutely over the moon. First artist on a new record label, and it's a hit. I was back in Swindon on a rare visit following the gruelling promo week, trying to pick up with my old friends from when I'd left off. It didn't really work. When I got the call from Mark Goodyear in the Radio One studio telling me I was number one I was about as far removed from my life as 'Billie' as I could get. I was parked up by some ruins called Castle Combe just off the M4 in a mate's Ford Cosi toking hard on bucket bongs. Nicely toasted speaking live on the radio. I got lucky – I think it went unnoticed. But the whole thing was very, very strange. I went home, had a cup of tea and went to bed. Somehow I was expecting to wake up the next morning metamorphosed into a whole new being. It didn't happen. I stayed the same, and I found that quite alarming. But after the number one I jumped a whole new league, so I had no time to think about the fact that I didn't seem to be 'feeling' any of it.

Suddenly I was doing shows like *Live and Kicking* and *Top of the Pops*! Oh, hallowed ground. The green room for *Top of the Pops* was full of famous people and I couldn't believe I was there. I was whisked away from sharing a bucket bong with mates to sharing a cranberry juice with Cher. She even let me try her ring on, like mates – or at least I thought we were mates. Surely ring-swapping meant we were bezzie friends? The following week I was on again, still at number one, and I got to meet the Spice Girls. I was bowled over. There they were, sitting in their dressing room, waiting for make-up, smoking cigarettes openly. They were all really nice to me, and after a glorious chat with them I left. I took one final look back as their door closed and saw with bizarre clarity not five superstars, but five ordinary girls stubbing out their fags into BBC polystyrene cups. Then the door closed and I banished the thought from my mind. I was looking for the magic everywhere. I wanted it to be like it was on the pages of the glossy magazines that I devoured. Like it was on MTV. I don't know what I was expecting, but I wasn't prepared for how very small everybody was in real life. Everything was smaller, in fact. The sets, the studio, even the sandwiches. It was all small and really rather normal. When I finished filming *Top of the Pops* for the third time I made the mistake of waiting around to see them shutting off the lights in the studio. Bit by bit it became a room like any other. Take the lights and the people away and it was an empty room – a bit shabby, a bit dusty, a bit small. They were really terrifying, those first feelings of anticlimax. Terrifying and hard to admit to. So I didn't, and kept on working.

As I got more into the touring scene, I made other friends outside my own little tour group. There were other acts I came across time and time again. B*Witched became good friends because we constantly crossed paths and were often on the same bill. Though we were friends, I was aware that their single was stronger than mine and would probably be number one for longer than mine. It was a pop song, not a nursery rhyme. Like at Sylvia Young's, we were all competing with our peers for our slice of the marketplace. B*Witched were my friends, but I was secretly jealous of them too: they were in their late teens and early twenties, which is of course where I wanted to be.

I also met Kavana, who was huge at the time. When I was at home with my subscription to *Smash Hits*, he was everywhere. Now it was all over the press that I was in love with him. I fancied him, sure, but he was like one of those guys in sixth form who'd come over and cuddle you and say, 'Ah, you're so cute', and you were a little mascot and they were cool and old and just spreading their gold dust around. He certainly didn't want anything from me because I was far too little. My mentor and friend Hugh Goldsmith had made it abundantly clear anyway – whatever you do, don't commit the ultimate crime and go out with a boy from a boy band because you'll be hated by your core market.

Shortly after releasing 'Because We Want To', we started on a European tour. Got England – now to conquer foreign lands. I'd only been to Tenerife and America before, so for the first two months I loved it, re-energized by the thought of new places. I spent my days being jolly, happy, trying to be inspiring and, more importantly, trying to look pretty. No wonder I wore so much rouge and Touche Eclat. In the absence of contributing creatively I was happy to take on the role of salesperson, especially since my pitch was working and we were shifting records and everyone was pleased with me. I was good at the job – selling the product was the part I felt most confident at. I knew I was being given an amazing opportunity and so I carried on, wanting desperately to believe in it as much as everyone else seemed to. I wanted to be positive, so I squashed the voice in the back of my head that was saying, 'I don't think this is what you really want to be doing.' I did my utmost to ignore that gnawing feeling that I was going through too many wrong doors. In fact during the day it was easy, because they were so busy, so manic, that I didn't have time to think. And I liked it that way.

By the time I returned from Europe at the end of that summer I was running on empty. It had been eight months of non-stop work, I'd barely been home, I was tired, I'd split up with my boyfriend in Swindon and I'd had to deal with my first period with no one to confide in. I was operating on overload. But there was no chance of slowing down. My second single was about to hit the shops, so if anything we were going to up the pace. I can recall the endless photo shoots, the videos, and the crazy faces I pulled all the time. I've been through the old press boxes and every shot of me shows a wide-open tunnel of a mouth gawping out from the magazine pages – looking at them now I wonder what on earth I was thinking. But deep down I know what I was thinking. I was thinking, 'Act like a pop star.' I copied what I'd seen other 'pop stars' do. Flick through a back copy of the *Live and Kicking* magazine, and every single one of us has our mouth wide open catching flies. I thought maybe that's what they wanted, that's what they were expecting. It looks a bit crazy so that's what I've got to be. Crazy Billie. Crazy kid. Occasionally, for a laugh, I still pull those faces. Me and my mates will get dressed up and pose for photos with my Smash Hits awards. Trust me, this is never done seriously or sober.

# 5ive

## A Stadium in Germany

I had briefly met the members of the boy band 5ive a few times at roadshows and the SMTV television studio. They would usually swan in and then be whisked away because they were the main act, the stars. I had been at school with Scott, one of the guys in the band. He was such a lovely, unassuming, down-to-earth guy – in fact he had shown me where I needed to go on my first day at Sylvia's. 5ive changed him, as the music business changed all of us. We were in Germany doing a show like the Prince's Trust, at which acts from all over the world are invited to perform. I was on with 5ive, B*Witched, Cleopatra, Westlife and other acts from America and Europe. It was a huge festival and I was feeling a bit cocky. I had had a number one single straight out of the box, and things looked like they were going the same way for 'Girlfriend'. I was beginning to feel I could hold my own in this world and with my sixteenth birthday fast approaching I felt a bit more grown-up, a bit more sexy. I felt I was getting a bit more respect. It was probably around this time that I started to let things go to my head. I didn't feel I was winging it but that I deserved it, so I was probably not quite so grateful as I should have been.

We were all rehearsing, followed by hours and hours of press junkets. When I saw Rich with Scott in a corridor I stopped to say hello to Scott, then kicked Rich up the arse. It was so playground – hurt the one you fancy. I'd never even met him. Kicking him was my way of showing him how unimpressed I was. See the weirdness. I couldn't understand why people were different around me, yet I was being different around someone else who couldn't understand why people were being weird around them. Actually 5ive were pretty famous by this point, so I'm fairly sure they weren't feeling quite so grateful either. Anyway, it was my cheeky, sexy way of saying, 'Hi, I'm a pop star too.' Rich gave me a really big hug. We all moaned about how tired we were, and competed with things like, 'We were on the road till four', and 'Hey, we didn't get here till six. . . .' Usual crap.

The business is a strange one. At that time there was a glut of young acts who'd all been plucked from obscurity, then buffed and preened and encouraged to believe the hype. To believe that you above all others were the special one. And then worse, to believe that special means better. Of course you have to have a base line of self-belief in order to put yourself out there in the first place, but anyone in the music industry will tell you that true stars are the ones who realize it's all a bit of a card trick. Yes, they have talent, but it doesn't make them better than other people. It must be pretty hideous to watch when a person whom you have found, shaped, fashioned and basically created is rude to the make-up artists and rude to people in the TV studios and rude to the stage managers, – all of whom are, after all, only trying to help further that person's career. I put the hours in and felt I deserved recognition for all that hard work, but I never felt the world owed me a favour.

The people I worked with at Innocent have said that, though there were moments when I threw my toys out of the pram, and an awful lot of tears, I never forgot the basic rules: say please, say thank you, and treat others as you would be treated yourself. I most definitely have my mother and father to thank for that. Rudeness was not tolerated in our household when I was a kid. Once I called my mum 'old dear' in front of my dad and was given a good smack. Manners have been drummed into me and have stayed with me. The people who forgot the basic rules soon learned the hard way. We were all vacuous pop 'acts' – few of our careers were going to hold the test of time. And when it ended, those who had burned too many bridges would lie in a crumpled heap wondering why people weren't coming to their rescue.

Rich and I met in the backstage bar after the show, pumped full of after-show adrenaline. We manoeuvred ourselves so that we could sit with each other and he brought me a drink: sweet white wine – the cheaper the better. Because 5ive were really successful in Germany there were girls everywhere and it made me nervous. I was very conscious of what Hugh had said and I really didn't want an irate posse of birds after me. 5ive's fans followed them around the world – God knows how they financed it. The attention was making it impossible to chat and so, fearing a backlash, we escaped up to his room. Just the two of us. We kissed for ages and it was lovely – I thought he was amazing. No clothes were removed, whether you want to believe that or not – we just rolled around on the bed together and talked. I instantly felt safe with him. I could talk to him about what was going on in my head and I knew that he understood. I believed he was on my side. In my corner. We spent all night holding each other.

Of course he had to leave really early the next morning and I didn't see him for ages. As soon as Rich was out of the room I rang Mum. I was so bowled over that I'd snogged someone I'd watched on MTV that I had to tell someone. I knew my record company would be furious, but Mum would understand. I wanted to share the excitement with her, and it was nice, because she got excited with me. Mum was the person I told everything to at that time. Who else could I tell? I didn't want to be accused of boasting or getting above myself. It must have been hard for her, with three young kids and a husband who was away a lot. For a few minutes she'd get to live my life with me, vicariously, via the phone, at the odd concert, then I'd tell her I was off out with 5ive and Boyzone . . . and away I'd skip without a thought for Mum back at home, putting the phone down in the kitchen and returning to the fish fingers, worrying, worrying, worrying. Is she all right? Is Billie OK?

I said, 'You know that boy from 5ive, the one with the big blue eyes? I stayed in his room last night.'

Mum's first question: 'Did you have sex with him?'

'No, Mum . . . I didn't.'

Our relationship was still close. I think my fingers had been burned by the odd story seeping out of Swindon – not particularly flattering ones at that. So as my friendships in Swindon started to give way, and before I had made proper friends in the business (apart from people on the payroll), I still told Mum everything. Dad hadn't been around that much when I was growing up, he was always on the sites working his arse off, so I was used to talking to her openly. We were such good mates that, when I was first offered drugs, I called her immediately. It was my first MTV awards.

'Mum, I've just been offered some coke!'

'Oh, that's nice.'

'No, Mum – coke!'

She was horrified, but I thought it was hilarious. I replaced the phone and went cavorting back on to the dance floor having the time of my life, while Mum lay awake all night fretting. I don't know if I told her about the next time I came face to face with drugs. It was my sixteenth birthday and the record company threw a party for me at the Cobden Club. I got a special outfit, a green suit, and drank champagne – it was very exciting. But that was the night I saw people taking coke for the first time. Mum was there, but this time I didn't tell her about it – I wasn't sure how she'd react. I didn't want any criticism voiced out loud because there was enough of it going on in my head.

I regret so much that I never asked her how she was, or how the kids were – I was just calling her up and telling her how excited I was or how miserable I was. So much has happened and we've become so divided that I don't know how to ask those simple questions. How are you, Mum? Everything all right with you? It feels loaded, heavy on the tongue. I'm too busy waiting for the barbed response, the sly criticism to put me in my place, when all I really want her to do is say, 'Well done, Bill. We're proud of you.' But I've made it so hard for them. They got no upside. There was never anything, no big house, though everyone thought they must be loaded – all they had was a chance to be proud. And I didn't even let them be that in the end. I shut them out. There are many things I want to say sorry for, because my career changed everything for them. I could get away from them, but in Swindon they couldn't get away from me.

I went home for a quick break shortly after the European

trip and Rich would call me on my mobile from some exotic location. I'd tell Mum to answer it, so she got to speak to him. She was happy for me because I was working, successful, doing what I wanted – back then we secretly couldn't believe my luck. But my record company was adamant that I mustn't get together with him as it would reflect badly on my record sales. But I liked him so much and we were getting on so well. He wasn't worried about our relationship becoming public knowledge and that gave me confidence. But of course he wasn't worried – it wasn't going to affect *his* sales, only mine. So on the sound but ill-received advice of my record company I hid the relationship. Not that there was a great deal to hide. We didn't see each other for ages – he was always in some country touring. In the end we had to look at our schedules and work out when we could meet. In fact Debbie, my PA, scheduled our meetings for us.

More than that, Debbie, who was like a sister to me, let me meet up with Rich 'in secret' at her house. Nothing sinister – we just wanted to hang out together in a normal environment. That was the story of my life. Everything was done through middlemen. There was always that extra person. I trusted them without question – if you're doing that job you have to be reliable and trustworthy, and you wouldn't last very long in the business if you weren't. As I became more adept at the game I would ask people to lie to my parents, and would ask my parents to lie to the record company to get me out of things I didn't want to do. I took advantage of them. It was a bit like having divorced parents: I played both sides.

I liked it at Debbie's house. I liked hanging out there with her boyfriend, making myself a cup of tea or beans on toast. I was getting sick to death of hotel rooms. Rich was coming back from a trip and off again the next morning. We hadn't slept with one another – just that one night in Germany. In fact since David back in Swindon there hadn't been anyone. Actually that isn't strictly true. Prior to my sixteenth birthday there was one older lad at the record company with whom I had a three-week affair – he had a classic MG sports car and took me to Brown's nightclub and for midnight walks through Hyde Park. I thought we had a great time. But I've since heard that he told tales about me around the record company boardroom, so I've decided to reduce him to a couple of lines. It's amazing who gets on the kiss-and-tell bandwagon. A couple of tales came out of Swindon, but I understood that because the person who sold his story was addicted to drugs and would have sold his mother for a hit. However, as far as Rich was concerned there wasn't a story to tell. We were grabbing what we could when we could, but it wasn't very much.

Leaving Debbie and her boyfriend downstairs we went and hid upstairs and smoked Marlboro Lights, my cigarette since moving to London. That was how my life had changed. From twenty B&H to Marlboro Lights – no wonder people back at home thought I was getting ahead of myself. Rich and I lay on the bed and talked, trying to exchange all this information about each other before he had to go again – it was lovely and desperate in a romantic sort of way. We were both huge fans of music. He was a rock-head before he joined 5ive, into Pearl Jam and Nirvana, and suddenly he was singing, 'Get on up, when you're down . . . did um, did um, did um. . . .' We would giggle about it. At last there was someone to whom I could voice my doubts out loud, someone who knew what it was like to feel a charlatan. He was undoubtedly a better singer than I was, he played the guitar and had a desire to write songs. In fact he fought to write songs for 5ive, but two of the others seemed to get all the writing credits. I think he had written a few by the end so he made some money, but not as much as he should have and not as much as he spent.

We didn't sleep at all. All night we swapped life stories, trying to squeeze it all in. Then it was back on the phone. I was spending all my cash on phone calls, talking to him late into the night. Some time just after my sixteenth Rich came home for a rare break and invited me round to his new flat in Kilburn in northwest London. I'd spent the day in London with my dad and he took me there. Rich was really nervous because of all the things I'd said about Dad and past boyfriends. He had a lot of nervous energy about him and was quite jumpy. They shook hands – Dad judges people on a handshake. Rich was good and made the grade – or so I thought. I was so excited that I'd been talking about him non-stop, and told Dad I was going to move in with him. Dad took it on the chin pretty well, considering I was just sixteen and announcing I was going to live with a guy. But according to Mum he rang her as soon as he was out of the flat and told her. They were both shocked, but Dad said I looked so happy that he didn't have the heart to say anything, and they thought maybe it was better than rattling around a hotel on my own in Maida Vale.

# Shoot Up Hill

## A Very Unfurnished Flat

I moved in straightaway, when of course we still didn't really know each other, but as far as I was concerned it was a done deal from that night. That's what I do. When I fall, I fall hard. I rang Mum to tell her myself. When I told her the flat was in a place called Shoot Up Hill, she cried and wanted to know why. I told her I didn't know – but I knew well enough. We were far from millionaires' row, but it was a nice enough block of flats with a swimming pool downstairs and round-the-clock security, and it was perfect for us. Paul Nichols lived next door, which Mum was well excited about. Rich had literally just moved in – there were no curtains, and no pictures on the walls, we had no sofa for about four months, and we slept on a mattress on the floor. Because we had so little time between us, the last thing we wanted was to spend our one day off shopping in Ikea. And to be honest we didn't care. The only sixteen-year-old I know who keeps his room immaculate is my brother, and clearly he's an anomaly. Rich and I spent a long time on the mattress in the back of the flat, in this shell full of boxes. Since he was fourteen he'd had a tiny TV with a huge aerial. He always burnt a candle on it, so it was covered in wax. We never had time to make our homes home – they were just places where we stopped off to empty our bags and then reload them. That was how we lived, and it was really wonderful at first.

The thing is we felt safe in our little haven, and by then that's all we wanted to feel – safe and away from the world. We started to become quite reclusive when we weren't working. Finally I had someone to talk to who didn't have a vested interest in the Billie enterprise, something I had undoubtedly lacked before. It changed my relationship with my parents, of course. Earning my own money and having a job was one thing. Living with a man and playing house was something else. Though, of course, we weren't playing house. We lived like absolute pigs. Even if we had time to shop, we didn't have the inclination. Sometimes Rich would go to the petrol station and get us some teabags, but other than that we'd have food delivered. Why cook when you can order in pizza? Why phone home when you already have someone there to talk to? This idea – girl stepping away from confines of her family with a new love – is nothing new. It's what the character of Rose in *Dr Who* is based on. Indeed, I was doing what many other sixteen-year-old girls were doing around the country. The only difference was that they weren't up on stage every night.

That's when I started feeling like I was thinking for myself. How my parents dealt with me officially moving away from home, still a child but living an adult life, I don't know. But they couldn't stop me. Since I was a child no one had ever been able to stop me doing what I had set my heart on, whether it was going to dancing lessons or acting class or going out with boys my dad didn't approve of. Now, if they tried to tell me off or tell me anything I didn't like the sound of, I said, 'Hey, I live in a flat, on my own, with a boy,' and instantly disempowered them. They couldn't tell me off – I was a working woman with my own money. They couldn't say, 'You shouldn't have done that, Billie. You're grounded.' I was out of their orbit, no longer their remit. I handed my emotional self over to a boy of nineteen, who in fairness wasn't even able to look after his own emotions, let alone mine.

I got on particularly well with Rich's brother, who was great. He worried for us, as both our families did, because they saw how much the music business took hold of everything and how paranoid it made us all. I think we could have handled everything so much better if we'd just been given some more breaks and time to recover. But we never had any R'n'R – we were walking wrecks, averaging five hours' sleep a night. And that was without trying to cram a little bit of normal life in between. I started to feel cheated because I had no life to myself – I wanted to be able to hang out with my boyfriend without some time constraint bearing down on me. We'd try to squeeze in a party for a couple of hours at the end of a long day, just to feel normal. Wake up to coffee, coffee, coffee and Red Bull, Red Bull, Red Bull. It was ludicrous. As Hugh says, the business is demanding. It asks a lot of its artists and promises much in return. None of us was doing this against our will. We all wanted fame and fortune and opportunity.

If you are under that amount of pressure – up late at night, up early in the morning, working eighteen-hour days – you need to be eating well, sleeping well and exercising well. You need to be a power house. Of course, ironically, the people of whom that is expected are also the people who are in a position to run riot. So the candle is well and truly being burnt at both ends. The music industry is a competitive market and expects a lot from you if you're going to sell records around the world. And this high-pressure lifestyle wasn't just restricted to the 'artists' – the management, the video-maker and the make-up artist all kept the same hours and all of them would say that if it wasn't the worst hours they'd ever kept it was up there in the running. The only difference was that they had breaks. When they went home, life returned to normal. We didn't have that.

When Rich and I told our respective labels that we'd moved in together neither was best pleased. I think our managers spoke on our behalf. I don't know what they talked about or what they agreed, but from then on for quite a while we simply lied our heads off about our relationship and denied it was happening. We went out separately and weren't allowed to be seen together at events. We told bare-faced lies to every journalist who ever asked about our relationship and hid when they came knocking on the door. It makes perfect sense that we started to become reclusive. We couldn't go out together. We wanted to see each other. So that was the only way.

But our affair was starting to hit the gossip headlines – are they or aren't they? – and people started to get wind of it. We were outed. And then, just as Hugh had predicted, threatening letters started to appear through the letter box. Not ours. Mum and Dad's.

As for me, I was sick to death of denying it. I didn't believe girls would turn on me because of my boyfriend, but no one said, 'Don't worry about it.' Everyone was worried, and as it turned out they had good reason. It was all being dissected and micro-managed like everything else in my life. We lived in fear of the *News of the World* – one of us would go out early every Sunday morning to check it. It was stupid of me, but at that time I cared deeply about what people were saying. It was confusing. Everything I did was commented on. I think probably because I was so young I became what's known as a 'tabloid darling', though there wasn't anything very darling about it. It was my life that was being judged, my feelings that were being tossed about – did she look fat, did she look thin, was that outfit a good choice, a bad choice, what's she done to her hair, she used to be sweet, now she's wild, she used to be dull, now she's interesting, what on earth did she think she was wearing! Another glamorous night out, another party, another limousine. They were talking about this person with my name who didn't really have my life. So much was written that was untrue – I was just a convenient vessel for the paparazzi to live their lies through. Over time I became paranoid. Locking myself into the flat and smoking a lot of weed probably didn't help.

We had a great time together, Rich and I. It felt like a mature relationship in comparison to the one I'd had with David Price, my ex-boyfriend from Swindon. Rich introduced me to a wider range of music, and in fact that was one of the best things to come out of it. He understood me. He was my rock when I didn't really have anyone else because I'd pushed my family and old friends away – so I relied on this one person who was in exactly the same position as myself. It was also the first time I'd been out with someone who discussed the meaning of life. I really looked forward to slowing down for a moment and therefore, conversely, I started to enjoy my working life less and less. The truth is, we didn't really have the sort of money we would have needed to do otherwise. We couldn't drive, which meant we had to pay drivers. And we couldn't get the Tube, because we'd be mobbed. So we stayed in and got stoned, and the more we did that the more paranoid we became about leaving the flat, so we stayed in and got more stoned and more paranoid. We were just trying to create a little world for ourselves but we ended up like Howard Hughes, hardly ever going out but just sitting alone in our squalid little flat.

# In the Red

## Looking at a Balance Sheet

If living with Rich taught me more about music, he also gave me an insight into the industry. He became my ally, the person to whom I could moan, 'Do they make you do this?', and he in turn would say, 'What the hell are you doing that for?' He wasn't that much older than me, but seemed to be. He thought I should be touring (up to then I'd only been doing promotional tours, which you didn't get paid for) and doing sponsorship and merchandise deals. The Billie Belt alone could have covered it. But I wasn't thinking like that. Nor was I aware of how much money I was haemorrhaging. In fact I assumed I was *making* money.

Those words that I had heard but not understood on the day my record deal was signed now came back to haunt me. I was working eighteen-hour days, but the money I thought I was earning was actually turning into an ever-increasing debt. The artist starts to get paid when the record earns out – when the profits become greater than the original advance payment. Even with two number ones behind me I was far from breaking even. All those 'recoupable' costs had been eating away at my advance, so that one million had now shrunk to no more than a couple of hundred thousand. And still more costs were coming in. So I learnt the hard way what 'recoupable' actually means. It means they give you an advance but out of it you have to pay for all the recording costs (each album can set you back a quarter of a million quid) and half the video (another hundred thousand at least), and you have to make a contribution to any television advertising. Very quickly your 'unrecouped' money can be up at £600,000. When I finally discovered all this. I was staggered – and angry. I thought I'd been robbed. Maybe Rich wanted me to be pissed off with my record company, or maybe he wanted to be the good guy, the one dependable one, because he never told me, or at any rate I don't remember him telling me, that my deal was the same as everyone else's in the business. From Robbie to the Rolling Stones, everyone pays the same.

I know producers are now looking at the whole model of a record contract, because it is getting harder and harder for anyone to make money these days. What I understand now, but didn't then, is that in fairness to the record company it's hard to get any change out of a million quid before you even know if you're in business – before you've even sold a single tune. Once you've paid the 'artist', made a couple of videos, paid all the marketing and promotional costs, transported everyone around the country or flown them around the world and paid the hotel bills, you're down a hefty chunk of money. Even with two number one singles and a platinum album behind me, Innocent weren't making any money. They were netting about £3 an album. At that rate you've got to sell at least half a million albums before each of those three pounds has paid back the initial investment. Until you hit that magic number, all you're doing is filling a hole. After that point, however, everybody starts making money. The artist is getting close to recouping and the record company is looking at the chance of a return.

My first album went on to sell 450,000 copies. I was the biggest selling youngest female artist in pop history – we had a great platform. But that's all it was. A platform. A beginning. Maybe something big was going to happen later. But no one was making any money: the balance sheet was firmly in the red. If I'd gone on and reached the dizzy heights that Hugh reached with Blue and Atomic Kitten, things would have been different. Blue's albums sold 1.3 million copies in the UK alone, another 1.5 abroad, and then they steamed ahead. *That's* when record companies make their money. More than the artists, it's true, but since nine out of every ten endeavours fail, when the companies hit the jackpot it has to be big. But don't feel too sorry for the 'artists': once they are that big, once they have recouped and are being paid royalties, a whole new income stream opens up to them which the record company does not participate in. Touring, publishing, merchandise – all nice little earners. Especially touring. But I didn't get there. I bolted long before. My second album didn't get as close as my first, and who knows what would have happened to my third – if I'd even made one. With my sort of numbers Hugh probably would have been under pressure to drop me, which I know he wouldn't have wanted to do, but if the numbers don't add up . . . they don't add up. I had put so much into that first big push that I don't know if there would have been anything left anyway.

My problem was that I never put my foot down, I never said, 'I'm not doing this.' Mostly because I didn't feel I was in a position to do so. I didn't want people to think I was a prima donna – I didn't want them to think I'd changed. I felt the record company had given me the best opportunity of my life and I wanted to serve them well. And I was living in a fatigue culture. I'd meet other bands on the road and we'd sit in the bar and bitch and moan about how tired we were, or more often we'd sit there with nothing whatsoever to say. I've never been as tired since. The hours I have kept in my subsequent career, even on two weeks of night shoots for *Dr Who*, have been a breeze in comparison.

Am I exaggerating? Maybe – it all seems so long ago. But then again, recently I bumped into a make-up artist whom I'd worked with a lot during the promotion for the first album. She said she had never fully realized at the time how hard I was worked. She said she calculated that during the time she was working with me she was averaging four hours' sleep a night, so I must have done the same. It was the toughest two years of her life. And mine. And then it happened again with the second album. For me the strangest thing about writing this book was when it came to piecing everything together into an ordered timeline. I know the dates when the records came out (they are set in stone), every September I got a year older, and every Christmas came and went – but when I look back on it all I am amazed that I did so much. Everything happened so quickly. I keep thinking that it couldn't have taken place in just over a year, but it did. Two weeks off, eighteen-hour days – and I wondered why I was so tired!

I call this period of my life the dog years. I wanted to call the book *Billie Piper – The Dog Years*, but the publishers didn't think it would sell. It wasn't just that I was working like a dog, but that every one of my years felt like seven. Actually, looking back on it, maybe it was more like time-travel. I entered a Tardis called the music industry, lived a whole lifetime, travelled to different continents, only to emerge and find my dinner still hot on the table. How did I do so much? How did I fit in so much? How did I visit so many places and see so little? I was working. Promotion for my third single, a tour to Japan, then to Miami to shoot the video for 'Honey to the Bee', then on to LA, Canada and NY, and in between that back home for the February '99 Brit Awards.

B*Witched, Steps and I did an ensemble Abba number. I wore a garish red flared all-in-one suit with cut-out sides, which did wonders for my girth. Walking around the party I overheard a presenter saying I'd looked fat in my red outfit. I'm a broad girl, no doubt, but *fat*! Jesus, what did they want from us? I was gutted. I'd been becoming more and more aware of my 'image' – you can't be photographed as often as I was being photographed and not be. I'd kept the 'body conscience' monster at bay, but no sixteen-year-old can hear a comment like that and not be diced by it. The '99 Brit Awards was Robbie's night – he wiped the board clean and took home an armful of gongs, and deservedly so. I got no award, although I was nominated for Best British Newcomer – but the prize went to Belle and Sebastian. I went home that night feeling less sure of myself than ever before. People thought I was fat, I didn't look as good as the others, nor did I sound as good as them. The process of being mic'ed up and put through rigorous sound checks for performances like the one at the Brits, only for it to be switched off the moment I started singing, was beginning to take its toll. Those little voices of doubt were getting louder.

# She Wants You

## US of A, April 1999

The third single from the first album had only gone to Number 3 in the UK. 'She Wants You' was pipped at the Christmas Number 1 post by 'Goodbye' from the Spice Girls. That was a quick dose of reality. Number 3 wasn't good enough. At Number 3 I could feel people panicking around me. A murmur. A tremor. I started to feel I had to get back on top of this or it would go. So in March the promotion went into overdrive. There wasn't anything I wouldn't do. I'd been a control freak about my sales from the beginning – not my finances, just my sales. I learned the lingo, talked the talk and tried to be taken seriously, and in doing so I'd asked enough of the right questions to know what the figures coming in meant. I knew who was giving me airplay, who was continually skipping it, how many times my song was being played. I thought learning the business was my way out of trouble. I knew what I had to do to get the only thing that mattered: a Number 1.

So, not for the first time, I busied myself with stepping into the role of salesperson – it was my way of keeping control, staying sane. I knew we had to get every single to Number 1. It wasn't about celebrating the song, it was about hitting the target. My job was to sell the product. And with a record at Number 3 I obviously wasn't doing that very well. While I kept the smile on my face in front of everyone else, hiding my doubts, my fears, my self-flagellation, when I faced myself in the mirror I was angry. In fact I was ridiculously hard on myself.

'She Wants You', however, was responsible for taking me to America. A dance remix had broken in Miami and spread over the dance scene. With three hits behind me and a Number 10 in the States, my first US tour was planned. I was ecstatic. I packed my bags once more and in April headed west to celebrate and capitalize on our Stateside success. First stop, the Miami Winter Music Conference. I was asked to join a panel of musicians, DJs and musicologists to discuss dance music. I was sandwiched between the incredible singer CeCe Penison and Eric Morrila, a wicked DJ. Umm . . . Help! I had no recollection of what happened. None at all. Was I interesting? Profound? I very much doubt it. I remember walking off in a right state, unable to speak to any of the pluggers who were responsible for putting me up there in the first place by distributing my records to the stations.

My one memory of America up until that tour was Disney World with my parents, before my brother was born. I was then a confident seven-year-old in love with the world and all its potential – a really, really happy kid. America was where Madonna came from, and she was my all-time heroine. America was where dreams came true. . . . Maybe I'd feel it over there now? Maybe that was what was missing? America. But I was knackered when I left the UK because the promotion for 'Honey to the Bee', released in March, had been tough – tougher still because of the previous slip with 'She Wants You'. I had given it my all, but it hadn't been enough. 'Honey to the Bee' went in at Number 3. What I should have been doing was resting up, but once again I could not find it in me to say no. Number 3 again. I told myself I had to do more, not less.

The plan was to do a four-week tour of local radio stations. That sounded pretty good and not too taxing. And there is no doubt that it was fun for a while, especially Miami, which after the conference was wild. Then we went to LA – the place that as a kid I had been so determined to return to after having made something of myself. And here I was, back in the City of Angels having made something of myself – and *still* I couldn't feel it. I buried the disappointment, got into another bus, car or plane, and arrived in parts of middle America that I didn't even know existed. Texas was fun because everyone really does wear stetsons and cowboy boots – all that was missing was Sue Ellen from *Dallas* slopping whiskey down her front in a Hooter's bar. I liked the energy of the Americans at first and felt like I could do anything – I took their compliments at face value and believed I was going to be a success there, that all the work I was putting in would be enough. Work? A few radio stations? Hardly very taxing. . . . Let me give you a snapshot day.

Steve, my manager, would be calling me every five minutes to get me up and out of my room by 6a.m. (And before I continue, let me add that everyone around me was working ridiculous hours too.) We would be picked up and driven to a radio station somewhere in town. There, more often than not, I'd have to do a live performance of a song or a section of it. I always chose 'Honey to the Bee', my fourth single and the title of the album, because it was best suited to my voice. That was probably the main reason why that tour sucked the last of my confidence dry. You don't mime in America – you can't. That's why you get the big bucks. You can't fake it because they want to know you can do it for real. Do you remember the outcry when it was discovered that Milli Vanilli mimed on stage? It was the same for every radio station, however tinpot it was. Every single one of those live performances terrified me, and I was doing it twice a day, day in, day out.

That ordeal would be followed by an interview. I would be searching the face of the DJ wondering whether this was the one who would bust me, out me live on radio as a fraud. I would smile until my cheeks hurt, try and dazzle them with my charm, to make them forgot that I hadn't quite hit this note or that. It doesn't matter how many times Hugh told me that I had a lovely tonal range – and he still does today when I remind him what was going on in my mind back then – but when you're up there, exposed like that, words of encouragement aren't enough. I can sing – I am aware of that. But being able to hold a tune and being able to cut it as a singer are two very different things. I hadn't been in the recording studio for a while so I'd almost forgotten that I couldn't do it. I had allowed myself, on the surface at least, to believe the hype. But standing in those radio stations with the cans on my head made it all come back to me. The voice of doubt that had whispered to me way back in Jacobs when I first started recording was laughing at me now.

After the interview we would take the entire staff of the radio station out for breakfast, when I'd seat-hop every ten minutes so that I could talk to twenty-to-forty-year-old pluggers, DJs and consultants and try to get them to play my records. We'd do the same at lunch at another radio station, drive, then the same at dinner at a third venue, then get on a plane and fly to a different state. Or drive for miles – through the night sometimes. It was hectic because we were trying to cover so much ground. We'd arrive at the next hotel at midnight and start again at six. All those bloody meals and saying the same thing like a wind-up dolly over and over again. After the first week I stopped thinking about what I was staying. I felt deaf and dumb – I wasn't listening to them and I was responding automatically. I felt numb with exhaustion. The only person who made me feel alive was

Rich, and he was thousands of miles away. I missed him so much. At the end of the day I just wanted to curl up in bed and talk to him on the phone. But because of the time-lag, when I got to bed he was asleep and when he was waking up I was asleep. Or, worse, I'd stay awake so that we could speak and then get even more tired.

Being alone out there was hurting me. Trying to seduce these people into playing my records was killing me. And on top of that, it wasn't working. I felt the record company was becoming distant because we weren't getting the coverage they wanted in the territories they wanted, so I was whoring myself out for nothing. As the fabulous Justine Bell puts it in her own inimitable fashion, 'It was a f*****g aimless exercise!' I think we all agree now that I should have stayed at home and used that time either to rest or to consolidate the market we had worked so hard to build up. Why did I feel like I was whoring myself out? For all the same reasons I had tried to hide from myself at home, magnified a hundred times. I wasn't writing the material, so I didn't feel passionate about it or bound to it in any way. And I hadn't been born with the voice of Mariah Carey or CeCe Penison, so all I was essentially doing was getting dressed up and letting lecherous DJs kiss my cheeks, seducing them until they agreed to play my song. The whole thing was horrible and left a really bad taste in my mouth. Every photo from that tour is the same. My eyes are still, locked on. They don't connect with the rest of my face. I'm smiling but there's no movement in my face. No light in my eyes, no laughter. All I am is this vast, enormous mouth, which pretty much summed up how I felt about my music career at that point. All mouth. No soul.

Hugh thinks I never put quite enough work into my voice, and yes, in theory I could have done with a lot more voice coaching, but I think we would all agree that in practice it wasn't really a possibility because there wasn't the time. A bit like my studies. I still had a tutor out on the road with me, but I hadn't done a stroke of school work for months. She was only there for show: as long as we could say I was keeping up my studies, it was enough. The whole thing made me feel bad. I had never worked so hard in my life before, and nor do I intend to again. I felt used. I was dog-tired, miles from home, and the only person I had for company was my fifty-year-old manager. I was still only sixteen years old.

When I finally got to my hotel room I would put on my headphones and try to shut the world out. I had got into pop rock because of my boyfriend, the rocker in boy-band clothing, and now in America I started to search out as much of the darker stuff as I could lay my hands on. I remember calling my mum on several occasions and saying, 'I can't stand it . . . I'm losing it . . . I don't know what's going on. . . .' Mum, naturally, would lie awake at night worrying. She was desperate for me to come home, but – and this may lie at the very crux of our relationship – didn't feel important enough to speak to my managers, let alone to get them to act. She didn't feel she was part of my life any more. She sensed she didn't count.

It was a situation of my own making – no one wanted to see me as a grown-up more than I myself did. But I couldn't have foreseen the consequences. I engineered that independence because I wanted it to be like it was in my imagination, back in my bedroom in Swindon, dreaming, dreaming, dreaming of being on stage every night. But in my dreams I hadn't had a mic in my hand. In my dreams I was doing something I loved and was good at. But in America I really wasn't. By forging ahead to the place I thought I wanted to be I had left the people who cared about me in my wake. Now I was alone. Promotion in the UK had been hard work but fun. The focus was on the dancing – all I had to do was get the steps right and mime in time to the tape. This was different. It was just an endless struggle of live performances as I tried to break in the USA a British act which, though packaged well, at heart wasn't good enough. They kept referring to me as the 'artist', a word that conjures up impressive images of creativity and originality. What a joke! I felt empty inside. We were trying so hard, but it just wasn't happening. All the work was for nothing. On a good day I'd feel relief that I'd got through it; on a bad day I felt terrible. And there were a lot of bad days in America: a lot of DJs to kiss and a lot of notes to visualize. America was so vast and so far away from home that I thought I was going mad. If I hadn't been able to feel my success, why did failing hurt so much?

My manager knew it wasn't working. He'd been watching me retreat into my shell but was incapable of reaching in and pulling me out. None of it was what I thought it was going to be, and when you are feeling tired and used and lonely, with only your own bleak thoughts to keep you company, listening to negative music, something bad may well happen. And it did, in a hotel room in Chicago.

# The Windy City

## Another Fucking Hotel Room

By the time I arrived late one night in Chicago I was utterly despondent. Here I was in this amazing hotel, staring out of the window and knowing that what lay before me was an incredible city, but equally that once again I wasn't going to get to enjoy it. More live performances. More hairy DJs leaving their saliva on my cheek. More fucking smiles. I'd been on the road for three gruelling weeks. At the time I was listening to the New Radicals on my headset, loudly, hoping that something would finally resonate and get me out of this stupor. I stared at the television which was on in my room, watching the endless terrible commercials and wincing at every bad edit. This anger started to well up inside me, the music got louder, the walls of the hotel room started to come in on me and I realized that I wanted – no, *needed* – the whirlwind to stop. But I had no clarity of mind, so I couldn't work out what I had to do to slow things down. I was out of control, living on other people's schedules. I didn't want any of it any more, but I couldn't get out of it. I had started the whole thing, but there was no way out – I think that's why the walls closed in on me. Then it dawned on me. There was one way out. Kill myself. Make it stop.

I had hit a concrete wall and simply had no energy to continue, no desire to do so, no spirit or fight left inside me. Rich wanted me home, and I wanted to come home, but I couldn't get home. Rich got angry, while I felt powerless. The tour was a failure. Success was ethereal. My dream had come true, but I was caught in a nightmare. Like the city that lay twinkling below me, I could see it but I couldn't feel it. Chicago was pivotal, the moment it all collided. I freaked out. I'd brought these pills called Melatonin which you use for jet lag but I, being sweet sixteen, thought they made you sleep. I had no idea how to take an overdose, but because I thought they were sleeping pills I felt all I had to do was swallow them. I was holding this bottle of pills in my hand while this voice in my head, my own voice, said, 'Take them! Go on, swallow, then, you stupid cow.'

I couldn't believe I was entertaining such a thought. How had it come to this? Somehow I managed to pick up the phone and, though I was practically hyperventilating, called Mum and Dad. It was about four in the morning, but they answered, and all I could say was that I wanted to kill myself. Those were the only words I could get out. Over the previous year I'd called in various states of distress, but this time it was different. I was incoherent and crying my eyes out, holding this bottle and wanting to neck all the pills and die. Mum and Dad were trying to calm me down by asking me questions. What had happened? Where was everybody? Why hadn't I called before? Why wasn't I being watched? I couldn't answer any of them, but just cried and cried and cried. Dad called my manager then and there while Mum was still on the line to me, too scared to break the connection, and demanded, 'Bring my daughter home now!'

And so we cut the tour short and the following day I flew home to rest and recuperate, and take my GCSEs. But in the event none of that happened. In fact, it just got a whole lot worse.

# Act Two

*Living a Life*

# Billie Paul Piper

## A Maternity Ward in a Swindon Hospital

My mother met my father when she was fifteen and he was twenty-one, and fell crazily in love with him. That is something Mum and I have in common – when we fall, we fall hard. In many ways we are very similar, but, sadly, similar doesn't mean easy. The relationship with my mother is one of the few things that can reduce me to pulp. It isn't one-sided – we do it to each other. And in writing this book, I think I may have come a step closer to understanding why. I love my family, but the truth is I don't know them.

I wasn't planned. Dad hadn't quite settled into the role of doting husband – in fact my parents are still not married. Though Mum may have resented that in the beginning, now she loves it. For a while her maiden name gave her some much-wanted anonymity. When Mum found out she was pregnant she was overjoyed, though she must have felt some trepidation. Dad was away and she wasn't sure if he was coming back. Still, she loved him regardless. On top of that she was a child herself. But she never even questioned keeping me.

From the moment she knew she was pregnant, Mum called me Billie. When I was born a girl she still called me Billie, even though everybody kept saying, 'You can't call her that – what if she ends up wearing tartan trousers and NHS glasses?' So in a drunken moment I was registered as Lianne Piper, but thankfully after she sobered up she realized her mistake, went back and re-registered me. Mum simply couldn't bring herself to call me Lianne because, as she says, 'It didn't ring true.'

After eighteen hours of painful labour, on 22 September 1982, Billie Paul Piper was born by Caesarean section. 'Eye of the Tiger' was Number 1 in the charts, and three months earlier Princess Diana had given birth to Prince William. Like my mother and her mother before her, I was born in Swindon. A few days after the birth, against the express instructions of the maternity nurse, she stole down the corridor of the hospital to get a proper look at her first-born child.

### Billie's Mum V/O

'She was perfect. There wasn't a scratch on her. She had these huge dark eyes that stared right back at me, and thick jet-black hair. I leaned closer to her ear to tell her that she was the most beautiful baby in the whole hospital. And I believed it. I thought the others were hideous in comparison. I felt sorry for their mothers – how was I to know that all the other mothers felt exactly the same? Suddenly I felt this overwhelming sense of responsibility. It frightened me a bit when I realized that I had to take care of her for the rest of her life – but mostly I remember being excited by the prospect. I stood there thinking, "I am going to take care of you and love you no matter what, whoever you are, for the rest of your life." '

In due course Mum took me home and doted on me. For seven magical years it was just her, Dad and me. Life was sweet. I went to the local school, and my aunt and gran lived around the corner. I knew my cousins and played with the neighbours. I was a pretty cute kid, all teeth and pigtails and a smile that stretched from ear to ear. Mum was young and had masses of energy – she would play with me, show me off and do all she could to encourage me. I was her one and only, so all the attention came my way.

But I wasn't spoilt – it wasn't like that in our house. Dad has a very strong work ethic and every penny he's earned is valued, as is his time off. He was always away working or enjoying a few shandies. I know he was working hard to pay the bills, but from the beginning he lived by his own rules. I was given pocket money, but I practically had to hand over accounts to show him what I'd spent it on. Dad is a grafter.

He was a labourer who worked his way up from the building site to running his own construction company in Swindon. Before moving to Spain, P.V. Piper was one of the biggest firms in Swindon. And it wasn't just Dad. All the men in my family are hard workers, and their women wives and mothers. My parents are working-class through and through, but towards the end of my childhood Dad had worked so hard that we had a nice redbrick house in the new part of Swindon with a conservatory and double glazing. We also had a family car, and Dad kept two classic cars in the garage. So as far as I knew, hard work paid off. And I was prepared to work hard.

Mum says I was creative from the start, constantly dressing up, prancing around the living room, putting on plays and shows. I had no brothers and sisters to play with, but was happy to create my own world. Imagination and make-believe were my playmates, and I relied heavily on them. With only one child to care for Mum had the time to observe me, and one of the things she noticed was that as soon as any music came on the ever-playing radio I would start to dance. So, either because she saw potential in me or to get me out from under her feet for five minutes, she enrolled me in a local dance class. I loved it from the beginning and begged her to let me attend more and more.

My mother was a beautiful young woman herself, who loved to sing and dance. The two of us would watch all the musicals that she adored and sing along to them. After a couple of glasses of Bacardi she'd grab a hairbrush as a makeshift mic and be off. You should see her on the karaoke – she's brilliant. She was always better than me at singing. But that was cool – I was more than happy to dance along. Singing and dancing were a big part of our life at home. Mum could turn the front room into something magical, something exciting, and I was happy – queen of all I surveyed and the apple of my parents' eye. Then two things happened. First I went to London. Then I went to America.

# Bright Lights, Big City

EXT:

## London, LA

When I was five my gran took me up to London to see Trooping the Colour. I vividly remember coming up the stairs at Oxford Street Tube Station, seeing adverts for McDonald's on the rise of each step and thinking it was beyond cool. Remember when those golden arches got you all riled up over the thought of burgers and chips? It was something else. I don't know why it made such an impression on me, but it did. I guess it was because it was the first time I realized that things could be different, like they were in my imagination – limitless. London was limitless and Swindon suddenly felt very small – even to me. The sight of the horses, the soldiers and the people of all shapes and colours had a dizzying effect on me. We walked past theatres, enormous shops, elaborate wrought iron gates –

it was like the stuff in story books, but it was real. I could touch it, smell it, taste it. The unique rumble of the London buses was music to my ears. When my gran took me back to Paddington Station I started to cry. I didn't want to get back on the train. I didn't want to go home. London was the best place in the world and I didn't want to leave it. My gran took my hand and said, 'Don't worry, Bill. You'll come back – if you want to.'

While I relied on my imagination to keep me occupied, I also relied heavily on the adults around me. I played up to them, performed for them, made them smile and clap, and was happy in their company. Then it all changed. Mum finally got pregnant again. She was over the moon. Charlie was a much longed for baby because she had started to fear it would never happen.

When Mum told me she was pregnant I ran out of the room crying like a spoilt little shit. I actually remember being calculated about it, going for maximum effect by running upstairs and throwing myself on my bed. Mum and Dad came up and sat on the bed with me and slowly caressed me off the ledge. My tantrum had worked. I had their undivided attention. To appease me, to cheer me up, or for a last hurrah, they decided to take me to California with them before my new brother or sister was born. That trip to Disney World and the Universal Studios was another pivotal moment in my life. It opened my eyes to a world beyond even London and far, far beyond Swindon. To a world of magic. To a world where dreams come true. By the time I came home, my dreaming had started to take over my life. And so it was until boys came into view.

Because we were going to America for over three weeks I had to be taken out of school. I was overjoyed. No lessons. No homework. School was not my most comfortable environment: my writing was hopeless, my concentration worse. I wish I could blame it on dyslexia, but that was never diagnosed. I was certainly more creative than academic. I think I was more excited about missing school than about going to America – until I got there, that was. Dad, on the other hand, was not pleased that I would be missing school and devised a way to keep me focused. He had left school at fourteen. What he didn't have, he wanted for me – and indeed still wants for my younger brothers and sisters. That's why he was always so severe when it came to school work. He wanted me to take my education seriously. It was a tool in life he didn't possess, and I think he still finds it frustrating. So he made me write a daily diary of our trip and make a scrap book. Every morning I would have to sit on the balcony of our hotel, staring down at the kids laughing and jumping into the cool, glistening blue pool below, while I wrote about everything I'd done the day before. They were the longest hours of my life and I hated it. But Dad would sit with me and help me, and now we have lots of pictures of us together which I love. In fact, that scrap book is probably one of my most treasured possessions.

There were other things on that trip that have stayed with me. MTV was obviously huge. We didn't have it in the UK, which made it even more amazing. Hanging out with me in the hotel watching MTV – or, more likely, watching me prancing about to MTV – was probably a nice way for my pregnant Mum to put her feet up. We had a ball, singing along to the Fine Young Cannibals. The other eye-opener for me was being invited into Dad's world. It was a really big deal that he was showing me his life. As I said, I'm not the only trailblazer in the family – Dad was doing it long before I did. He went to LA and Germany to work, and he'd often go off travelling and leave Mum and me at home. He did his own thing; he was his own man. Once he ended up kipping with twenty blokes from Swindon in one rented room on Hollywood and Vine. In fact I think he was in LA when Mum was at home pregnant with me, so I understand why he took so long to come home. It's an incredible place – a place where, if you work really hard, things can happen and dreams come true. It was a heady mix and I loved it.

In LA I was invited into an adult world, and I leapt into it without so much as a flicker of doubt. Mum and Dad would take me to these big parties and I would mingle with older people, totally at home. I have a photograph of me having put one of the biggest, burliest men's hair into bunches. Cheeky, certainly – but always with a smile. They were a real bunch of characters with names like Piggy, Tiny and Spider. I vividly remember going to a party given by a man called Champagne Charlie. He met us at the door. I stuck out my hand and said, 'I'm Billie Piper from Swindon in England' and he replied, 'I'm Champagne Charlie from anywhere and everywhere. Do you want to come and see my one-eyed shark?' It looks odd on the page, but it was completely innocent. He wasn't a pervert – he really did have a one-eyed shark. In a tank. I spent all evening watching it. That holiday was pure joy. On the way home all I could think about was how I was going to get back out there, into the world where dreams come true.

# 10 by 8s

## Reception of the Tanwood Agency
## (for the precocious)

Not long after coming home, possibly even before Charlie was born, Mum and I were watching TV while she ironed. It was a Sunday, always the shittiest day known to man. Dad would do sports and lager all day, come home at five, eat dinner and fall asleep on the sofa. If you tried to change the channel he'd wake up and say, 'Oi, I was watching that!' I'd always hated the routine of it, but after LA I hated it more. Anyway, this particular Sunday we were watching a documentary about a young girl who was trying to be a model. I never wanted to be a model, but I did like the idea of working and what struck me about that programme was that the girl had an agent. I didn't really understand the concept, of course, but I was aware that it was the agent who got the girl work. So I turned to Mum at the ironing board and, quite sure of myself, said, 'Right – you've got to get me an agent.' And somehow she did.

It was the Tanwood Agency, a local place in Swindon that Mum knew about. She rang them and made an appointment. We went together and met Molly Tanner, the mother, and her daughter Polly. The entire room was covered in large 10 by 8 photographic prints of gorgeous kids. Really amazing, beautiful, perfect children – I'd never seen real children like that in all my life. I was quite dazzled that such people actually existed. I was far from perfect. Yet to grow into my big features, I was all teeth and brows and really did resemble Chip'n'Dale, Disney's chipmunk rescue rangers. I'd asked my gran to cut my hair like Martika, a singer with a very distinct look and wonderful shiny hair. So she cut a wedge at the back and, though it was a horribly unsuccessful haircut, off I went full of bravado. I have never been picture-perfect – I shall never match up to those girls in the 10 by 8s that I saw that first time in the Tanwood Agency, though it took me a long time to work that out – but I had something else. Apart from a prominent jawline, that is. Cocky, maybe? Unusual, possibly? Small, undoubtedly. Whatever it was, the first job I went up for I got. It was for an American cereal called Honeycomb. I'll never forget the audition. My gran took me to London again, this time to a big studio somewhere in Soho (though frankly anything would have seemed big to me then, since I was miniature). There was a bell and lots of lights, and an oversized TV made from foam, and people everywhere with clipboards and mobile phones. Even the smell was exciting. It seemed like there were hundreds of other kids up for the part, but it didn't bother me. I had a chance like any other. I ate a lot of sugary cereal, smiled into a camera and rubbed my tummy, and then it was over. I was buzzing all the way home: 'Do you think I've got the part? Do you? Do you?' My gran tried to be circumspect but, devoted as she is, she probably thought they'd be mad not to take 'our Bill'. Luckily they weren't mad – Molly Tanner called Mum and said I'd got the job.

I went back to the same studio, this time running ahead because I knew where I was going. It was brilliant. They suspended me in a harness and made me eat cereal for hours. It was ludicrous, but I loved it. They could do as many takes as they wanted – I would have dangled in that contraption for days and found it utterly wrenching when I had to leave. I just wanted to stay and do a million more. I was so fearless at that age that I was a sponge. The director said, 'Do this' and I did. I didn't have to question it – it all came naturally. Needless to say, I had the bug. Badly. I rushed back to Molly Tanner and begged for more. I didn't want to model, though I did bits and pieces; it was about working. I made her promise to put my name forward for anything that came in. Not long afterwards an American drinks company was looking for a 'face' to re-energize their marketing campaign.

So I auditioned and got the part to make a series of Coolaid ads. This was the big time. Though unknown here, over in the States it was the biggest drink. One swig of that toxic orange candy-floss and I was bouncing off the walls for days. What I loved most about doing the advert was that there was some dancing involved. I couldn't wait to show off my skills, but what I was even more excited about was that I got to step inside the legendary, iconic Pineapple Studios. I stood open-mouthed (quite a sight when you've a mouth the size of mine) watching dancers limber up. They looked so slick, so cool. They'd cut the feet and crutch out of their tights and were wearing them as tops – frankly, you couldn't get much cooler than that. I went back to Swindon, told my best friends and we promptly cut up the contents of our ward-robes.

This advert was a whole production, with a cast, a choreographer, crew and make-up. I was in seventh heaven. One of the other kids in the ad was a real actor, John Picard from the sitcom *2.4 Children*. He told me about drama classes. Drama classes? That sounded interesting. A place where you could learn to act and get to do more of this stuff? I went home itching to tell Mum about it. Then I started to beg them to find me a drama class to go to. And in the end, as always, they relented.

The Coolaid ad was huge in the States, but on the ground my life didn't change. I was so bright-eyed, so in love with it all. Pineapple was like Nirvana to me. I just wanted more. I wanted to stay. I wanted to disappear into that world and

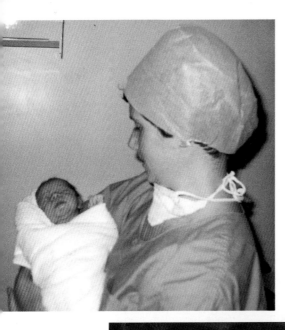

Half a minute old, but never mind that - what about the nurse's tash!

Perfect portrait, minus my wandering hand.

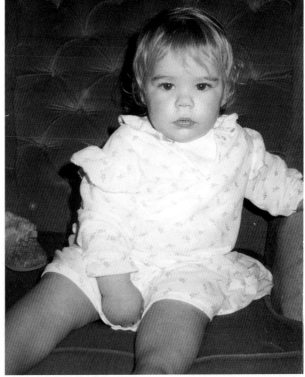

Growing up with
Bear, the family dog.

Wannabe Madonna,
headset and all. (Mum
covering her ears.)

Charlie and me,
first day at school.
Speaks volumes.

Wing Attack.

Down on Sandbanks with the family.

Three of the Rockley Babes. All hands on
the Toblerones.

Ma and Pa.

Caravan kids. Me, Ellie, Harley and Charlie.

Boarding in Barnes with Laura Evans.

Blowing kisses with my best friend Sally Price.

not come back. I yearned to be able to go back there. I would go to my room and practise, practise, practise. I always get quite emotional when I think about it. I was this tiny kid with an enormous dream, and I was determined to make it back.

# Baby Blues

## A Terraced House in Swindon

On 30 November 1989 Charlie was born and I lost my audience. I was dreading him coming home but actually he was gorgeous. He smiled all the time, the happiest baby in the world. I used to pretend he was mine and sneak him out of the cot, rock him like Mum did and try to copy how she spoke to him. We had baths together all the time, and I just wanted to take care of him like Mum wanted to take care of me. It was lucky I felt that way about my brother, because the years following Charlie's birth weren't really my mum's best. None of this is anyone's fault – it's just what happened. Mum was pregnant again four weeks after Charlie was born, and must have been beyond knackered. But she was young and fought it for a long time, so the baseline tiredness that was consuming her took a while to manifest itself. And then came Ellie, hot on Harley's heels, just to finish her off. It had taken seven years for my parents to conceive their second child, then three came along in three. By the time I was ten we were living in a madhouse. I don't think it is unfair to say that my mother went a bit crazy around that time.

Whereas my every move had been watched, applauded and encouraged, my brother and sisters were a job lot whose upbringing was more to do with crowd control than anything else. Mum was depressed, but didn't know it. I helped where I could, keeping the kids occupied, entertaining them, playing with them. But I also threw myself into my dance and drama classes – and, frankly, anything else I could get my hands on. I loved school assembly, hymn practice, nativity plays, harvest festival – anything with some kind of performance attached to it. I remember creating a nativity play that was so detailed it practically lasted the length of Christmas. Pity the poor unsuspecting kid who walked in through our front door. Within minutes they had a towel on their head and had been thrust into a play of my making. I have to thank Mum and Dad from the bottom of my heart for sitting through my endless plays and performances, which I thought were marvellous. They all had a beginning, middle and end, and the longer the better – anything to escape the chaos of three small kids.

For my tenth birthday, Mum agreed to take me and my girlfriends to Planet Hollywood. Unfortunately the bus broke down on the motorway and we ended up sitting on the embankment by the M4 waiting for the AA. We never made it to London. I can't remember this, but I can believe it: when we got home I had an absolute fit. My birthday had been ruined and here was Mum, as if nothing had happened, standing at the ironing board, staring at the TV, running an iron over and over the same piece of clothing. While I screamed and kicked and cried that the world was plotting against me, something happened to Mum. She started shaking, her mouth went dry and her arms went numb – she was terrified that she was having a heart attack. Her head was throbbing, her hands were sweating and she honestly thought she was going to die. As she says, 'After that I sort of lost the plot for about two years.'

It was a panic attack, but Mum didn't know that then. She was in trouble, but she didn't know that either. Nor did I. Ellie was just a baby, but post-natal depression was not something that was talked about then, or even admitted to. Dad was quite sergeant-major about life then, so I'm not sure he would have been that helpful either. And I was only ten. At the age of seven I'd been playing mummy, but three years later the game got a bit more serious. Mum leaned on me more: she needed me to help with the children because she really couldn't manage on her own. When I came home from school I would make sandwiches for everyone. Sometimes I dropped Charlie off at playgroup. I would entertain the three of them until bathtime while Mum took a nap upstairs. I took them to the loo. I changed nappies. I made up bottles. I did everything I could to help my mum get better. My journey into adulthood was speeding up.

Another terrible drama was unfolding in the Piper family at the time. My aunt Norma, Dad's sister, was diagnosed with a melanoma. One mole went bad, and six weeks later she was dead. Norma didn't even look unwell, yet she sat across the table from Mum and said, 'I'm going to die.' Mum couldn't cope with that on top of everything else; it was beyond her. She kept saying, 'No, you're not. No, you're not,' though it was futile. Mum was losing weight fast, and when she dropped to seven stone she started panicking that she wouldn't be able to continue the keep-fit classes she loved to the point of obsession. I had no idea what was going on at the time – all I remember is Mum constantly checking me over for moles while I was talking to her because she was obsessed with the thought of dying. To be honest, she's still checking the kids for moles – in fact I think Charlie has been sent up to the local hospital a number of times because of his. That's reasonable; what was happening at the time of Norma's death wasn't. Mum was manic then, on the absolute edge. She didn't know what was going on in her own body – she kept feeling this tingling down her arms. So while Norma was lying in hospital, dripped up and coming in and out of consciousness, Mum, convinced she herself was dying of a brain tumour, took herself off to see a brain specialist.

Once she was sitting in his office, as she puts it, she broke down. The specialist was absolutely lovely and seemingly unfazed by this crazed woman sitting opposite him with nothing physically wrong but emotionally all over the place. He didn't dismiss her. He listened. And when she'd exhausted herself he said, 'I can't help you because it's not my field, but I will send you to someone who can. Go home and I'll call you when I've set it up.' Well, Mum didn't go home. Norma, who was desperately ill by then, had been taken to the hospice. So Mum went straight from the hospital to the hospice and stayed there until Norma died later that day. The lovely brain specialist called home incessantly. All I could say was that Mum hadn't come back from the hospital and no, I didn't know where she was. It is a testament to the terrible state my mother must have been in that the longer she didn't come home the more he worried and the more frequent the calls became. I think he feared she'd done something to hurt herself, or worse. Whatever, from then on Mum got help. Brilliant help. And it wasn't just Mum who was in pieces. Dad had lost his sister, so he was broken too. It was the first time I'd seen a man cry. Men never cry in Swindon – unless England go to penalties.

At first someone came to see Mum every week. His name was John, he was great for her, and she was grateful to him. She accepted help because she knew she needed it, knew she wasn't coping. Often she just went to bed – I remember her being in bed a lot of the time. When the one-on-one therapy ended she started going to group therapy, and I think that was amazing for her too. Foremost because it got her out of the house. At group therapy there were all these different people with all these different problems that simultaneously opened up Mum's world and closed it down. She wasn't alone, and she wasn't the worst. There was one woman who was so scared of flies that she spent all day spraying her house with insecticide and wouldn't go out. As she tells the story, one day she was cured. It sounds miraculous, but it wasn't – it had taken two long years. By the time Mum was back on her feet I was collecting the kids from school, making their dinner, feeding them, playing with them, bathing them, brushing their teeth and putting them to bed. Don't get me wrong – I loved those kids, they were my playthings. I would bribe them with chocolate and they would let me dress them up and give them parts in my plays. I was forever dressing them up. At Halloween I'd do all their make-up and help design their look and Nan, who makes wedding dresses and prom dresses, would make these incredible outfits out of a bit of green nylon. We'd play games – it's amazing what you do when you don't have alcohol or computer games. There was no internet – we were active ourselves. Looking back on it I realize that Mum's depression bonded me to the kids, but in a weird way it also separated me from my parents. But even that is over-simplifying the situation. My brother and sisters and I weren't a unit because I was constantly being singled out. I was the oldest, the grown-up one, the responsible one, so actually I wasn't being grouped with my siblings but with the adults. Was I a child with adult responsibilities? Or an adult in a child's body?

Mum says one of the worst things she did was to give me the video *In Bed with Madonna* to watch while I was still very young, just so she could have a break while the other kids were asleep. She knew well enough that anything with Madonna in it would keep me quiet for hours. I loved Madonna. She was my absolute idol, and later I copied her work ethic. But Mum didn't realize how horrible that video was because she hadn't vetted it. She remembers me coming into the kitchen and saying, 'Mum, what's Madonna doing with that bottle?' She was horrified and never let me watch it again. Which I then couldn't understand, since I'd already seen it. I think my position in life became a bit confused, and I ended up in no man's land. I can't blame everything on the kids, or on Mum's depression – even before all that I was out of step with my own age group. I wasn't into the normal stuff kids were into. I never played with Barbies, except for a short but fun affair with them when I was eleven. I wasn't doing Stikkle brick or Lego or Meccano, Sindy or My Little Pony – I didn't do any of it. My time was taken up with dance classes, drama classes and the kids.

I was doing some form of dancing – tap, jazz or modern – at least three nights a week. I loved squeezing myself into a shiny Lycra cat-suit, scraping my hair up into a high pony-tail, and limbering up like I'd seen the real dancers do at Pineapple. I'd spend the whole of Sunday making up routines to Madonna and Prince for my family's delectation. In fact I distinctly remember rewarding myself for my hard work with little tea breaks. I'd get the first verse and the chorus down, then give myself a Kitkat break, then go back for the next verse. Work and treat. Work and treat. I thought the world worked like that.

From the age of seven to twelve – the mad-house years – Saturday morning was dedicated to drama class. I was absolutely committed to it. The drama class that I'd begged Mum and Dad to send me to after doing the Coolaid commercial was the utterly brilliant Swindon-based 6th Sense. It was run by the wonderful Julia Dickenson, to whom I owe an enormous thank you. I loved dancing, but I began to realize that my heart belonged to acting. It came to me naturally, and once again I fell hard and fast in love – with the teachers and with my fellow drama students, in both my age group and the set above. Especially the set above. Not only could I escape from my home life with screaming kids and a mum who was permanently stressed out, I'd found something that I was getting praise for. I loved talking to the older kids about the plays we were reading, and I loved hearing them discuss films and their favourite actors.

People go to drama classes for many different reasons. Some go because they love showing off, others because their parents have run out of ideas and need to exhaust their exuberant, high-energy kids. Yet others go because it's like therapy for them, an escape. I went because I wanted to act. I know it sounds mad, because I was so young, but I really did love anything to do with drama, dressing up and performing. Yes, I probably was a bit of a show-off too, and had inexhaustible energy ready to throw at the task, and I loved the feeling of being part of a bigger, older family. So I was a combination of all three, but more than anything I wanted to learn the craft. There were people there who were passionate about the theatre. I felt comfortable in their company and I could be with them on my own terms. Like any keen kid with their heart set on the stage, I watched films over and over again, read plays, dreamed in scenes and acts. At drama class we talked endlessly about those plays and films and no one would laugh at my thoughts and interpretations. Being different was something to be encouraged, enhanced, and I basked in that kind of response. I come from a family where praise is thin on the ground, so it was a bit of a revelation to do something well and be applauded for it. At home I was competing for attention, but at 6th Sense I stood out.

Home life went on in its usual happy, child-centred, chaotic way, and to balance it out I made sure there was order in my bedroom. When I wasn't with the kids, dancing or acting, I was rearranging my room. My favourite time to clean and rearrange it was during the Top 40. Mum would often have to come in to retrieve the cleaning products that I'd stolen to do the skirting boards with.

I used to display everything I owned as if it was in a shop window – I thought my room was Laura Ashley or the Body Shop. My china dolls sat, immaculately dressed, on a shelf above my bed. When I started babysitting in the evenings I loved it because I had the house to myself and got paid. I would put the kids to bed and then maybe a friend would come over and we'd stay up and watch scary movies and terrify the life out of ourselves. But after I saw Stephen King's *The Dolls* I was never able to look at my collection of dolls in quite the same light again – I thought they were going to kill me. Every night I used to take all my teddies into bed with me but the dolls remained up on the shelf. After watching that film, though, I was convinced they were actually staring down at me thinking, 'Why aren't we allowed in the bed too?' and they were going to get their revenge. I brought one down, but it wasn't enough. In the end I was sleeping with twelve china dolls in my bed.

I was pretty weird about my bed, too. I had the most beautiful pine four-poster that Dad had bought for me when I was little, with curtains made by my aunt, which made me feel like a princess. I used to spend hours making it with proper hospital corners. When my friends came round I'd make them sit cross-legged on the floor because I didn't like my bed getting creased. Did I do all this because there was chaos in the house, or is it in the genes? My mum and gran are both very houseproud, so I don't know.

When Ellie, my youngest sister, turned two I started to take her everywhere with me. She was my real doll. She used to sneak into bed with me and I'd wake up and she'd be sucking her thumb and stroking her eyelashes, just staring at me through her huge green eyes. We were best mates for a while. I don't know what it did to her when suddenly I wasn't there. I've never asked. I daren't. She was such a gorgeous kid, a really lovely child, and everyone adored her. When I took her into town I'd pretend she was my own baby, which didn't look out-of-place in Swindon. Women having children young was common around there. My mum was twenty-one when I was born, and her mum was even younger. But I must have grown out of all this maternal stuff after practising on Ellie, because by the time I started at secondary school I wanted to break out of the cycle and out of Swindon.

# Lynx Africa

## A Comprehensive School

Like all my other friends, at the age of eleven I left primary school and went to Bradon Forest Comprehensive. It's the school we all wanted to go to. In fact all the Year Sixes dotted around Swindon wanted to go there. I don't know why – it was word of mouth, I suppose. My dad wanted me to go to another school, but as usual I was adamant about what I was going to do. It had a great drama department and a space they used as a theatre. But it was also out in the sticks in Perton, half an hour on the bus. That was the bit I hated. It was a time for bullies, a time to be picked on and intimidated. I thought prefects were there to protect us, but it turned out they were just sixteen-year-old arseholes with too much power. The only bullies on the bus were them. With hindsight I would now say that the two most empowering things to give a human being are a clipboard and a badge. Once you've got either of those two you feel as though the world is your oyster, yours to rule. Well, the prefects ruled the bus, and made all our lives a misery.

They sat at the back and would pick on one of us every day. There were all these little kids climbing on to the bus, trying to keep themselves to themselves. Then one of them would get picked out and the prefects would make her get up in front of everyone else. Some of the kids would laugh nervously along with this bullying because they were supposed to, but most of us just stared into our laps. Some got picked on more than most. There was this one kid with terrible eczema, who was also a Jehovah's Witness. That combination is lethal, a bully's idea of heaven, and what was so awful was that we couldn't do anything about it because we were just as terrified ourselves. I *wanted* to stand up to them but, like all the other kids, in the end I was just grateful it wasn't me that day. It was the first time I was aware of feeling compassion, and of feeling that there were forces beyond my control. I got away lightly considering I could have given Frida Kahlo a run for her money and my mouth was bigger than Wookey Hole. Luckily I soon found a group of friends, and from then on I was safe.

Going to secondary school was a strange time. I was so looking forward to it. I thought it meant freedom, that I was going to be liberated from a house full of small children and be among older kids whom I looked up to and respected. And I so wanted to be part of it. What I didn't realize is that you get picked on, rejected and excluded, bigger kids take your money and you get blamed for things you haven't done. I heard the rumours about the terrible things that were done to new kids, but I didn't really believe them. Then sure enough, day one, someone ended up with their head down the loo while it was being flushed. It was a massive smack in the face, a massive wake-up call. On my first day I was sick with fear. It was my brother's first day at school too. Primary school. There is a picture of us which says more about the contrast than any words. I am straight and stiff, hiding under my fringe, next to my brother who clearly can't wait to get there, looking so confident, all smiles and bravado, with his jumper tied around his waist.

I had one best friend from primary school who ended up at Bradon with me. She had an older sister who was part of a really cool crowd of beautiful girls. The look at the time was all about scraped-back hair and scrunchies, from which carefully selected strands would hang like tampon strings down the side of your face. The other look was the stiff quiff. Our fringes were held up with so much Harmony hairspray that in the end we didn't need it – they just stood up on their own. We spent hours fraying our ties like the big girls and carefully dabbing Tippex on to them to look like accidental splodges. A lot of work went into that look. I managed to get in with this group through the sister link and it was there that I met Sally Price, who was to become my very best friend. Sally was my age but she'd been hanging out with this bunch of older girls since she was about nine. She was like that – way ahead of her years – and I was pulled into her orbit. Anything to seem older than I was. Sally was always going to be the rebel out of us all. She'd always be the one to bring the booze and the fags. She'd always know where the party was. She was a lovely girl and, though I liked her because she was a bit mad and a bit out there, I also recognized that she was a sweet person underneath it all.

Sally's parents were a lot less strict then my own and if you can do anything you like at that age, you will. I had Dad to protect me from myself – hated it at the time, of course, but I'm grateful for it now. Sally's parents, on the other hand, were divorced. She had learnt the fine art of playing one parent off against the other, and most of the time she wasn't where they thought she was. Her dad was always at work so we used his amazing house as a party venue. He was well-off, Sally's dad, and had bought an old farmhouse outside Swindon. It had been derelict for ages and a group of hippies or a cult had got in and squatted there. If you lifted the carpet up in one of the rooms there was a huge ouija board painted on the floor – we spent hours playing with it and trying to raise the spirits. It was actually quite a weird house anyway, even without the hippie touches. Her dad did house clearances after people had died, so the place was full of the strangest clutter: make-up from the twenties, stuffed animals, huge chests. But it also had a swimming pool. On Friday nights Sally and I would put on *Immaculate Collection* and dance around it. There was a bar next to the house and we'd pour ourselves glasses of Pernod and drink shots like we'd seen in *Raiders of the Lost Ark*. It was really fun. Over the next few years it got increasingly out of control as we progressed from wine and Pernod to smoking bongs and doing 'hot knives' (where we stuck resin on to the end of a knife, burnt it and inhaled the smoke directly – very good for the concentration). Then it was poppers. It sounds sordid, but it wasn't. We weren't escaping anything – we were experimenting – we were doing it because we wanted to, because it was fun. It was innocent.

After the initial fear of the bus I really enjoyed it at Bradon Comp. and felt very grown-up. I loved being able to have a burger at tuck at ten in the morning. Sitting in the canteen, chatting between lessons, felt like you were in *Grease*. Of course, what energy we had left after spraying our hair and Tippexing our ties went on the boys. Whose mad idea was it to put girls and boys together at a time of hormone rush just as you need to start taking education seriously? What would I rather do? Long division, or write boys' names on my bags, notebooks, pencil case and any other surface I could find? And how important was stationery back then? And wait, what about the joy of a new geometry set? Protractor, compass, 15 cm ruler, crappy pencil and a rubber that never worked – blue and grey, I mean *really* blue and grey. Of course it was going to leave a mark on the page. But did I care? No. As long as it all sat neatly in the box, each item in its allocated space. Sheer joy to someone as anally retentive as me. And what was the triangle thing called? I never knew.

Far, far more exciting than even stationery were the boys.

You knew you'd arrived when one of them wrote your name on their hand with a compass point. That was great. Especially when it scabbed over – then they could pick it, so it would leave a small pink scar of your name on their skin. Great for us. Not so great for the boys, since so many of their hands got infected. But it was a time of rejoicing. Yes! He carved my name in his flesh! It was such good fun. Your friendships were so solid. Your mates meant the world. Secrets and dramas filled your waking hours. I was having a great time – but I was still set on leaving.

Sally and I got involved with the drama department straight away. She had an incredible voice – still does, despite smoking twenty B&H a day from the age of twelve. I only had to listen to Sally to know that singing wasn't my strong point, but it didn't matter because acting was my thing. I got on really well with the drama teacher, who was extremely encouraging, over the top and as an added extra one of the fittest male teachers at the school. He inspired me. Once he wanted us to do a book reading at the local library – in fact he wanted us to turn it into a play and script it. So we adapted the story and performed it. It was a great success. The thought of adapting something now fills me with terror, but back then I wasn't held back by self-doubt or self-criticism. I just threw myself into it, like everything I did back then. Drama was the one thing I was consistent at, concentrated on, committed to. I hoped it was my future.

I didn't tell anyone at school I'd been in an advert or anything like that because Mum and Dad had told me from the very beginning to keep those things under my hat. I was already being picked out quite often to play the lead in school plays, and they didn't want me to make it worse for myself, to bear the brunt of too much envy. They just wanted me to have a happy time at school.

There are so many things I remember about school: the smell of a Bunsen burner, the smell of ink ingrained in the skin, the smell of crisps on my friend's hands – Monster Munch and Space Raiders I remember particularly, at ten pence a bag. But the most vivid smell of all – no, not cabbage, though that was the underscore for all the other aromas – but Lynx Africa. My God, those boys must have soaked themselves in it! It was everywhere. Occasionally you'd walk through a mist of Joop, Charlie Red, ! or White Musk from the Body Shop, but Lynx Africa hung like the LA smog in the corridors, enveloping them all.

On the weekend you'd get wind of a house party and seek it out. Sally and I once stole two bottles of red wine from her dad's cellar. I was worried, but I remember her words of reassurance: 'He won't miss them – he's got loads.' We drank them on the way to the party. Of course once I got there I promptly puked up. In fact I spent the rest of the night spewing and finally passed out in one of the rooms. A low point. But not as low as when their cat, who was deaf and blind, came and spewed on me too. And then there were under-eighteen discos, 'nappy nights' with crappy live acts. No alcohol was on sale at them, but obviously that didn't stop some of us smuggling it in.

My best male friend from Bradon Comp. was Rob. We became friends when we bumped into each other in the hallway. He said, 'I heard your name was Cookie.' And that was that. Friends for life. He has such a good spirit – he's so excited by life. I think we had a bit of a crush on each other for a while, but I was in Year One and he was in Year Four, so 'Wha'cha gonna do?' On one occasion when Dad wouldn't give me the money to go to a nappy night Rob posted five quid through my letter box in coppers, plus twenty Lambert and Butler. What a mate! Everyone loved Rob – Mum and Dad would have loved it if something had happened between us – but I was about to discover a whole new world. First love.

# First Love

## A Shopping Precinct

David wasn't like other boys I knew. He wasn't into football, didn't idolize Eric Cantona. He was a bit chubby, a bit aloof – a bit weird, I suppose. Savvy. He didn't fancy girls with big tits who'd started their periods. (I don't know why starting your periods was so important to the boys, but it was. Kind of ruled me out as girlfriend potential since I didn't start mine until I was fifteen and my nickname was Toblerone Tits. I wanted a bra to hide the triangles, but Mum said bras were for women.) Anyway, I was seeing a bit of David because of his sister, my mate Sally, and we were getting on well. There's a strange moment when you fancy someone and they fancy you and you both realize that you want to talk to that person and to no one else. One day after school I was watching him spit crisps at a wall, and shortly after that I asked him out. Going out basically meant snogging your face off at lunch, 'twosing' up on an Embassy down the bottom of the field and doing naughty things because he did.

It was a very strange time to be a young woman. Part of me still wanted to play with my secret Barbie collection, but I was old enough to kiss boys. I was bridging the gap between childhood and adulthood, and sometimes it was a painful stretch. When I first read a Judy Bloom novel I was so relieved to find a voice that I understood – and that understood me. Mum and Dad weren't happy about David and me. Dad thought David was trouble. And in Dad's defence, I did start messing around. We'd bunk school, spend hours avoiding the prefects, more hours sitting outside Asda smoking Lambert and Butler's and Embassy Number One. Once Sally got over the weirdness that I was going out with her brother we became an inseparable threesome.

David and I were true love. We did everything and went everywhere together. He became the main man in my life, and he didn't ground me or tell me off but held my hand and stroked my face. My favourite things were being held in spoons or lying close and staring at one another. We'd groom each other like a pair of monkeys. We could touch each other anywhere and it was OK. This was the first time I stopped thinking about my family and about my immediate world. The first time I stopped listening to my dad. In fact it was the first time I saw my dad as a bad person. It cut him up so much that I was going out with this guy, even though he was friends with David's father. Dad saw arsehole potential in my new boyfriend and often had him up against the wall. David was big into smoking resin – we couldn't afford weed – so I started getting into it too. There was this farm with a big tube tyre-swing where masses of kids from Swindon would go and hang out, and for some reason the farmer didn't mind. He kept some static caravans on the farm and me and a group of mates all chipped in and rented one so that we could go there and toke on bong for hours. We just laughed our heads off and enjoyed taking the piss out of each other, finding our senses of humour and discovering how we fitted in. For all of us it was our first official circle of mates, and that first feeling of love for my friends made me high with excitement. That and the soapbar hash.

I would be with David all day at school until cut-off at nine, and then we'd speak on the phone for hours. We used to fantasize about getting out of Swindon, living together, having babies and getting married. The fantasy that a man would rescue me from my home life and provide a better one was powerful. My man would never turn bad, never leave me for his mates and hang out in the pub, never drink too much or raise his hand in anger. He would always love me as he loved me now. David and I both believed in this fantasy. I wasn't the first woman to fall for that old chestnut. Nor was I the last.

Part of me wanted my own little family, something to nurture and love and take care of, and I also wanted someone to be good to who would love me unconditionally.

I thought I could get it right and that David was the perfect person to get it right with. He would never have an affair. He always chose me over his Umbro-clad posse – we were a pair of soppy gits. I thought it would be different for us. And nothing would change that.

Sally, David and I spent a lot of time sneaking out to the field for a cheeky fag, and eventually I did get busted for skipping school. Dad wasn't impressed. As I said, because he had had no real education himself he was a tyrant when it came to his kids' schooling. He expected good results and no excuses. Missing school was bad, but not as bad as smoking, something that both Mum and I were doing behind his back. He hated smoking, my dad – except for his odd cigar. I was forever being grounded, or so it felt. For her thirteenth birthday I took Sally out to the Chinese Experience, a huge restaurant set on a lagoon in the new part of Swindon. I spent my entire contact lens allowance on this special evening. Sally was finally a teenager so we got smashed. We went straight to the top shelf and enjoyed many scotch on the rocks – God knows how we got served. Anyway, of course, when Dad asked me about where I'd been – slightly teasing, tongue in cheek – I lied. Unbeknownst to me, his mate had seen us falling all over the tables. Once again I got grounded. Those were the sort of games Dad would play with me. He'd always try and make a grounding a bit of a laugh. For him, anyway.

Comedy was the last thing on *my* mind when I got busted with cigarettes. I wanted to stay at home to intercept the letter that the school were sending my parents to inform them that I'd been caught smoking, so I burnt my head on the radiator to make Mum think I had a temperature. I remember once listening to her on the phone talking to my aunt when my cousin got meningitis – she said his eyes were rolling into the back of his head. Rather than thinking, 'Shit, my cousin's really ill', I thought, 'Great! Now I know how to freak out the parents.'

I needn't have gone through the trouble, because, as with everything else during that time in my life, I confided in Mum. And then for some reason she told Dad, even though she'd started sneaking fags herself. She could be vicious at times and would get me into trouble, but, looking back on it, we were maybe just competing for Dad's attention. I don't know. If I was his princess, what was Mum? Still, I was furious with her. It was just so hypocritical – but then I was only twelve, so I guess she had a point. It certainly underlined the ambiguity of my relationship with my mother. Sometimes she was the sibling, sometimes the parent, sometimes the friend, sometimes the enemy.

Dad was furious about the smoking and I was grounded for six weeks. He wouldn't let me out of the house even though it was summer, really hot, and I was in the garden trying to entertain myself as well as the kids. I could see my mates walking to the bus stop and shouting, 'Are you coming to the Cricklade Street party?' But I couldn't go. I'd cry every day but he stuck to his guns. I hated him because of it, and Mum was shouting at me for getting under her feet – which I was, nagging her to get Dad to change his mind. I should have known better. Dad is strict and there was no way he'd go back on his word, and since he was out of the house most of the day it didn't make any difference to him anyway.

By then I was also beginning to steal things – very badly, mind you. I'm easily led (I know it's no excuse), but I was hanging out with girls who shoplifted and I thought I'd give it a go. The most I ever stole was a sticker. Everybody else was stealing lip liner, but I was too scared of getting caught. It took me about an hour to pluck up the courage and then, just as I put it under my shirt, my Uncle Danny walked in and I thought I was going to pass out.

Up until that time I was still going to all my dance and drama classes, which covered almost every night of the week. While my friends were out getting drunk after school, I was often at a class. But during that first year at Bradon Forest I had started to tire of acting because the girls didn't think it was cool. And I wanted to be with David, I wanted to hang out with the tube crowd, or go to nappy night with my friends. Eventually I told Mum I didn't want to do drama any more. She said, 'Please, Bill, stick it out,' and urged me to do one more year: 'Just so you can look back and remember what you've achieved.' Maybe she was talking from experience, maybe she saw drama as an anchor which would keep me from floating adrift as so many others did, maybe she knew I'd regret it because that was how she felt. Whatever it was, I listened. I completely attribute my continuing relationship with drama to my mother. She didn't let me lose interest when I so easily could have. In fact she taxied me around to all the classes, even though she was frantic with the kids. So the drama and the dancing continued – as did getting stoned in the caravan, bunking school, hanging out with my mates and generally testing the boundaries.

But slowly, as Mum and Dad had no doubt predicted, the emphasis on what was important in my life started to come full circle. I fell back in love with dancing and acting just as I started getting bored with the tube crowd and nappy nights, and even with David who was beginning to change. Hanging around outside McDonald's has its limits. I saw repetition ahead, and it scared the shit out of me. I started to feel trapped, fearing there was only one life available to me there, and I didn't want to do what everybody else was doing: be born, live and die in Swindon. I began to find that concept suffocating. Then two very significant things happened. David chucked me, and my drama teacher at 6th Sense showed me an advert for a stage school in a publication called *The Stage*.

Being chucked happened first, and I shall never forget the feeling. It was the first and worst time ever. It happened at the bus stop, and I was waiting for the number five bus when David told me it was over. I thought I wanted to die. It was the most painful thing I had ever experienced. I honestly thought there was no point in going on living. I didn't make it easy on myself. I immediately went out and bought the single of Annie Lennox's 'No More I Love You's', then proceeded to sit in my room and listen to it for two weeks. I shed many tears, but hey what's new? It drove my dad insane. I quite enjoyed indulging my misery. It wasn't healthy, but it wasn't uncommon either. My dad hated David even more now for making me so sad, even though he was pleased about the break-up.

Obsessed with my own heartache, I'd go into the chemist and spray myself with Africa Lynx to remind myself of him. Since every other girl was doing the same about her 'special someone', either because they were together or because she was mourning the end of the world as I was, everyone smelled the same. I would wear the clothes that David had given me to bed, and try to work out what he'd been thinking when he'd given those garments to me and why we weren't together. It took a while to work out that he probably hadn't been thinking anything except, 'She needs a T-shirt to wear.' I stayed in and listened to music: Eternal, Kylie (who was being a bit cool during her whole Michael Hutchinson phase), Chaka Demus and Pliers and any bad reggae compilation I could get my hands on. I was misery personified at home and finally, exasperated with me, Mum packed up the car and headed to Bournemouth for the holidays, hoping that a stint with the Rockley Babes would cheer me up.

# The Rockley Babes

## A Caravan Site on the South Coast – Sunny

Rockley Park is a static caravan site in Bournemouth, and from the time I was eleven we went on holiday there every year. Half the caravans were owned, as ours was, while the rest were rented out. It was right on the edge of a field overlooking the sea. With four kids there was no way we were going abroad for holidays any more – it was just too expensive. So we now went to Bournemouth for all our family holidays and, to quote one of my favourite films, I had 'the time of my life'. The owners of the site had their own separate swimming pool and, because we went there every year all the kids knew each other really well. Me and my mates were the queens of the caravan site, a bunch of fully made-up, tottering, hair-sprayed girls. Obviously there was a lot of talk about boys, a lot of batting those Maybelline-mascara'd eyelashes, but mostly we were just a group of girls loving each other. It was hot down there. Or so I remember. Then again, when you're young all summers seem to be long and hot.

The rented caravans got new blood every summer, and we'd meet people from all around the UK: cockneys, northerners, some oldies and hundreds of kids all piled on to this one site. It was very self-contained and safe down there, so Dad let me do what I wanted within the boundary of the site. Of course I did occasionally sneak out, but the positives vastly outweighed the negatives. Every year this big group of girls, gradually making our way to puberty, would sit around the pool chatting and laughing and listening to music, reading *More* magazine and staring open-mouthed at the position of the fortnight. It felt as though there was no better fun in the world to be had. Our gang became known as the Rockley Babes and oh, the tears at the end of the holidays! We'd all be crying our eyes out, hating the idea of being ripped apart by our evil parents and hideous school. We always wrote to each other during termtime and were so excited when the holidays came around again.

This was a whole separate part of my life, something away from the constraints of urban life, which encouraged us to be outside and active. By day we were playing Frisbee, catching crabs and playing basketball. By night there'd be cheeky fags, lots of 'getting off', occasionally giving a boy a hand job or letting a boy 'tit you up' . . . and, scandalously, there would be odd moments of heavy petting behind the swimming pool. But mostly it was about being part of a group of girls. At night the Rockley Babes would take the clubhouse by storm. We spent hours getting dressed up, back-combing and crimping our hair, putting on a face full of make-up – serious work went into our look. Occasionally we'd get pissed, sometimes we'd steal booze from our parents, sometimes we'd be with people who could legally buy alcohol. Alcopops did the rounds, of course, which was like drinking pop so that we could get pissed without having to taste the alcohol. After the clubhouse I'd share a fag with an eighteen-year-old northerner and think it was the coolest thing in the world.

It was my uncle who named our gang. Of course we loved it, and then as the years went on we really bought into it. Twelve blonde girls (some more assisted than others – oh, the joys of Sun-In), all the daughters of owners, spending all our money on making ourselves pretty. But we weren't a *real* gang – there was nothing aggressive about us. We were sweet to everyone's grannies, we weren't bullies, we weren't rude and we knew everyone by name. We even knew the security guys. We *especially* knew the security guys – it was with them that we had the cheeky fags. Smoking was our thing. It made us feel grown-up and sophisticated. Also it punctuated our evenings – each cigarette was a massive operation. I remember eating lip balm when I didn't have gum to chew to disguise the smell, and once I had neither and scoffed a load of leaves. Dad had all these techniques for testing me which I was quite aware of – like making me sit on his knee and talking to me really closely. We outwitted one another, but he always won in the end.

There was a guy at the caravan site called Tim, who was older than me. He looked like the Marlboro man, perfect for healing a broken heart. He'd come and go and I'd always be waiting for him – he was my Mr Big. I could see that he thought it was weird and that I was too young. But also that maybe he secretly wanted to play too – he was only a few years older than me, after all. It wasn't that bad, but it was frustrating. I'd be the one sitting there trying to convince him it was OK. Everyone else was snogging boys their own age, but I'd always be lusting after the guys at the bar with the pints. I soon realized that older boys weren't mean, and didn't tease you and say evil things like the boys my age did. Older guys were nice – they had so much more going on that they didn't have the time to be rude – and they were interesting, a fascinating study. I'd been hanging out with older people so perhaps it was just what I was used to, or perhaps it was something to do with hero-worshipping a dad who was away a lot, or even perhaps it was because I was growing up fast. Sometimes I tried to lie about my age and wore my gold £18 Miss Selfridge dress when I went out with the rest of the Rockley Babes. I loved that dress, but it left nothing to the imagination. It was way too much for Dad – he sent me home from the clubhouse to change. He needn't have worried: Rockley Park was the perfect place for his daughter to spend a safe, fun and carefree adolescence.

When I went home at the end of the holidays I had to see

David all the time through Sally and at school. He'd jumped on the bandwagon of lusting after girls with tits, and that upset me even more because I was still flat as a pancake. But I had a ploy to get him back: I was always wearing really sexy clothes whenever our paths crossed. I distinctly remember a boob tube I bought for eight quid from Pilot because I saw him looking hard at me, and I thought, 'Hey, this works!' But luckily before the boob tube had a chance to work its magic and redirect my attention my drama teacher had shown me that tiny advert I mentioned earlier. Talented young people were being invited to audition for a scholarship to go to stage school, a place where I could dance and act every day. A new obsession took over.

I owe a great deal to Julia Dickenson of 6th Sense, who was rooting for me from day one. She knew how passionate I was, while Mum and Dad probably only saw the acting thing more as a hobby, a way to keep me off the streets. I hadn't known the magazine called *The Stage* existed, or I would have asked for a subscription for my birthday. According to this ad, I could do all the time what I loved most in the world. Absolutely hooked, I ran home and showed my mum. I started to pray about going to drama school – it became my religion and the inside of my head turned into a whole world full of plays and performances and standing ovations. As so often before, I badgered until finally my parents acquiesced. So we sent off the forms and waited anxiously for further instructions. Eventually we received a reply. I could audition for a scholarship place.

All I had to do was perform a classical acting piece, a contemporary acting piece, one song and one dance. It seems quite full on for a thirteen-year-old, but back then I could have done five of each in five different accents. I was a kid on a mission, and Mum and Dad's encouragement, Julia Dickenson's tutoring and my own tenacity were about to pay off.

# And Now for Something Completely Different

## Sylvia Young Theatre School for the Perversely Dramatic

When the audition day arrived I went up to London on the train with Mum. I had rehearsed with Julia twice a week at her house for the previous month, and was quietly confident. Without a boyfriend to fill my time and thoughts, I had dedicated myself wholly to the cause. Julia's support gave me that extra bit of self-belief that I needed to make this giant leap. I was nervous about the academic exams in the morning, though. I knew I wasn't at my best in the straight subjects, and I was absolutely sure I wouldn't get in on maths, science or French – I had a habit of going blank the minute I had to apply myself in that area. Sitting those morning exams was hellish, but somehow I managed to get through them. And the best was yet to come.

With the taxing stuff over, I almost ran to the auditioning room. Then suddenly everything changed, and fear came and gripped me. We all had to stand in a queue outside the main studio, but you could hear everything that was going on through the doors. These girls with epic voices were going in one after another after another. It was like standing next to a string of Bette Midlers all singing 'Tomorrow' or the ballad from The Little Mermaid. I remember looking at the girls standing either side of me and thinking, 'I've got Etta James behind me and Whitney Houston in front of me. I have no chance.' My piece was 'Where Is Love' from Oliver, and I knew before I went in that it didn't hold up to 90 per cent of what I'd heard. It was awful. I don't know what we'd been thinking – it was far too high. Next it was dance, which was fine, then drama. For my classical I had chosen Helena's soliloquy from A Midsummer Night's Dream. I cannot remember for the life of me what I did for the modern. Didn't matter. As far as I was concerned I didn't have a hope in hell of getting in. And, frankly, nor did my parents think I would. I came home on the train despondent. I'd given it everything, now all I could do was pray.

On the day that the letter with the Sylvia Young crest on it arrived my dad gave it to me to open, even though it was addressed to them. I took it upstairs and sat on the floor – the bed was looking too good to sit on. Inch by inch I slowly opened it, then couldn't believe the words I was reading. I had a place! Not the full scholarship that I had wanted – only half the fees would be paid – but a bloody place nevertheless! Now I had to get my folks to let me go. And what a convincing performance that was. Even as I ran down the stairs screaming with excitement I was plotting how best to persuade them to pay for the rest. I knew they were prepared to spend some money on my education, but I wasn't sure if they could stretch to that. But I had no shame, no thought for the difficult situation I was putting them in. They had three other kids to consider, but I was begging them not to. Dad approached the matter as he approaches everything to do with business and money. Methodically. He got on the internet. He thought about boarding, but didn't want me to live with other people from school or with a family we didn't know. It was excruciating. We'd inch towards a yes, then lurch back towards no when Dad imagined me on the train alone, night after night. Then Mum had a brainwave.

Fortunately my mum's aunt and uncle, who lived on a council estate in Barnes in west London were used to taking in exchange students and other lodgers, so Mum rang them and sure enough they came through for us and said it would be fine for me to live with them.

Apart from that Mum and Dad hadn't really had a hand in any of it – it was Julia who had put me up for the scholarship. My parents had thought there was no chance I would get in. But after all the discussion, after all the to-ing and fro-ing, the fact was that I *had* got in. Between the two of them they decided I had done my bit, I had persevered, and now it was their turn. As Mum says: 'How could we tell Billie that she couldn't go because we couldn't afford the other half of the scholarship? She was having none of it – she was so determined. So of course we let her go and we found the money to pay for the other half, but it was bloody hard.' And it wasn't just half the fees they had to cover – it was my living expenses, my travel costs and my food. There was a uniform, too – I'd suddenly gone from buying it from Asda for twelve quid to having to fork out for a blazer with a crest.

I remember practising the journey that I would have to make to London every Monday morning and across London every day come September. My parents gave me a panic button and a rape alarm. First we'd do the journey together, then after a few times they'd let me do it on my own, with Mum waiting at one end of the platform and Dad at the other. Then they let me do it completely on my own. At the age of thirteen I started commuting to London every Monday morning and I wouldn't return home until Friday night. I remember sitting alongside hundreds of men and women in suits. I would stare at the tiny little columns of numbers on the pink pages of their giant newspapers, knowing that everyone on that train was striving towards their own goals. I liked that I was part of it, I don't remember feeling scared.

Mum thought I might hate it and was fully prepared to let me come home if I was too lonely – but she also knew that when you've been given a chance like that, a chance that doesn't come along very often, you take it. I don't think any of us were thinking of the consequences of attending a school like that. Maybe I'd stay there until graduation and then get a normal job back in Swindon. Maybe I wouldn't stick out the year. Maybe they weren't thinking at all. As Mum says, 'We never thought we shouldn't do this. To be honest, we were so busy with three other children that I didn't really think it through. With Billie away at school, there was one less person to worry about.' As far as she was concerned, I was being given a chance to follow my dreams and do what I passionately loved.

As for myself, I was so bloody happy that I was completely fearless. I wasn't scared of leaving or of telling my friends that I was going. I was still going to be home for the weekends and, since I'd never been allowed out in the week much anyway, it didn't feel that dramatic. Dad always liked me to spend time with the family even though he couldn't always be around. I was just really excited about starting drama school.

Sylvia Young's was a different world. It's a huge town house in Marylebone, converted into a school. The first three days of the week are given over to academic studies, and the last two days are vocational. Pretty much all of us gave only lip service to our academic studies: we longed to get out of science and into our tights. The school was full of kids with the same objective, ambitions and desires as me – and every single one of them set for stardom. I knew as soon as I got there that I had to raise my game. At 6th Sense I had been the only child who wanted what I wanted, and suddenly there were 120 kids who had the same dreams as I did. It was overwhelming. I felt I had to raise my game just to match them: only after that was it about bettering them. I wasn't alone – we were all thinking like that. Bubbling underneath everything all the time was the knowledge that to get to the top you had to be the best, and that meant beating your friends. It was very competitive and probably went against making friends. I did have friends, but not like the Rockley Babes. Not like Sally.

And as for the teachers, I'd never seen people like them. They would tell us tales of when they danced in *Cats*, worked the West End, did all the things that we really wanted so desperately to do. More recently I met a woman who was chaperoning a Sylvia Young girl on the set of the *Sally Lockheart Mysteries*, and apparently the teachers are still there telling the same old *Cats* stories and bursting into 'Macavity the Mystery Cat' at any given opportunity. There was Peter the pianist who played with a perpetual fag hanging out of his mouth, dropping ash all over the keyboard as he banged away. I had a crush on him, of course – he was older. Then there was Jackie Stoker, our LAMDA teacher (the prestigious London Academy of Music and Dramatic Art) – an eccentric fifty-year-old who'd throw your pencil case out of the window if you were caught playing with a pencil and not concentrating. She'd even throw chairs. She was brilliant, fiery and temperamental, but if you worked hard she gave you her everything. I'd never seen a teacher like her. At Bradon they'd all been so beaten down by life, by the system, that they no longer enjoyed being teachers. But these teachers were outstanding, and really wanted us to better ourselves.

There was so much brilliance at Sylvia Young's that for a moment I was dazzled. I'd lost my footing, my U.S.P. I had one girlfriend called Laura Evans who sang like Mariah Carey. She was humble and adorable and sweet. But those traits were rare. Most of the other girls were terrifying: they all looked great, and possessed the sort of Stevie Nicks hair you could sit on, with not a kink in sight. They had perfect fringes and perfect brows and talked about iambic pentameters with their perfect vowels. At that time I was still wholly unrefined. The mono-brow arced the width of my forehead – I hadn't even thought about changing what I had, or the way I looked. But I soon started to become more aware of weight and image. And I started to be aware of being popular, being liked. That had never been a problem before, but I felt like a right pikey compared to the Stevie Nicks girls. Looking back on it, I realize that what I was seeing for the first time was girls with some serious issues. My nonchalance for my own appearance soon changed. I noticed after about a week of being there that the girls just didn't eat. In fact they'd go to the toilet to escape the smell of food wafting out of the canteen. There were kids walking around with ankle weights strapped to their legs and no one would say anything. Girls were instructed by their parents to eat carrot sticks at lunch and drink soya milk – I had no idea what soya milk was. Along with Granola bars and smoothies, it was all new to me. I felt common as muck when I joined that school. I felt like I belonged on a caravan site. And you know what? I did.

The parents who would accompany us on outings were so different from my own. When I was doing shows in Swindon my mum and dad might drop me off, go for a pint and a fag and then pick me up with a cursory, 'How was it?' I never got a grilling about whether I'd put a foot wrong, etc. None of that. They weren't pushy, living vicariously through their children. Mum wasn't a beauty pageant mother. No way. She wasn't ambitious for me, I was ambitious for myself. This was a whole new world plus I'd never seen money like it. There were these extraordinary rich women who fancied the idea of their child being famous and had limitless funds to finance it. Suddenly I was surrounded by children who were being pushed rather than pushing themselves, though I suppose it amounts to the same thing and the disappointment surely feels the same.

Of course there were cliques, and of course I wanted to be a member of the long straight-haired gang, the bitchiest of the bitches. I would lie in bed at my great-aunt's dreaming about being part of their crowd. I would find my way in, plotting, planning and executing my manoeuvres, a shameless cling-on. Life is full of people who you think have something special about them, who hold themselves above the rest of us, but when you get up close you realize that they are actually quite bland and have very little to offer. When I think of the planning that went into joining that crowd, I don't know why I bothered. I haven't seen one of them since. Eventually I did settle with a couple of my own friends – older than me, naturally – called Ebony and Emma. They were fun, normal and keen, like I was.

Some of the girls scared me because they were so leery, so rich, so superior. There were no rules with them – they didn't seem to give a shit. The school was already pretty lax and you could get away with a lot of bad behaviour, but they were off the scale. It took me a while to realize that the reason why they were there was less to do with fulfilling their dreams and more to do with their parents having no other options. I was staggered when I saw one pupil pinching a teacher's bum. Having been in the naughty set in Swindon, I now retreated from that crowd. I knew how much this school was costing Mum and Dad and I wasn't going to piss it away. And, as always, Dad expected good exam results in all subjects, not just in dance.

Not only was it the first time I had met kids who came from a background of shitloads of money, I also now met my first camp kids, black kids, Asian kids, cockney kids. Suddenly a guy would come up to me and touch my hair and say, 'I really like what you've done with your colour.' I was amazed – I'd never knowingly met a gay person before. But for all the wonders of these new experiences, the school knocked me at first. I'd gone from being a big fish in a small pond straight to the deep, wide ocean. Not even a fish any more – just an amoeba. I didn't think I could manage it. I knew from the audition I wasn't the strongest of singers, and suddenly my dancing, which had been my second strongest subject up to that point, went haywire. I think it started in ballet, which had never been my best area of dance – I was a tap, modern and jazz girl. I certainly wasn't built like a ballerina. And boy, did I feel it there. I was constantly being told I should be lighter, smaller, thinner, longer . . . it freaked me out. That trickled into my other dance classes. I had always been a strong street dancer, but suddenly I lost my bottle in that too. The jazz shoes didn't last very long. Have you ever tried to street dance in jazz shoes? My brain wouldn't connect with my body. Routines that at one time I'd been able to do after seeing once I now couldn't get into my head at all. I'd been so looking forward to going to Sylvia Young's, but the first thing that school did was stifle me. Perhaps I needed to be stifled, I don't know. But it was going to take me a long time to rebuild my confidence and I needed help to do it. So I went home, where I could jump back into that small pond and regroup.

SCENE NINE:

# Cherry Picking

INT:

## A Haunted Room

David and I got back together, all the more ardent for our painful split. I was so happy he loved me again that I didn't really question my motives. You can imagine how happy Dad was about that. I'd cried my eyes out over David. I'd told Dad all about the horrible things he'd done to me, then I expected him to forgive and forget and welcome my boyfriend back with open arms. Not bloody likely. My mates, however, were delighted. It was strange: in a way, everyone else took ownership of our relationship. We were their love mascot – we'd conquered splits and separations – and it was all ridiculously dramatic, as everything is at that age. For some reason my friends and I decided that David and I would finally do the deed. We were going to have sex on New Year's Eve upstairs in his dad's bedroom while all our friends sat downstairs and waited. Bonkers, but I loved him. I was thirteen. And a quarter.

We went upstairs and lay on the bed, wondering how we should go about it, neither of us wanting or knowing how to initiate it. I got cold feet lying there. Not literally – I think I was still fully dressed. But I just looked at him and said, 'I'm so scared.' It was such a relief when he said he was too. I told him I didn't want to do it and he said he didn't either, then we lay on the bed talking about it for an hour or so. Still fully clothed.

Finally I said, 'What are we going to say to the people waiting downstairs?'

'Let's lie,' said David.

So that's what we did. We went downstairs and lied. In fact we parted company, I to the girls, he to the boys to discuss what had happened. Sally was asking me what it was like, and I told them it really hurt because that was what I'd heard the big girls say. I think we all got pissed then. It was New Year's Eve 1996–7 and I ended up back at my parents' house being sick, which was a sorry beginning to what would be an enormous year.

I never even told Sally that we'd lied. Actually I didn't have to, because soon afterwards David and I did have sex. It was spontaneous and unplanned. In fact it was on the floor, surrounded by antiques, in a room we were sure was haunted. All I really remember was feeling really little and cold. It hadn't hurt like I thought it would, but it wasn't all that great either. Anti-climax? Certainly. We were only

Kick starting my pop career.

Sylvia Young Theatre School

HEADTEACHER: M. T. MELVILLE. B.A., CERT.ED., L.R.A.M.

Rossmore Road
Marylebone
London NW1 6NJ
071-402 0673
Fax No. 071-723 1040

Sylvia Young *Director*

### Audition Report:  Billie Piper – D.O.B. 22/09/82

**Stage Scholarship 1995 – 5 & 10 March**

**For entry to Year 8 September 1995**

**Drama** – Billie performed an excerpt from "This Property is Condemned".  She used an American accent which was very good. She has a good voice, uses space well, has a very expressive face and shows excellent potential.

**Dancing** – Has good dance potential and would respond well to further training.

**Singing** – She sang "Where is Love?"  Her voice is clear, strong and she held the tune well.  Well presented. There is more to come.

**Appearance** – She has an interesting face, rather beautiful and a good slim figure.

**English and maths test**  – She shows average ability.   This is backed up by her school reports which put her at level 4 in English.

**General comments** – Billie comes across as a pleasant, hard-working girl with a real desire to train in the performing arts.   She has talent and would respond very well to training. Excellent potential.

*M.T. Melville*   22nd June 1995

*Proprietor:* SYLVIA YOUNG THEATRE SCHOOL LTD.   Regd. No. 1812483   *Directors:* SYLVIA YOUNG, N. A. RUFFELL, M. H. SHELTON
*Registered Office:* 12 PETERBOROUGH ROAD, HARROW, MIDDLESEX

My audition report from Sylvia Young's.

kids and we didn't have a clue about what we were doing. In January I went back to drama school. David and I would cling to one another when I was home at the weekends, then I'd leave again. It felt like such a grown-up relationship. I had a man in my life, a man I could depend on, a man who was all mine and who loved me. We'd have crazy fights when it felt the whole town was getting involved, but mostly it was me, Sally and David having a laugh. The New Year of 1997 was good to me. At Sylvia Young's I slowly began to find my feet, and a new kind of ambition took hold. An ambition to be better than my peers. An ambition to be the best.

I used to come home on Friday night and, as ever, tell Mum all about it. It was her favourite night of the week, with Dad at the pub and the kids in bed. It was Mum's and my night and it was such fun. We'd put records on, sing, dance and do some acting. I'd tell her all about school and what we'd been doing, and all about strange new characters I was meeting, and we'd end up on her bed rolling around with laughter. It was all good, and she was happy that I was doing what I wanted to do. I think she missed me, but not that much. Not because she didn't care – she did – but because, she was just so darn busy with the kids.

Ambition worked its way into my consciousness slowly but once it was there, like every new dream, it took hold. I honestly didn't go to that school with the intention of getting famous. I was there because I could act every day. The burning desire came later, as my confidence grew and the competitiveness of the place got to me. My innocent desire to act was replaced by a calculated need for recognition. I wanted to be Sylvia's favourite, I wanted to be the one called up by an agent for auditions, I wanted to own a Filofax and compare gigs and dates like the others, and I always wanted to be chosen to perform leads in the school plays. I wasn't the lead very often, and I felt robbed every time. Nothing like a bit of rejection to get your hackles up.

I had started off as this really goofy kid with huge eyebrows, lank, mousy hair and big features that I hadn't grown into. But because of what I'd witnessed, I started to manage my own image a lot more. My Molly Tanner 10 by 8s were replaced by the spotlight photos that Sylvia Young organized for all the students who were automatically run through the agency at the school. In fact that was probably why 'getting work' was constantly being drilled home to us. We were not there to be normal kids, we were there because we wanted to be part of the entertainment business. Emphasis on *business*. We wanted to learn, we wanted to improve on what we already had, but we wanted to get out there too. And when we did, we made the school a bit of extra money. We were paying the school fees, and they were taking a commission. And of course every Sylvia Young kid who made it propagated the reputation of the school. For the first few years my name appeared in the press the names of my fellow SY alumni were always listed next to mine. Denise Van Outen. Emma Bunton. The All Saints Girls. Samantha Janus. Dani Behr. Scott from 5ive. So by the time we had our new photographs taken I'd got with it. I'd finally plucked my

Getting ready for *Top of the Pops* with all my men!

On the road with
Nikki and Paula.

Celebrating a good year Down Under.

Backstage on the
*Smash Hits* roadshow.

Mum gets a
makeover backstage.

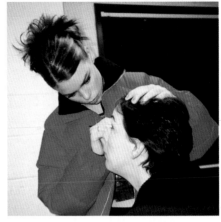

*Smash Hits'* Poll
Winners Party with
my perfect perm.

Happy days with
Rich. Boxing Day,
1999.

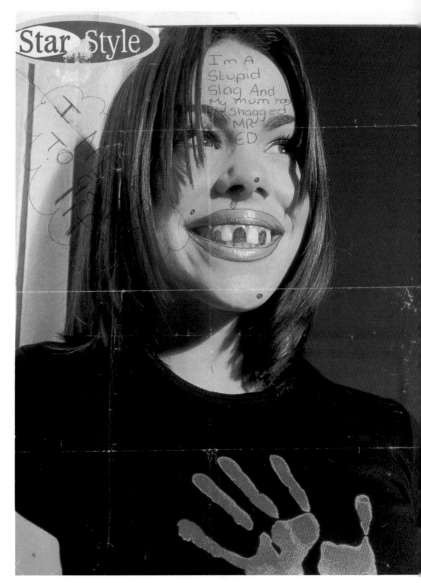

Hilarious hate mail.

Slipping into Old Faithful.

Leaving Titanic in a bit of a mess.

Back on *Top of the Pops* with 'Day and Night' at No.1.

Celebrating my 18th birthday.
'Dad, you're crushing me!'

On my way to
*TFI Friday*.

eyebrows and had my hair cut into a bob. I was looking much more appealing and a lot more sellable.

As if by magic, the calls started to come in. And as I got auditions I began to feel more capable, more confident, less like an impostor. I got into the drama school mind-set. I camped it up. I could be dramatic, tactile, over the top and no one told me off. In fact it was actively encouraged. We were almost coached to be cheeky to the teachers. It was all about sharp wit, showing off, grabbing the limelight. We'd even sing at lunchtime, and if there was no teacher to tell us to get off the table we'd be on it, out-shimmying one another. At times it was like *Fame*. Can you imagine a kid from Swindon dancing on tables, going to auditions, being picked for parts, owning that hallowed Filofax? It was beyond my wildest dreams, so once again my dreams changed accordingly. I wasn't getting lost in the crowd any more. In fact I started to stand out against the same kids who'd overwhelmed me in the beginning, and as soon as that happened the teachers took more notice. And it wasn't just the teachers. Somewhere in the offices of Emap a discussion was taking place about relaunching the magazine *Smash Hits* with a new young edge. They started looking for a face that would appeal to a generation, called the Sylvia Young agency and asked for some 10 by 8s. Sylvia sent mine.

There must have been something in the photos that fulfilled the criteria they had set because they phoned the agency and I was called for audition. But I hadn't really taken on board what it was all for. No one told me I had to be funky or trendy, so I just turned up in my grey pleated skirt and squeaky clean bright red V-neck school jumper. I walked into this room in my uniform and someone put on The Prodigy and told me to dance to it. So I did. In my uniform! I danced around to 'Firestarter' and the Spice Girls feeling like an absolute prize monkey. Had we known what the combination of a school uniform and a heavy bass could do, things might have turned out differently.

I got the job! I had a reason to get a diary! The teachers were really pleased for me and everything started to change. It was really beginning to happen. I couldn't quite believe it. I didn't tell my friends in Swindon about the *Smash Hits* ad because I didn't want them to think I was getting above myself. And I didn't tell my friends at Sylvia Young's that I'd had sex because I didn't want them to think I was beneath them. I already felt common as muck – these kids didn't go home and do hot knives and drink hooch and have sex, they went to festivals and put on shows. I started to feel less and less comfortable at home. I thought I had seen something different in David, but maybe he couldn't see it in himself. The curse of a little bit of money? Nothing compared to the kids at Sylvia Young's, but David wasn't exactly going hungry. His dad was doing OK. David was happy doing the same old thing, whereas I wanted to work. He had always partied harder than the rest of us and liked feeling out of control, but I was beginning to realize that work and getting stoned were mutually exclusive. I started to drift away and the bond started to fray.

From time to time David would go dark on me – cynical, negative and angry. It must have been hard for him, having this absent girlfriend. He never laid a finger on me or anything like that, but his words upset me. Trouble was I loved him so much that I forgave him. I told myself it wasn't really him, that I understood why it was happening. I think I just wanted him to love me like he had when we first started out. But I was kidding myself. One of the reasons I so wanted to get out of Swindon was that I had seen wonderful women turn weak by allowing inferior men to take over their lives. And here I was, doing the same thing. Why do you always think it's going to be different for *you*? We split again. Just about the time the call came from Emap that they'd chosen me to be the face of *Smash Hits*. I couldn't fucking believe it.

That campaign changed the course of my whole life, because somewhere in London another meeting was taking place in a coffee shop. The managing director and the A'n'R woman for a new label, Innocent, got out a piece of paper to list what it was they were looking for. He wrote, 'a new, exciting, solo female that we can turn into a British Madonna'. 'Young' didn't even come into it. They just wanted a solo act to put up against the tide of boy and girl bands that had swarmed into the industry. They weren't in any hurry, but they'd made a note to keep a look-out for someone who might fit the bill. Within days the *Smash Hits* campaign took off. Everyone says this business is as much about luck as talent; I'd say it's more so. The gods must have been looking favourably on me, because on 23 August 1997 that ad for *Smash Hits* was on the cover of *Music Week*. Every record producer in the land reads that magazine, which is how I came to be pointing my finger into the face of Hugh Goldsmith, manager of Innocent and in search of new blood.

# Innocent, My Arse

## A Very Swanky Office

**Hugh Goldsmith V/O**
'I just thought wow – she looked full of something, she just came off the page at me, this out of control, crazed young lady, and I noticed it. Then the *Smash Hits* ad came on the Box and I saw her again, this time looking different. More like a pop star. And absolutely cute as a button. She was blowing up a huge bubble and when it popped she smiled and said "Pop." '

These two things had a big impact on Hugh and he decided to track me down. In fact he had to be interviewed by Sylvia before he was even allowed to meet me. What she said to Hugh at that meeting was this: I was an excellent actress, a great dancer, and a good singer. In that order. And of course she was concerned that I was so young. Hugh wasn't put off. A week later Hugh came back to the school and met Dad and me.

### Hugh Goldsmith V/O

'She was delightful. Really so lovely. You are just drawn to her, there is just something there. She was buoyant and bright-eyed of course and unbelievably young, yet very mature at the same time. No doubt, having success in the entertainment world was her single-minded objective and yes, she wanted to investigate this music thing further.'

I just remember being summoned to Sylvia's office and him asking me what music I liked. He wanted to know who my inspirations were and what bands I was into, so I told him. R'n'B. Soul. Motown. Janet Jackson. Michael Jackson. TLC. Mariah Carey. But my closest love was the Spice Girls and Hanson. Then he asked me the million-dollar question. Would I be interested in a singing career? In making a demo tape? He had no idea whether I could sing or not. I knew I was good at acting. I could definitely dance. But could I be a pop star? Well, there was no harm in making a demo tape just to see.

Hugh recommended some people he knew who could cut a track for relatively little money. How exciting was that? So Dad and I agreed we would go away and make a demo tape. I started trawling though the radio stations to find a song I could use that would convince them I could deliver what they were asking of me, and decided to do a cover of a song called 'Get Out' which I heard on the chart show. It was Number 37 and I thought it was right for my voice. I then met Wendy Page and Jim Marr at their house-cum-studio in Clapham in southwest London – though it could have been Apple as far as I was concerned. They had all the sound systems, all the kit with the sliding buttons – it was amazing. It didn't bother me that the mic was strapped to the banisters and that I was singing on the landing, right outside the bathroom door. I was blown away. As for Wendy and Jim themselves, I adored them from the moment I met them. Wendy was this wonderful, beautiful woman, a blonde Kate Bush with a lovely dreamy quality about her. A singer/songwriter herself, she actually released her own records. Jim seemed like a giant to me – a big, handsome Lurch who spoke softly and got the best out of me in a calm and gentle way. We'd stop for lunch and have crumpets and beans on toast and cheese, then go back to work. And what work! I was with adults, people I could learn from, people I could look up to, people whom I desperately wanted to be taken seriously by, people who thought that thinking differently was actually thinking the same. I didn't have to hide my desires from them. I still drive past that house and stop and look at it, remembering that happy time, the promise of what was to come, the phenomenal excitement that potential creates. If they thought it was mad to cut a demo tape with a fourteen-year-old, they never let on.

I went home to Mum and Dad and we sat around the kitchen table playing the song. It sounded really good and we all started giggling because it was so mad. Once again Dad, worried about backlash, urged me not to tell anyone at school. The next day was back to normal. We packed the car and drove to Bournemouth for the summer. This time Sally was coming to visit. In fact David had turned up on my doorstep looking for a reconciliation. I told him he could come and see me in Bournemouth, then promptly forgot all about it. Down at the caravan site there were new pastures to sample. I think I told one of the Babes about the demo tape, but mostly I kept this whisper of a promise of a whole new life under wraps. It was my delicious secret to think about when I was alone, and when I did tremors of excitement would rush through me.

Despite having been the face of *Smash Hits* and on TV I wasn't treated any differently on the caravan site. The person on the ads wasn't the person I was. It didn't feel real. I feared that my success was a temporary arrangement and that the holidays would take place as normal, then I'd be back at school having to chalk up Hugh Goldsmith and the demo tape to experience. I did my absolute best not to let the fear of rejection ruin my holiday. Cue Harmony hairspray, figure-hugging dresses and flirting with the security guards.

Ah, the guards – they could almost make you forget about the music business! Matt Rose was one of them, and he was one of the sweetest guys I have ever met. He was twenty-three. And yes, again it was me having to convince a man that it was OK to go out with me. I'd been giving Matt the eye, but I thought he'd never fancy me because I was too young. So I tried to dress like I was older by wearing specs and pencil skirts, as if I was about to go to the office. I was always wearing my mum's clothes back then.

One night when I was dressed like a secretary a whole gang of us had sneaked out of the caravan site. I think it was one of the occasions when we'd got a bottle, filled it up with whatever was lying around our parents' caravans, swigged it down, then spun round and round until we fell over. Which was very quickly. This particular night we were busted on Ham Common by the police. Matt hugged me and said, 'Hide me. They've got a warrant out for my arrest.' Total bullshit, of course, but I quite liked the chat-up line. What followed was a very grown-up affair but without any sex. I was too scared to have sex with him because he was that much older and I was aware that it would be a different ball game. We weren't two kids doing it together for the first time, and I was scared I wasn't going to be good enough or know the techniques. He never pushed it. Not once. I'm sure everyone thought we were at it. But I had told my mum that we weren't and she believed me, maybe because this time I was telling the truth. My poor father, though! I vividly remember buying a chocolate brown dress that was so tight it stuck to my body. We were in the clubhouse and I was watching Dad watching Matt stroke my body and end up on my arse. I told Matt he ought to leave. Dad had got David up against a wall a few times, and although my parents really liked Matt, who was courteous and polite, I wasn't sure he was safe.

That year was a really fun holiday with the Rockley Babes, one of the best. Sally came down and we had this mad idea that we were going to do up a boat. Not so daft, you might think – except the boat was moored way out in the middle of the estuary. We'd been lying on the beach when we saw it. It looked like it had been abandoned, and our radical idea was to turn it into a party boat. Sally had brought 100 B&H so we put our fags into plastic bags, blew up a couple of rubber dinghies, raided mum's cleaning products from the caravan and set sail. But the current just whisked us straight out to sea – it was so fast it felt like the dinghies had engines. We ended up clinging on to a mooring post for about three hours waiting to be rescued. We hadn't realized how far out it was – I don't know how we imagined we were going to get everyone out on to our party boat. We were so less concerned about nearly drowning than we were about losing all our fags, which were soaking wet. Our genius idea had turned into a disaster because the bags had holes in them.

Unfortunately I had completely forgotten that David was coming down and then it all kicked off. He was beside himself, crying, heartbroken. I'd replaced him with someone who was older and who had a car. It was what I thought I wanted, what I thought I could handle. Matt took me to nice restaurants. For my fifteenth birthday we went to Alcatraz in Bournemouth and had a grown-up meal with wine. I didn't think I looked ridiculous, but I must have done. Unless, as Hugh Goldsmith had said, I seemed older than I was. Or I acted older than I was. Whatever I may have thought, I wasn't old on the inside. Matt and I finished because I started to feel uncomfortable about the age gap. I remember sitting in a science class back in the beginning of my second year at drama school and thinking it was wrong. I wasn't ready to have a full sexual relationship with him, and yet I knew that at some point he was going to expect more than I was prepared to give. It was the school again – I was very aware of not wishing to be seen as a slag. It was bad enough that I'd lost my virginity. So I went back to David, back to my safe place.

I don't know why I never found anyone at Sylvia Young's. I think the guys there were so different from the kinds of boys I knew. Most of them weren't interested in girls anyway, but even the ones who were had a tendency to preen. And that's never been my bag. I like confident men who are slightly off the rails – men like my dad. They should eat pies, not salads. Drink pints, not cocktails. But maybe I'm being too harsh – maybe the real reason I didn't really care for the boys there was self-protection. Because in truth I never felt I was good-looking enough to be with those boys. They were in a league of their own.

Finally, after a nail-biting wait, news came through from Innocent. They loved the demo tape! I thought that was that. But there were terms and conditions to agree to, and just like with the decision over stage school, Mum and Dad would inch one way, then slip back another. There was a lot of to-ing and fro-ing between the record company, Mum and Dad and the school. I would occasionally be picked up by Justine and driven in my school uniform to meet the rest of the company. I'd be shown around the publicity department. Meet the people from marketing. Every trip made it more and more exciting. One day a coachload of people arrived to see my parents at home. There were lawyers, press officers, record company executives, the whole shebang. Mum had made everyone tea, and then she and Dad sat down and had to tell them everything that had ever happened to them, everything they'd ever done. Innocent were checking whether there was anything in the family tree that would harm their investment. It freaked Mum and Dad out a bit. Fine to make sure *they* weren't dodgy, but did they have to go back a generation? Who would be interested?

I was desperate for it all to happen. Absolutely desperate. All the tasters were brilliant, but made it so much more agonizing. I'd got a peek of what my life could be like and it looked amazing, as long as everyone agreed the terms. Finally there was a record deal on the table. For a million quid. They were going to make me into a star! It was without trepidation that I got into the car that the record company sent for me, and drove to the Innocent offices. There with my parents, in a boardroom bigger than our front room, we sat looking at a record deal with my name on it. The world was my oyster. The deal meant no more school – I could start making my way. It was everything I had dreamed about since being suspended in a harness scoffing cereal at the age of seven. The deal meant I was off the starting block, out of the box, ready for take-off. I was so close. The only thing I needed was a signature. I lowered myself into the enormous leather-backed chair, chewing the inside of my cheek with anticipation, and stared at the empty dotted line.

# Act Three

*Living a Lie*

# Pipes!

## Back on Shoot Up Hill

When my plane touched down at Heathrow after that disastrous promo tour of the States which brought me close to suicide I finally exhaled. I was so glad to be home, so glad to be out of Chicago and away from those terrifying lonely hotel rooms and lecherous DJs. Dad was waiting to drive me home to Swindon, and I curled up in the back of the car, just a pathetic heap. Mum was desperate to take care of me; she wanted to wrap me up and feed me and tuck me into my four-poster bed where my teddies and dolls still sat waiting for me. But I didn't live at home any more. I'd made myself another nest with my boyfriend. I had needed Mum and Dad to get me out of America, but it was Rich I wanted to see. So, sixteen years old, I returned to London, to an unfurnished flat on Shoot Up Hill and a very busy boyfriend. Our relationship had intensified dramatically. I thought he was the only one who understood what was happening to me and the pressures I was under, and I knew he wouldn't judge me.

Rich and I got engaged at the beginning of that summer of 1999. Secretly, of course. Rich was on tour in NY and went shopping for a ring with his hairdresser. Rich was big into yellow gold, but his hairdresser was a lovely guy with great taste and he pushed Rich towards the white gold display case. When he came back from America he held out this tiny black jewellery box and proposed to me in our flat. In the box was a perfect white gold ring set with a very simple but perfect little diamond. It made me feel like a real woman. It's amazing what diamonds can do. Every time I left the flat I'd be sure to move it to my middle finger and turn it round, because it was our secret. I didn't tell people for two reasons. First, I didn't want to upset any of Rich's deeply loyal pre-teen fans, and secondly I was probably a touch embarrassed. I knew what the folks and my friends would say if they knew: 'You're too young!', 'It's not right!', and 'He's a madman!' So I didn't tell anyone. It became the one thing in my life that wasn't up for discussion. But I did bring my fiancé down to Rockley Park to meet the Babes. While it was a laugh it was also a collision of my two worlds, and sometimes it made me feel a bit cheesy – like trying to mix friends at a party.

We were in the pub. Rich snuck outside for a scented cigarette and my Uncle David went out and had a fag with him. Rich wasn't happy. He hadn't wanted a witness – a witness could get him into trouble. Because he was angry with me, I got angry at them. I shouted at my mum – why Mum I don't know, because of all people she didn't deserve it. I have the hideous notion that I might have said something like, 'Do you know who he is?' What I should have said was, 'This is my family we're talking about, not some honey-trap.' But I was probably frustrated, feeling torn and got my loyalties a bit crossed. No matter how desperate you are to stay 'normal' there is a moment when you start to believe that you are a pop star, that you can wear opaque shades in a darkened studio and no one will tell you otherwise. Of course they won't, because most of them are on the payroll and too busy kissing arse. Mum never kissed arse. She says I didn't speak to her for two months after that. I feel a hole open in my belly when I think of that and all the other times I dropped my family like a stone.

I don't really remember what I did for the first part of that summer except swan about in cat-suits and all-in-ones, but I know what I didn't do. I didn't do my GCSEs with the rest of my year. I had already told Mum I wasn't going to do them and she was naturally disappointed, but she soon got over it. I thought what I was learning was so much more valuable, and in a way it was. But it means there are gaping holes in my knowledge of history and I still struggle with my four times table. I'm useless at maths – I'm convinced I'm dyslexic with numbers even though three tests have told me otherwise. But even if I had taken my GCSEs I would probably have got terrible results anyway. It makes me slightly cringe when I think of how I behaved, though once again the people at the record company said they didn't witness any 'brattish' behaviour (and they should know, since they had some extreme versions of it on their own label). I probably reserved my worst behaviour for my family. Isn't it always the way? You take it out on the ones you love. Or, in my case, the ones who I knew would love me back. Loyalty is a tricky subject at that age. Boyfriends, friends, family – it's usually quite a volatile mix, especially when you are trying to discover who you are. Throw in a work commitment and a dog (more about the dog later), and I continually got my knickers in a twist. My family wanted me home, my fiancé wanted me with him whichever day, hour or minute he had off, and my company wanted me back out on the road.

What *I* wanted was a dog. I wanted a bit of normality, something I was in control of, that I could love and that would love me back. I knew the dog thing was going to be a handful – walking, training and playing with a dog were activities that weren't going to sit well with our schedules. But, as always, my impulsive streak won and led me to a local pet shop where Milo was snapped up. We found a dog walker for those days when we couldn't make it to the hill. His name was Peter and he would turn up at our block, Jubilee Heights, with a handful of dogs all waiting to greet Milo. Poor Justine was also endlessly sent to the flat to take him out when our schedules meant that neither of us could get back. I don't know how many dog poos she picked up, but even one would have been more than she should have done. I took him to some studios occasionally but that wasn't any better. Milo would poo indiscriminately. Actually he would poo discriminately – whenever it was most inappropriate. Justine eventually put her foot down. 'Pipes! *Your* dog, *your* shit. *You* clean it up!' So in between having to look like a cool pop star, I was discreetly trying to shovel dog poo into plastic bags.

Occasionally, however, our schedules did tie in, and we would take Milo up the hill to the park and try to be normal. But the downside was that we started to get spotted more and more and by the end of that summer there was no more denying it – we were a couple, a 'celebrity' couple at that. I've been reminded that it was Rich's people who decided to 'out' us – an official leak as it were, but I'm not sure if that's right. Either way, there was a picture in the press of us together and that was that. By this time I was actually relieved. I was bored with hiding it, bored with lying. Maybe we'd be left alone. That just goes to show how naïve I was. Everything that Hugh predicted came true.

# Cry Baby

## On stage at the Smash Hits Tour –
## Middle England

It was August, and I was back out on the road doing a *Smash Hits* tour. You don't get paid for a tour like that, because we needed them more than they needed us. And anyway, who was going to turn down the chance to play in front of eight thousand kids every night? Performing was the best bit about being in the music industry. That's what it was all about – especially for me, who didn't enjoy the whole studio/singing thing. We would endlessly rehearse the dance routines, perfecting them on the stage during the day and having a laugh with the dancers at night. We'd sit through the tech rehearsals having a camp old time, with the dancers drawing on fags like zealots and sinking endless diet Cokes. I didn't want to be called fat by anyone in the audience again after the Brit Awards. Tell you what, by the end of that tour 'fat' would have been just fine.

I was touring with 5ive, Atomic Kitten, B*Witched, West-life, A1 and Steps, and it was truly a blast. We'd all hang out in the bar after a show and get good and pissed. Sometimes we'd venture into town and soak up the night life of New-castle, Manchester or Leeds, wherever the tour took us. We weren't looking for anything exclusive – just a Walkabout or a Wetherspoon's, somewhere we could dance our arses off to Wham and Chumba Wumba while throwing tequila down our throats. Quite often the wilder dancers on the tour would encourage the entire bar to do the conga or *Oops Up Side Your Head*, and the punters would capitulate. Granted it wasn't throwing TVs or ourselves out of the window, it wasn't drug-induced orgies or men dressing up as women. It wasn't terribly hedonistic at all in fact, but it *was* a bloody riot. We went all around the country, staying in the same hotels, and of course there was some corridor creeping – Rich and I for one, Kerry and Brian for another. And it wouldn't be the music industry if there wasn't a smattering of groupies. Gradually over the tour I'd begun to notice that the crowd had gone from really enjoying my show, copying the moves and singing along to pretty much ignoring every word I sang. I wanted it to stop, of course. I wanted them to enjoy it like they had before. I knew that some of the songs were weaker than others and not as good as those of some of the other bands, but by then we could certainly hold our own. Personally I always thought our set was a winner – it had an edge and of course there was a cat-suit! I had a great dance partner and we did some terrific lift sequences to funked up remixes of 'Girlfriend' and 'Honey to the Bee'. All good tunes for an environment like that. I just wanted them to stop ignoring me.

It all kicked off on the day that Mum came to see the show with the kids. Charlie, Harley and Ellie must have been so excited at seeing their sister on stage for the first time – there was a great atmosphere and they loved all the acts. Manchester is always a tough crowd to work, so I was prepared to go out there and give it my best. And that's what I was doing when I first heard it. The booing started somewhere in the middle of the audience. I thought maybe I'd misheard, or it was a chant, or some problem had erupted in the crowd, so I ignored it and carried on with the performance. But it got louder and louder. The problem quickly escalated, all of them encouraging each other to jeer at me and drown me out. My brother and sisters kept looking round in confusion while Mum tried to tell them it was something else, but there was no getting round the fact that their sister was being booed off stage. The glo sticks were no longer in the air swaying in unison. They were hurtling towards the stage. At me.

I came off the stage with a family of frogs in my throat. I tried to ask the dancers whether they'd noticed, but I could barely speak. I kept whispering, 'Did you hear that?' They told me not to worry, said it was one or two silly girls and I shouldn't give it another thought. Even Mum tried to pretend it hadn't been that bad and I tried to make out it hadn't bothered me, but all I had to do was look at the expression on Charlie's face to know it had been even worse from where he was standing. Even now Charlie hates going anywhere with me in public – hates it to the point of phobia. I took him and his mates to the V Festival, which was brilliant except when we were walking through the crowd. He was expecting people to start chucking their fags and tinnies at us, but it didn't happen. The only thing coming my way was smiles and hugs. Funny that!

Standing backstage, I was crippled with embarrassment – all the more because these were kids of my own age who were shouting me down. They were supposed to be on my side – we were supposed to be sharing this experience. But as at Sylvia Young's, it became a competition. A competition for Rich, for the affections of a boy that they didn't know and whom I was living with. It was mad and I couldn't understand it. Even after Hugh explained, I still didn't get it. It was so vitriolic, so personal. Couldn't they see I was normal? I was already becoming more sensitive to comments made about me (and there were plenty all the time), and about the way I looked. But regardless of that, the one thing I had always known was that my shows were great. Because we put so much work into them. The dancing was street, challenging, creative and tight, and I had mastered the art of miming. It was a slick show and it went down well. That was what I was doing it for. When the booing started they took away the upside, because it certainly wasn't the riches I was raking in. And it didn't stop there. As soon as the booing had been reported, it became the thing to do. I stepped on stage and after only a few seconds someone would start it off, and then, like before, it spread through the crowd. My hearing became sharp, dog-like. Every time a whistle went off in the audience I knew that any moment now a chorus of cat calls was going to start up. And like the dog that I am I would run in the opposite direction, trying desperately to avoid those teasing kitty cats.

I know now that it was all very playground – girls being mean to me, picking on me. I shouldn't have let it bother me, but facing a gang of hostile girls is a terrifying prospect for anyone – and these were girls who had the potential to destroy my career. I felt embarrassed, then threatened, then worried – worried that it would affect my record sales. I was still only sixteen and I took the rejection of these strangers to heart. And it upset my family so much: Mum hated it every time the press reported another incident. I started to lose my nerve. It would probably have been better to go on lying to all and sundry, but I thought Rich and I would last. So why couldn't I show off my boyfriend like everybody else?

The tour continued. So did the booing. As I remember it it got increasingly worse, but maybe I just became increasingly aware, increasingly humiliated. Once, I nearly turned up the volume on my mic to ask them what their problem was. But I never did. I wasn't brave enough. I wouldn't give as much of myself out on stage because I wanted to protect myself, which meant the energy of the performance – my trademark

– started to dip. Eventually I started getting stage fright, and then I had to question what the hell I was doing any of it for. The vitriol spread to other areas. Hate mail flooded in to my fan club, my website, any teen magazine with an open letter page was targeted by girls who hated me. And not just about my boyfriend. About anything else they could think up. My arse naturally got a fair amount of attention. My thighs. Well, they had a point. My David Coulthard jawline. My Shergar mouth. My songs. My clothes. My hair. My sales. Each insult pecked away at me until eventually Hugh took pity on me and gently suggested I lie low for a while, go back to the States, record the second album and wait for it to all die down. What a wise old owl.

SCENE THREE:

# Old Faithful

EXT:

## On the Open Road

So, five months after coming back from America, the scene of my pathetic attempt at suicide, I returned. Or did I run away? This time it was a tour with dancers, which was at least an improvement in that I had company. I was good friends with the dancers by now, especially two fab ones called Zoe and Nikki. We decided that on this trip we were going to get really fit because we all wanted nice defined muscles. From the off we would do a pretty hard-core gig, then go to the gym for an hour. The show consisted of five numbers, three hectic dance routines and then two slower ballads. Each one was followed by a massive signing with the crowds. The girls would sign autographs as well and we'd all talk to the fans in our 'sweetest' British accents. Then we'd go to our hotel or on to a plane to fly to the next location.

And of course, because it was the States we had to sing live at every venue.

The girls were eating normally. I, on the back of the name-calling, had decided to cut out the burgers and chips and stick to a healthy diet – fruit, salad, a bit of chicken. But I like instant gratification and I didn't see enough change in the first week – the weight wasn't falling off like I wanted it to. So then I thought I'd cut everything out and see what happened. It started as an experiment, seeing how long I could go before I really had to eat. I could get to four o'clock pretty easily if I drank enough decaf coffee and diet Coke and smoked enough cigarettes. Perversely, it made me feel better than I had for a long time. I got a buzz. I felt in control, and not just of my appetite. I felt in control of my life. After four or five days like that the scales showed a dramatic improvement. So now I had results. Unlike my diminishing sales, here was proof that I was doing something right.

I didn't hide it at first. The dancers knew exactly what I was doing, but weren't concerned. It wasn't unusual for someone in that business to cut out food for a while. We even gave it a name – 'old faithful', because it worked. If my 'old faithful' was anything to the others it was no more than a nuisance, a slight inconvenience. It meant I didn't want to go out and party because that would mean consuming calories. I quickly became obsessed. I would stay in and think about food and not eating while the others went out. I felt this awful, enthralling, pleasurable pain – a pitched battle against hunger, seeing who would win. My mum came and joined me for one leg of the trip, in New York City. I knew I had a photo shoot for *GQ*, so I wanted to look my best. Mum was bowled over by the city and wanted to explore. But I was spent. So she said she'd come up to my room instead, have a cuddle, lie on my bed, watch TV and order some food in. I hadn't seen Mum on my own for months. But I wouldn't let her up because then I would have to explain why I didn't want any dinner. She in turn didn't want to go out without me, so she probably went to her room alone. Actually I think she might have sat in the bar with the journalist from *GQ* and got pissed, but she certainly didn't see me. My excuse was always the same: I was tired. I truly believed I was in control of the situation. My mind seemed so sharp that I believed myself capable of doing anything as long as I had this one thing which nobody else was allowed to know about.

The awful thing about crossing the line between healthy eating and unhealthy dieting is that when you are healthy, the right weight for your body and well fuelled from the right food, you feel fabulous. Anorexics never do. You think, you'll just get to nine stone and then you'll feel good about yourself. But at nine stone you can still see the convex curve of your belly and you want it to go. So maybe eight and a half stone will do. OK, then eight. I just wanted to disappear.

The worst thing you can do is read other anorexics' diaries. I'd buy endless magazines along the way and look through them to pick up tips. It was a terrible thing to do. You're reading this story about a girl facing massive organ failure, and one half of your brain is thinking how awful that is while the other half is thinking what she did might be a good idea. One story was about a girl who ate tissues to fill herself up. As soon as I'd read that the ubiquitous box of Kleenex started to wink at me. There's one in every hotel room – tissues and a Bible. Eventually my curiosity got the better of me. I sat on the floor of my hotel room somewhere in America and strip by strip tried desperately to force Kleenex down my throat. To make the hunger pangs go away I used to punch my stomach hard. I picked up various other hideous little tricks to side-step hunger and searched out pictures of skinny models to spur me on. I searched out films with ultra-thin actresses in them and glared in disgust at anyone carrying extra weight; normal-sized women seemed revolting to me. But however bleak a picture I try to create – and it was utterly soul-destroyingly bleak and I wish fervently that it had never happened – some people reading this will want to do exactly as I did: pick up tips. So tough. The only tip you'll get out of me is this: the tissue thing was bollocks – it didn't work. Not only was I still hungry, I nearly choked on a ball of tissue when it momentarily got stuck in my throat. That would have been a nice way to go. The best tip anyone can give someone who is battling with any addiction is to get help. Because there are incredible, humbling, wonderful people out there who *can* help, but only if you are prepared to meet them halfway.

LA was a turning point for my eating disorder, but not a good one. We were staying at a place called the Park. We'd go up on to the roof and it was all very LA with lots of people-gazing, lots of fun – everyone looked famous or like they should be famous. The girls had managed to get tickets to this really cool club called the Sky Bar, *the* place at the time, but I didn't want to go. I'd now been starving myself for nearly three weeks, the tour was ending and I knew I was going on holiday for my seventeenth birthday. I thought I'd eat then, but for now I didn't need to. I was mesmerized by the concept of starving myself until that date. If I could reach that goal I'd really have achieved something. During the day I was surviving on diet Coke, decaf coffee with Sweet and Low, and endless Marlboro Lights. Then, if I was about to keel over, I'd have a little something at night. I distinctly remember asking a waitress to weigh my chicken, but more often I'd have a garden salad (basically just green leaves) with the dressing on the side. You can be an anorexic in the States and get away with it, almost be applauded for it in some places, and I was pleased with myself. It was all going well. The scales were dropping – not fast enough for my liking, but they were dropping. Then we met a hippie on the roof of the hotel and it all went horribly wrong.

He offered us a Philly Blunt – a cigar skin full of pure weed. A few drags of that was all it took for me to get the munchies in a major way. At first I managed to hold it down with Nikki by ordering a fresh fruit salad on the roof, but I was twitching with the thought of food. I went to my room and emptied the contents of my mini-bar: two Hershey bars, two packets of crisps, three jars of nuts (including cashews, which I don't even like), two flapjacks, one packet of m&ms, one packet of Reece's pieces, and all the juice I could wash it down with. I just couldn't get the wrappers off quickly enough. If you'd been watching me on CCTV it would have looked like the tape was running on double time. I was like Augustus Gloop. I ate and ate and ate until there was only the bottle opener left. Then *bam*! I got guilt so badly that I put on three layers of clothes and ran from Sunset Boulevard to the bottom of La Cienega where I knew there was a drugstore. And there I got hold of the first, second and third packet of laxatives that I'd ever bought in my life. I ran back to the hotel, took three laxative pills and then, still in all my clothes, went to the gym and worked out on the treadmill for an hour. As if that wasn't enough, I then sat in the sauna in my clothes waiting for the pills to work.

My friends found me in there. They knew what I was doing but couldn't say anything. I'd deny it anyway. If anyone ever did raise the issue of me not eating I would always say the same things, 'I'm in control . . . it's manageable . . . it's not got out-of-hand . . . I just want to lose weight . . . you're only jealous. . . .' My defence was well rehearsed. I used to watch everyone else eating and think, 'How can you eat so much and stay so thin?' I'd start to look at people and find flaws in them. When you're in this state you lose your head and disappear into a terrible vortex where everything is centred around weight. Yours, your friends', that of people on the street, on the telly. I adored the girls but in the mind-set I was in you can't really have proper friendships because you are at war with the rest of the female population and yourself – only the thinnest will win. That's why it can kill you. Zoe and Nikki took one look at me in the sauna and said I was mad. All I thought was, 'Yeah, and what are you going to do about it?'

When I had finished in the sauna the laxatives finally kicked in and I ended up on the loo for hours. That's why that evening's experience was a turning point: I had discovered the power of laxatives and was amazed at how well they worked. These weren't the gentle herbal ones – these were pure gut-flushing, dehydrating chemicals. I never found anything to beat it. The terrible long-term side-effect of laxative abuse is that it reduces your digestive system's ability to work normally. It's an absolutely stupid thing to do to yourself because you set up a lifelong battle with constipation, which is about as far removed from glamorous as you can get. I could no more stop my friend in Swindon selling a story about me to the press for a hit than I could stop myself prising out those little pills and swallowing them by the handful. You are supposed to take no more than one in any twenty-four-hour period until the blockage has passed. I had no blockages, but if I ever put food in my stomach I wanted it out as soon as possible. However I could never make myself sick. I tried and tried, forcing my fingers down my throat, and retched until my throat was sore, but I couldn't do it. So I took laxatives instead. It started with one. But the effect lessened over time, so I had to take two at a time. Then three. Then four. Then five. Then six. Then seven. Seven was my maximum. I couldn't watch myself in the bathroom mirror as I swallowed them because I hated what I was doing. But I loved the power of those little pills more.

I discovered I had the most extraordinary willpower which enabled me to stare down at a plate full of food, with my stomach gnawing at me to eat, and not pick up a morsel. And I pushed myself through absurd pain barriers. Not just hunger, but stomach cramps, kidney and bladder infections and diarrhoea as starvation and laxative abuse took hold of me. I was constantly watching the clock, waiting to tick off another hour without food. My life existed in minutes – it became all about me and time and calories. I was weighing myself constantly. Convinced that the scales weren't accurate in each new hotel, I would locate three or four different places to weigh myself and average the readings. I played horrid, destructive little games – for instance, when I wanted to feel angry with myself for failing I would move the little dial at the base of the scales and give myself just cause to miss another meal.

When I came home from the States Mum was shocked, I looked half the size I'd been when I left, but I told her I'd been working too hard and she bought it. I'm sure the dancers told everyone I wasn't eating, but no one said anything directly to me. It's very hard to confront these things, to look someone in the eye and say, 'You are anorexic', because we all had some kind of eating disorder and what was the difference between going on a 'starvation diet' and slowing killing yourself through anorexia? I thought I looked pretty hot, but there is a photograph of me coming out of a club called the Titanic doing a fine impersonation of Skeletor. I think that was when my name was first linked to drugs. I certainly looked like a model for the 'Just Say No' campaign, but the press were wrong about drugs. It wasn't drugs that were ruining my life, but a good old-fashioned eating disorder.

After my seventeenth birthday Rich and I went on holiday to the Seychelles for a couple of weeks, which was amazing. It was our first proper grown-up holiday and I'd never seen beaches like that before – except when I filmed the video for 'Honey to the Bee' in Florida, but there hadn't been any lounging around that time. We must have looked an odd couple. I don't think anyone asked me where my parents were, but they could have. We were children let loose on holiday without our guardians, and I binged big time. At no point did Rich comment on my loss of weight or my subsequent gain. Did he not care? Did he simply not notice? Or was he ignoring it, giving it power, ignoring it for my sake? Or for his? Eating disorders in the pop world are by no means limited to its female members.

When I came home from the Seychelles I went straight back on to the 'old faithful', and my routine over the next six months was basically this. I would try not to eat anything in the day, then allow myself a garden salad or a piece of chicken that would fit in the palm of my hand. I knew the weight conversion from pounds to kilograms. I knew about fat content. I knew how many calories a teaspoon of French dressing contained. In fact I knew the calorie content of *everything*. It consumes you, this lack of consumption – it doesn't only eat away at your body mass, it eats away at your mind. So in the end it's just you and your addiction. Eventually I confessed to myself that I had a small problem – nothing serious, nothing I couldn't control (the lies you tell yourself are extraordinary). But I was aware that the smaller I was getting physically the bigger I was becoming in my mind. What had been acceptably thin became, to me, exceptionally fat.

# Drugs – But Not as You Know Them

## Staring into a Toilet Bowl

If I had eaten more than I thought I should have, which was basically any solid morsel, I'd take laxatives at night. I would wake up at three in the morning with terrible cramps and spend an hour and a half in the loo crying and waiting for the next wave of cold sweat. Sometimes I thought it would never end. Every time I would vow that it would be the last, that I wouldn't put myself through this sort of pain again – enough was enough. It was out of hand. And then I would cry again, silently, clutching my stomach, because in those deep, dark hours you can't lie to yourself. I was in trouble. Sometimes I'd fall asleep holding my stomach because I was so tired. And I still had to get up to go to work in the morning.

I was recording my second album, and I had actually been given a chance to work on it myself. Collaborate. Co-write.

Things that could have helped me feel less like a puppet. One of the dichotomies of battling with an addiction like anorexia is that, while you are numb to a great deal, you feel other things very acutely. My mind was quite creative. Here I was on my own, surviving this addiction which I couldn't tell anyone about. I committed myself to solitary confinement, and in the absence of company my mind filled the space. I wrote a lot. When I'm sad that's what I do. After recording I would go back to an empty flat because Rich was still working as hard as ever. All I wanted to do was go home, curl up on a sofa and watch TV. I didn't have any energy to do anything else. But I did produce reams of tortured poetry.

There are tiny pulses all over my body.
Every inch of my skin feels like it's about to split.
It's the tipping point and I'm desperately hoping
it will happen imminently.

I want to help the process along.

I want to see the saturated fat oozing from every
pore. Finding, seeking out a new home in which to
sit and fester and grow like
a cancer.
Feeling this swollen makes me want to sleep.
In a freezing cold isolation room, without the
luxury of a bed.
I don't deserve a bed.

## Billie

I want to lie there and freeze.
The freezing would help me feel empty.
It would force my skin to tighten.

I can't be this obese any more.

It makes me want to grab at myself
Paw at myself
Bruise my ugly skin.

I want to stand and shiver and feel cold, stiff and
alone.
Just me and my body, at work, one.
Listening to each other
Studying each other
Exhausting each other
Loving and despising each other
Body and mind testing and teasing
Like two spoilt siblings fighting for their mother's
touch.
Which is stronger of the two?
Who can go longer without capitulating?
My mind watches and monitors my body's
behaviour,
Constantly disapproving and disappointed with
my poor body's efforts.
They no longer work in unison.
They no longer fight for the same cause.

174

There's no common objective.
They parted company a year ago.
Alone they struggle.
I struggle.
All three of us are weak.


Sometimes when I feel this full I fantasize about
taking a kitchen knife and making a
large incision across my stomach. I like to imagine
scraping away all that was there.
Forcing it out with the back of the
shiny blade.
Like filleting a fish.
Getting rid of the innards so the piece is purer,
lighter.
Much more appealing.
More desirable.
Oh, Mum.

3 laxatives tonight
1 gym session
7 days starvation
3 nuts if passing out
As much coffee and diet Coke as I can get down
Loads of fags

I indulged it, just as I did when I played 'No More I Love
You's' after David dumped me. I thought it was romantic,

this being alone in a dark world. What it was, in fact, was a waste of time. I should have been out with my friends having a laugh, enjoying being given the chance to do what I'd not been able to do on the first album. Typical of me – just as I reach the place I was aiming for I move the goal posts. It wasn't about writing a good track, it was about losing another fucking pound. I was writing about wanting to cut my stomach open and I thought it was romantic. It seems so far-fetched now, but still I have the words. They are there to remind me of the dark places I retreated to when I was in the grip of anorexia, the places I have no intention of ever visiting again.

Obviously, being kept up all night on the loo meant I just got knackered again. To compensate I drank gallons of black coffee and diet Coke during the day, and when that wasn't working I'd pop endless Pro-plus to keep me going. My 'time out' was just as hectic as ever. Songs needed recording, then videos had to be made. Other territories needed to be conquered. By the end of the day I was so wired on too much caffeine that I started taking sleeping pills. Also, just having no food in your belly makes you feel restless. The worst time was the first two months after getting back from the Seychelles. We had entered a new millennium and I was doing the same old thing. I really hadn't properly eaten for the entire time. I would take sleeping pills to get me to sleep, and every night I would dream about eating and end up biting my mouth. I'd wake up with sore gums, and callouses on the inside of my cheek from where I'd been chewing my own flesh. They say a human can go without proper amounts of food for five days – but actually you can go without food for months. Eventually your head becomes so strong that you can continue, or you think you can, indefinitely. But anorexia is like an auto-immune disease: eventually it kills the host, you kill yourself. But it can take years. I didn't get close to death because I was 'saved' long before that, but my periods did stop and so I had to go to hospital. Did that knock some sense into me? No. I was quite pleased not to have to worry about contraception.

As I got thinner, I developed a routine in front of the mirror on different parts of my body. If I could see pointed and angular hip bones I was happy. If they were slightly curved, or I could see any more meat on them, I'd be thrown into despair. The worst thing anyone could say to me was, 'You look really well', because in your head 'well' equals fat, warm, cuddly. If I look 'really well', then I must keep up the diet. If people say you look really terrible, you think yes! It's working! You can't win. What you need to do is find the *right* people. It's all about love. It's about someone giving you the biggest hug in the world and loving you. But of course you are being intolerable, pushing everyone to the limit, so you don't get the hug. What of the person who was supposed to be giving me those hugs? Well, things had turned nasty in that department too.

In the pop star pecking order, Rich was further up the scale than I was. While his schedule couldn't possibly be changed, mine was less rigorous (read important). I was trying to juggle things to keep him happy but, as in Rockley Park with Mum and Dad, I ended up pissing everyone off. Rich would get angry, mean messages would be left on my phone, and I was too young and too inarticulate to be able to fight my corner. In truth I probably didn't know what I wanted to say even if I had been able to. Justine thinks I was in love with the idea of being in love, which meant our foundations were built on sand. I once tried to rip my hair out with the sheer frustration of not being able to make Rich understand. I cried all the time – no words, just tears. I didn't know what to do about Rich or the possessive, destructive cycle we'd got ourselves into. Clumps of hair came out in my hands, and for a little while that made me feel better.

I don't blame him. I must have been a nightmare, because anorexics aren't fun. I was completely irrational most of the time and, frankly, slowly going mad. He was trying to control me, but I was out of control – all I wanted to do was to control food. We put up with a lot of each other's shit. Every separation was worse than the one before. Even before I got ill we had drifted apart, but we couldn't admit it. We had provided one another with such a lovely little safe haven for a while that we couldn't give it up. We wanted to be in each other's lives, yet at the same time hated and resented each other. We couldn't put anything to bed – we'd row, he'd leave and arrive in another country, and we'd pick up the row from where we'd left off. On top of all that things weren't going so well with the band who were all at each other's throats, and although Rich started out a sweet, passive, peaceful hippie the monster consumed him too. We were taking stuff out on each other because we had no one else to take it out on. We'd cling on even when our relationship was in tatters, but in the end even we couldn't weather the storm we'd created. We split up. We got back together. We split up again. Nothing was going according to plan.

None of the tortured poetry that I wrote during the first five months of 2000 went into the second album, but the producers did give me the more adult sound that I had secretly craved first time round. The kiddie chorus of 'Because We Want To' had lodged me firmly in the pre-teen marketplace that I wanted to break out of. On the first album I was singing about being them: nothing too challenging, nothing untoward. Now I know why. I've looked at the original 'Billie' market report and discovered that I was being pitched at twelve- to fourteen-year-old white girls living in the south – the pony club crew who had enough money to buy their own singles. The songs had to be safe so that Mum and Dad would like them. I think Hugh recognized the mistake we'd made with the first songs and was as keen as I was to leave the 'anthems' behind and create something more sophisticated. But while I was away with Wendy and Jim again, working on that new sound, a star was forming on the edge of the galaxy. She was a girl my age whose whole demeanour from the off was about looking ahead to the next step in life. It was 'aspirational'. It was sexy. She was still in school uniform. But she wanted out. 'Hit Me Baby One More Time' did everything that 'Because We Want To' didn't. The titles say it all. I had to up the ante dramatically if I was going to compete with the phenomenal worldwide success Britney had with her debut single. But I had one card up my sleeve: underneath those baggy clothes I'd been wearing I was thin.

# Thank F***

## A Helicopter is Seen Flying Through the Air

We finished recording my new album, *Walk of Life*, and the promotional train began to pull away from the station again. We were put through a twenty-four-hour video shoot behind the Hoover building in west London, with non-stop singing and dancing. After twelve hours I was about to keel over. Panicked by the dizziness, I resorted to cramming a Mars bar down my throat because I couldn't hold up the schedule and I couldn't tell anyone I hadn't eaten. I picked at peanuts until the shoot was over. The song got enough radio play to become an A-list record. The plugger was doing a good job. MTV were loving it and playing our video all the time. Britney had taken the board, but I was back in the game. Back on the map. In fact it put me on a whole new map. I clearly looked different. The grinning hamster in man-clothes had been replaced by a sultry, thin temptress in black leather. I was still young, but nothing like I'd looked when 'Because We Want To' came out. I'd had no credibility, of course, back then, nor did I deserve it at fifteen, but my God I wanted it! Like all teenagers, I wanted to be taken seriously. Maybe that's what my first song should have been called: 'Because We Want To (be taken seriously)'. Oh, the anguish of being misunderstood. Now I was being taken a bit more seriously, and I have to say I liked it. If I hadn't been in such a mess in my head from the eating disorder I would have enjoyed it. Perhaps that's a bit harsh – some of it was really, really fun, but always at a price.

'Day and Night' came out on 24 May 2000 and went straight in at Number 1. I had a new look (thin), a new image (sexy – because thin looks good on the page, and now I was all of seventeen and could go long on black eye-liner) and a new name. Billie Piper. Hugh threw one hell of a party for it, which really did make us feel like we were all back on track. It was at the über-trendy Papagayo. Paul Conroy, the president of Virgin, was there, and we all allowed ourselves to feel proud about what we'd achieved this time. It really was a great song backed by a great video, and everyone was happy. The starvation had paid off, and the publicity we got was huge. And we'd succeeded in crossing the divide from pre-teen to teen and beyond. It wasn't just *Smash Hits* who wanted me on their cover but *GQ*, *Loaded*, *FHM*, *Company*, *19* and *She* magazine.

We'd earned that party. The schedule of performances,

appearances, interviews and photo shoots was more intense than ever because now we were competing with Britney Spears and Christina Aguilera for the queen of teen pop crown. As ludicrous as those six weeks were leading up to the release of 'Day and Night', I wouldn't have changed a single frantic, knackering, stressful moment. Not because it was my third Number 1, but because it was 'Day and Night' that caught the attention of a certain ginger-haired TV god. Yes, Chris Evans wanted me, Billie Piper, to appear on *TFI Friday*.

I absolutely loved that programme. When I was at stage school I had sat having sneaky fags in Barnes, watching it being filmed at Riverside Studios. On those first weekends home from Sylvia Young, before Mum and I began to dress up and practise 'acting', we would watch *TFI Friday* as a family. I'd always really fancied Chris and, like all his thousands of viewers, could see something brilliant in him. But I thought it had to be a stitch-up. I'd already been asked to appear on *Never Mind the Buzzcocks*. I'd known what sort of show it was, but I'd thought I could hold my own when it came to discussing music. All I got was ritual humiliation. I think I was only invited on the programme to fulfil the role of 'stupid little pop star' and make everyone else look brilliant. Mum and the kids had accompanied me. I'd thought it would be a treat for them to sit in the green room, but instead they had to listen to lewd comments being made by some of the people watching the show from the green room with them. That wasn't much fun for anyone, so when I heard Chris Evans wanted me on *TFI* I thought it was going to be the same thing. I was terrified. We tried to get out of it by saying I was at Alton Towers that day doing a promo gig and there was no way we could get back to London in time. But he wouldn't take no for an answer, and the next thing I was being told was that a helicopter was on its way to pick me up! Now this was more like it. Excited as I was about the chopper, somewhere in my twisted head I thought it was all happening because I was thin. This must be my reward for starving myself, and it gave me impetus to carry on.

That flight was something I shall never forget. Justine and I were just screaming – God knows what the pilot thought. But as we touched down in Hammersmith the panic set in. *TFI* was live. Chris wasn't known to suffer fools gladly. I was a fake. Was I walking – flying – into a trap? I was nearly sick because I thought he was going to make me sing. We'd just stepped off the helicopter and I couldn't bloody breathe. Justine kept saying, 'Calm down, just calm the fuck down!' (Justine is now a mother of two, so obviously if her children ever read this then all expletives are simply me taking a bit of artistic liberty and your mother would never ever have used such atrocious language. . . .) She shoved a paper bag into my hand and told me to put it over my mouth and breathe in and out until I calmed down.

As we walked away from the helipad Justine and I started planning what I would sing if I had to. It was all very well having a 'lovely tone', but Justine knew that I couldn't deliver as a singer. That might have been fine most of the time, because most of the time it wasn't required. But just occasionally it was, and I thought it was now. By this time I had completely lost my bottle as far as the singing was concerned. I was being offered the chance of a lifetime, and all I wanted to do was turn and run. But I couldn't. How could I let everyone down? How could I let myself down? We chose the easiest bit of 'Day and Night', the bridge part, and practised it together, trying to get the tune right, trying to start off in a key that wouldn't go out of my minuscule range. Frankly, I was shitting myself.

Eventually my name was called. I left the safety of the green room and walked out on to the balcony that wrapped around the studio. The music was blaring, the lights were flashing, masses of faces were smiling and people were waving at me and shaking my hand. The energy of the room pulsated and I was driven along by it. As soon as I saw Chris's smiling face I stopped resisting what was happening and started enjoying it. I still had butterflies, but now from excitement. From the buzz. It was brilliant, absolutely brilliant. He made it so easy for me to be me that I completely forgot to be nervous. That's his gift. I knew I had it in me, and he allowed me to raise my game. During the break I said, 'I really like your shirt', and he said he liked mine, and we said, 'Why don't we swap when we come back from the break?' So we did. We stepped behind the curtain and stripped. That was the first time he saw me in my bra. It was a Calvin Klein bra, really sweet and very simple – funny the things you remember. He didn't say anything suggestive – we were just like little kids behind the curtain trying to hurry up before we went back on air. During the second half it was pretty clear that we were getting on very well – there was a natural affinity between us, an easy banter. I wasn't just holding my own, I was giving as good as I got. My overriding memory is that I couldn't stop laughing. The rest of the world shrank while the limitless world of Chris Evans opened up in front of me. I forgot about everything for those few minutes that we were live on TV. I forgot about the audience, the record company, my voice, calories, the jealous boyfriend – everything. But as soon as I came off the set, I reentered my life. The first thing I said to Justine was, 'I've had it when he sees this!'

# Packets and Packets and Packets

INT:

## Under a Bed in an Empty Flat

The story went that Rich had dumped me over the phone.
Poor old me. My family and management were over the
moon. Our relationship had been going from bad to
worse. Maybe the extraordinary sales for 'Day and Night'
were a consequence of sympathy – or were people feeling
a bit guilty for all the booing and name-calling? Or was it
just a great song and a great new look? The video is one
of my favourites. One mag rang me up and asked me
whether, given that in my interview I'd uttered that
cursed line about being 'more in love than ever', which
is almost worse than 'he is my rock', I would now like to
have a good old bitch. I didn't. He hadn't actually
chucked me brutally over the phone, it was mutual,
though he later claimed he'd said that in order to help

187

my record sales. . . . Hmm, I don't remember him being so altruistic at the time.

I wasn't heartbroken. I had been welcomed back into the fray with my new look and a surname, doors had been opened, I was older and could enjoy a few perks that a fifteen-year-old couldn't. I was edging towards my eighteenth birthday, and when people tried to tell me off I felt justified in telling them to fuck off. I was looking pretty good too, so being single didn't terrify me. My look at the time is ingrained in my memory. I designed it: high heels, backless shimmery top, low-slung jeans. I had no back fat, so I was taking my back out on the town. I was never happier than when people could see my ribs. As far as the business was concerned I was at the sharp end again, and who knows what little deals were being done between the press and the publicity people? Maybe they really were trying to boost my sales on the back of the sympathy card, or maybe a bigger, more famous pop star was in trouble and my story was being given as a reward for keeping stumm. That's how the business works. Don't print that, but I'll give you this.

What did I care? I was off on tour with my lovely friends the dancers, happily showing off my skinny back. 'Day and Night' had sold 250,000 copies and it all looked rosy. But then Britney hit back with the rush release of her second single, 'Oops I Did It Again'. It came out of the blue, and 'Day and Night' got tangled up with it. The most frequently asked question after 'Does Rich wear make-up?' was 'Do you feel threatened by the incredible success of Britney Spears over here?' Er . . . I hated her and Christina. The green-eyed monster had taken hold. I would say things like, 'What a whore! What the hell is she wearing? School uniforms are for children and dirty old men. At least my thighs are thinner than hers.' But in my mind I was thinking, 'The song's a smash. She looks fab and, yes, her thighs are thinner than mine and always will be because I have big knees you see and I'm never going to have svelte legs!'

Rich had left the flat by this time but needed to get back to retrieve his stuff. Mum went to let him in. He was in tears. It was awful for her because he was genuinely upset, but she'd heard some of his angrier messages and just wanted him gone. He took everything. Mum went to Ikea to replace the basics and then set to work cleaning the flat. It was a pigsty – we'd had no time to make it a home anyway, but now my clothes and belongings were strewn everywhere. Mum wasn't unused to coming to our flat and tidying up after us, but mostly she just did the washing up and took our dirty clothes to the launderette. She spent hours sitting in that launderette – she's a bloody heroine for doing that alone. Not just mine, Rich's too. But this time the flat was an utter shambles, so she decided to pull her sleeves up and get her hands really dirty. I think she found the first empty packet of laxatives under where the bed had been. The rest came out of drawers, from the backs of cupboards, out of washbags and plastic bags, under the sink. Boxes and boxes of laxatives, all half-full. I'd just forgotten about them. I had no one in my flat to hide them from and I knew they'd be used eventually – I always had to have a supply on me for when I succumbed to food. She called me on my mobile: 'Billie, why are all these packets of laxatives in your flat?'

My heart shot into my mouth. I wanted to tell her, and I nearly did, but then I lost my bottle and told her I had bad constipation. She found a way to believe me in the same way that a mother will believe her son isn't taking drugs even though it's obvious to everyone else. Maybe as a mother you can't admit it, even to yourself, because you think it reflects badly on you. Maybe I was a more convincing actress than I realized at the time. Maybe our close relationship from before, when I would confide all to my mother, was the relationship she wanted to believe we still had even though I had wandered far from those safe pastures.

Did it make me stop? Did it bollocks! I just made sure never to go to the same shop twice to buy laxatives. If you're anorexic, subterfuge rules your life. Of course I was having to buy more and more because they were becoming less and less effective. I was terrified someone would say, 'Sorry, Miss Piper, you've had three packs already this week.' When Mum found some a second time, when she was once again sorting out my flat, she told me that if I carried on doing them then she was going to take me out of the business. That time I just told her they were old ones left over from before and that I'd had them for ages. Mum was on to me, or so I thought, so I did what I've always done when my parents were getting too close to the truth, too close to asking the right question: I put a little distance between them and myself.

# Oops I Did It Again . . .

## A Bedroom, Location Unknown

For the promotion of *Walk of Life* I pushed myself harder than ever. I had no option. Everything depended on the build. The workload reached a whole new level, worse even than for 'Honey to the Bee'. It was beyond frenetic, and finally my body started to complain. I still wasn't eating sensibly, I was taking laxatives, I was going out and drinking, and I was working a minimum of sixteen hours a day. The problems started with cystitis. I should have taken antibiotics and given myself a bit of time to get over it. The trouble was I'd taken so much time off that I couldn't afford more. 'Day and Night' had been hampered by Britney, so I needed to capitalize on the gains we'd made and push on through. I couldn't let Hugh down.

On a not particularly special day I would get up before six

to be picked up by car and taken to a TV studio. There would be endless waiting around, smiling a lot, having a bit of a laugh in downtime but effectively being on show the entire time. In between takes a couple of mags would turn up to do a quick interview and take some snaps, then we were off to another studio to do the same all over again. We never sat down for lunch, but I was offered food wherever I went. The trick was to avoid it without drawing attention. 'I'll eat later,' was always a good one. But on some occasions I couldn't completely avoid eating with people, and then my head would race to work out what I could get away with eating without making it obvious. In those instances I always had the laxatives to neck straightaway – I couldn't let the food sit in my stomach for too long without getting paranoid that the weight was going back on. I didn't mind not losing any more but I didn't want any of it back – it was a battle just to stay as thin as I was. I tried to be sick, but however hard I tried I still couldn't do it.

Justine remembers me spending ages in the toilet wherever we went. She was aware of the laxatives, but I can't remember if she knew about the cystitis at that point. She said it finally dawned on her during a trip to Sweden that what I was doing to myself, the 'old faithful' was more than an occasional thing I put myself through before a video or a photo shoot. It was all the time. She was eating McDonald's and offered me some. I declined. We'd been together all day and I was starving too, but I wasn't going to eat that. She said, 'Are you honestly not going to eat anything?' No one had ever confronted me quite so blatantly about it before. So I just told her. 'No. I'm not going to eat anything.' What could she do? She couldn't force me. Occasionally she'd ask me how 'old faithful' was going, just to let me know she was aware of what was going on, but it really wasn't her business. What could she say? I told her what I told everyone else. I was in control. It was just until I did this video, that TV appearance, next week's award ceremony. There was so much going on with my eating that no one was privy to – once again the problem of being looked after by many and cared for by none. It was doubly difficult for Justine. She was a friend. I confided in her. We had a laugh together. If she suddenly put on her 'record company' face I would have been pissed off. And anyway, I was getting a bit bored of doing what people were telling me to do.

I wasn't only working harder than I ever had before. I was going out more and more to flex those flirting muscles. I was single, it was time to party and I knew exactly the girls to do it with. I stayed at Zoe and Nikki's house in North Finchley because I didn't want to be on my own in the flat that I'd once shared with Rich. All of this meant I couldn't starve myself so effectively and would end up eating. As long as I had my laxatives to hand, I wasn't too concerned. That's when things started getting a bit messy. I felt like I was in control again, though I clearly wasn't. I was now a lot more desirable because I was half the size I used to be, and every male magazine – *Loaded*, *FHM*, *Maxim*, *Sky* – wanted to set up a photo shoot. All it took was a few drunken nights to make me the tabloids' new 'wild child' – I was Aled Jones gone bad. Look, I'm not going to pretend that I was squeaky clean during my purple patch, but it was nothing like the papers suggested. I was having a bit of fun, or trying to anyway. I was seventeen, single, living in London, with my third Number 1 under my belt. It was a little bit crazy, but nothing compared to your average advertising exec. or press agent on a Saturday night.

I thought the boys would come flocking. But when you're super-thin and seemingly super-perfect, you're kind of threatening. You become unapproachable. Isolated. You wait for people to come to you. And if they don't come to you, you wonder why they don't like you. You feel you must get thinner. . . . It makes you needy. It makes you do things you might later regret. And that's why things got messy – I started doing stupid things with undeserving people.

It was my own fault. I sent out cold vibes because by the end of that summer I had no energy left to send out anything else. Food gives you energy and makes you feel alive – it's the most obvious thing in the world to me now. When you're starving yourself you have a personality bypass. You can't be bothered to think about being funny because all you can think about is being thin. When you live off fags and coffee you look like a mad paranoid jitterbug. And the men you'd like to be with can see it too. They know you're mad and they wouldn't touch you with a bargepole because you've got 'Nutter' written in neon across your forehead. So all you end up with are the ones who like that sort of mad-skinny-bitch thing – guys who are likely to fuck with your head and worry about their own weight and use you to feed their narcissism. There's no doubt about it, I was a donkey on the edge. And unbelievably paranoid. You think everyone is talking about you. That's how obsessed you become. It's so ugly. You never relax, never throw your head back for fear of triple-chin syndrome. You perch holding it all in, even when there's nothing to hold in. In my backless-top phase I used to make myself slightly hunched so that my spine stuck out through my sallow skin. I looked like fucking Quasimodo and thought it was sexy. It wasn't. It really wasn't.

I convinced Nikki and Zoe to come and live with me in my flat for a while, and things improved because I felt safer with them. We had some great nights. Dancing on table nights. Flirting with famous people nights. Sometimes a little more. Justine's hen night was a particular favourite. I'd got the hots for a certain R'n'B star who shall remain nameless to protect him from my dad. Somehow I got his number from the tour manager, rang him and went over to his exceedingly plush hotel room. Of course all the girls were laughing, telling me not to, but laughing more and loving it because it was a mad thing to do. And it was. I was driven into the underground car park and whisked up to his suite – and that's about all I can remember. The Strawberry Daiquiris had caught up with me. I recall being vaguely aware that he wasn't nearly as good-looking in the flesh but still ended up in his huge bath, smoking a cigar, while he serenaded me with his own songs. Maybe that was why I puked up on his bedroom floor. Classy. Hell, I'd been monogamous for a long time. And every pop star needs a few notches, even me. It was a mad, experimental time and yes, once I did do that rock-and-roll thing of going on telly having not been to bed. But I know presenters of those early morning Saturday programmes who've done the same, and they had to keep it going for longer than my fifteen-minute slot.

Trust me, no one gave me a harder time about my wilder nights than myself. I would run home, to my nan's, or to Justine's cottage in Bedfordshire, to self-flagellate. But though I hated myself for it, the papers seemed to like it. There was an absolute frenzy in the least classy red-top papers over my accidental 'flashing' moment at G.A.Y., an exceptional dance club on Tottenham Court Road in London. In the middle of a Michael Jackson moment I pulled the lapels of my jacket open and briefly popped out of my pink bra. I hadn't even realized it had happened until it made the front pages and a few of the centre ones the following day. I was accused of having orchestrated that little manoeuvre, but I really hadn't. Do you think I enjoyed hearing about Dad going into the builder's merchant's only to see *The People*'s 'full-page pull-out' of an eighth of one of my nipples with the added headline 'No Enhancement! All Genuine!' Everywhere he went he got 'Saw your Billie's tits in the paper today.' 'See your Bill got her tits out again.' Poor Dad – no wonder he packed up and moved to Spain.

I suppose the question wasn't just was I going bad, but how hard was I going to fall? Nothing like seeing a 'celebrity' implode to shift a few copies. If anything I was a good girl trying to forget bad times. Needless to say, it wasn't the way. But what did I know? It was supposed to be fun. Trouble was, I was getting sicker and sicker. I'd been starving myself for six months, I was swallowing laxatives by the handful, and I was living off caffeine and alcohol. The cystitis came back, each time more acute than before. Eventually it got so bad that I couldn't work through it, however much I tried. Every few weeks I'd be forced to cancel something, and every single one of those cancellations got reported. I was getting the reputation of being flaky – drunken and flaky. All they needed now was drugs, and I was going down.

# The Scene of the Foam

## Bar 38

On 17 June my body said stop. Five minutes after arriving at a bar in Soho, I collapsed. I'd ignored all the warnings, at my peril. The fact that my periods had stopped didn't bother me at all. In fact I was pleased, because I was on my way to where I wanted to be. I conveniently turned a blind eye to the hairy face and was loving my ribcage. But the combination of lack of food and late nights was wreaking havoc on my health. The bladder infection moved up to my kidneys and I started to pee blood. That was why I cancelled gigs. I thought kidney infection sounded better than haemorrhaging cystitis, but that's actually what it was. The day I collapsed in Bar 38 I'd been feeling particularly unwell – in fact the night before I'd had such bad cystitis that I kept wanting to be sick. Unwilling to sit at home in an empty flat, something I still struggle with today, I swallowed some painkillers, got tarted up and headed for Soho with the girls. None of us was wearing very much – they were in skimpy cowgirl outfits, complete with Stetson hats. I was hoping for another fun girly night out.

We arrived at Bar 38 and immediately I had to go to the loo, which was downstairs, so I left my friends at the bar. No wonder people thought it was drugs – when it was bad I had to rush to the loo every five minutes, absolutely bursting. But when I got there I could only manage a few acidic drops. My body was full of toxins. It would make me weep because each time it felt like I was peeing razor blades, not using them to cut up coke. That evening was no exception. I shuddered with pain, completely tensed up, and couldn't breathe. When it passed, I stood up. Usually I felt a window of relief after going to the loo, but that night I still felt sick and light-headed. I walked slowly up the steep stairs, thinking, 'It's OK. I can handle this', breathing very carefully, step by step. When I got to the top I felt my head suddenly get very heavy, and next thing I knew I'd collapsed. Hit the deck. Luckily I had a driver who was with me all the time (see what a hit gets you) and he carried me out. They took me to the London Clinic. A private hospital. I just remember being picked up by my feet and being turned upside down to get the blood to my head. They did lots of tests and discovered I was anaemic. I had been seeing a doctor who'd looked after me since I'd signed my deal – he was there to protect the record company as much as me, I guess. He came to the hospital to talk to me. I told him I had to pee, but I couldn't get up without help. I was in agony – I could barely speak but I didn't want to keep ringing for help. He said, 'Just pee in the bed, Billy.' So I did, crying every time with the humiliation and the pain of it all. My friends had to leave me. I needed my mother, but I told everyone not to tell her. Once again, I didn't want her to take it all away. I still don't understand what it was about this that I wanted to keep. I needed a hug. I needed someone to look after me. I needed my head examining. I needed someone to give me permission to stop and not be branded an ungrateful little brat for the rest of my life. I needed out.

What I got instead was my management calling up to tell me I needed to give the papers a statement. I could think of many. All started with 'F' and ended with 'off'. Instead I had to say some crap about being grateful for their concern – it was just a recurring kidney infection, combined with exhaustion, and I'd be back on my feet in no time. I kept saying over and over, 'It's not drugs. It's not drugs. I promise it's not drugs.' And I was telling the truth, though that very same press person had been happy to offer her own wares around when we'd all been on a night out. Two-faced isn't the word. My cowgirls left and I had to deal with the doctor alone.

He took one look at me and said, 'You're not eating, are you?' How could he see what everyone else had failed to see? Was it what my blood tests were telling him? Or the fat content test he did which revealed I didn't have any? Or could he just see by looking at me? I'm not saying that people purposely ignored what was under their noses, because I think I made it very hard for anyone to say anything to me. And above all I'm a broad girl – I have a physique that wasn't designed to be stick-thin, so from the front I still looked OK. Broad shoulders, wide hips, big head. But turn me on my side and there wasn't anything there. However hard and long I tried I couldn't make the square peg fit into the round hole, couldn't make myself into something that I wasn't designed to be.

I insisted the doctor didn't tell my mother. Absolutely insisted. So he didn't. He didn't tell anyone. He couldn't ask me any more questions because by this point I was in so much pain I couldn't actually speak. I just wanted something to make it all go away. I was prescribed morphine and slipped away from the phone calls and the press people to sleep in my own urine, happy that no one could get to me.

Mum woke the following morning and knew that something had happened because there were press outside. I always told her not to open the door when this kind of thing was taking place, and most of her didn't want to, but I was her daughter and she wanted to know what was going on. Since I wasn't going to tell her, this is how she found out what had happened to me. Did I consider this as I lay in my hospital bed giving statements to the press people? No. Mum opened the door and a guy called Jonathan who worked for the *Daily Mail* was standing on her doorstep. I think it was this charming journalist who at one point called Mum and told her he had a copy of her bank statements – such a favourite story in the Piper household.

He said, 'Have you heard about Billie, then?'

'What about Billie?'

'I can tell you don't know.'

'Know what?'

'She collapsed in a club last night – apparently something to do with drugs. But I can tell you don't know, so I'll let you get on to her people and I'll come back in five minutes.'

Once again she was in pieces. She headed for London straightaway, leaving Dad to get the kids to school. After that he went to work, but was back to collect them and look after them until Mum came home. The next day the papers printed a picture of my father loading his van, with the headline 'Dad Turns His Back on Billie' – something like that, anyway. It was completely untrue – he had to stay behind to look after the kids.

By the time Mum arrived at the hospital I had thought up a convincing lie. I told her that I'd taken the morning after pill and had had an allergic reaction to it. She believed me. Just to make sure, she asked the doctor. But he had given me his word – all he told her was that it wasn't anything to do with drugs. Mum wasn't aware of what was going on. She'd noticed how much thinner I'd got, but again, because I was never skeletal the working-too-hard line always seemed to work. Maybe it was easier for her to believe the lie. And since everybody in my 'camp' whom she asked said the same thing – kidney infection, tiredness – she had nothing to go on.

I absolutely loved being in hospital, and would have stayed there longer but for the fact that I was spending all my money on the bill and on top of that I was being sued for cancelling a gig at Greenwich University because I was in hospital. (Phone bills, hospital fees and one flat on Shoot Up Hill worth £280,000 – the sum total of the earnings of my music career. I had bought the flat by this time. Well, Dad had signed the mortgage papers because I was too young.) After Mum left I didn't speak to anyone. I just lay in bed pressing more and more morphine into my blood, in and out of hazy sleep. For once I wasn't thinking or worrying about work or what I had to do next. There was a big football match on – the European Championships, I think. I could hear everybody in Marylebone cheering, and I cheered with them because nobody could touch me.

It was Robbie Williams who warned me off drugs. We were friends, and he had told me in no uncertain terms to leave them well alone. When the news broke that I'd collapsed in a club and had been seen 'foaming' at the mouth, he called to see if there was anything he could do. I told him it wasn't drugs. We had a laugh about the foaming-at-the-mouth thing and wondered who these eye-witnesses were – from then on it became known as the Scene of the Foam. Apparently the story dominated the press. Another story came out that day too. It was claimed that Rich had had a dalliance with 'Natasha – the naked Russian' while we were still going out. On top of everything else, I was devastated by that. Nevertheless I slowly got better in hospital. Well, the cystitis did thanks to a week of antibiotics and no booze. But I also got worse. I liked the numbing effect of the sleeping pills and started to find ways to get my hands on them after leaving hospital.

# Cheek to Cheek

## An Award Ceremony

I'd play on my mother's weaknesses. I'd go home skinny as a rake and tell her that I couldn't sleep and that I was having a nervous breakdown, knowing that she'd take me to the doctor's. The doctor in Swindon had fixed her nervous breakdown, so they'd fix mine. Once there, I wouldn't let her come in with me. I was going to her when it suited me, keeping her at arm's length when it didn't. Well, it didn't take much to get me some sleeping pills. Temazepam became my new best friend. I told Mum I didn't like the effect, then took them home with me thinking that at least Mum wouldn't worry (or catch me). I found a very good use for them. If there was an award ceremony coming up my anorexia would go into overdrive. I'd start to think that I could be that extra bit thinner and that sample-size dress I'd been sent wasn't quite cutting it. So I would take the Temazepam and sleep my way thinner, delighted with my own brilliance: if I was asleep, I wouldn't have to eat at all.

Before one award ceremony I decided to sleep for the entire weekend and cut out three days of food. But when I woke from my drug-induced state I was absolutely convinced that somehow I had eaten something in my sleep. I'd dreamt it and it had been so real. I could remember chewing. Remember swallowing. Remember the taste. In actual fact I had not put a solid thing in my mouth for five days and what I'd been eating in my dreams was not food, but the inside of my cheeks.

I became so paranoid about feeling food in my stomach that I picked up the phone, as I had in Chicago, and sobbed incomprehensibly to Mum. What could she do? Any hint of her coming and hauling me out I'd resist, then shut down all lines of communication and run away. Mum just could not comprehend what it was I so desperately wanted to go back to. She thought, rightly, that it was a crazy world I was living in, but it was mostly one of my own making. And I never thought it was wrong, even when I was knocking myself out so as not to eat. I had become everything I'd loathed. I was a manic, neurotic, high-maintenance woman who felt put upon by everybody. Why did I go on? Because I thought it was working. I thought I was getting all the attention I'd ever wanted, and so I did more.

I had new management by that time – I went through managers like knickers. At this point it was Nicki Chapman and Nick Godwin from Brilliant. When they met me they thought how very endearing I was. They were impressed by my work ethic, and saw me as nicely ambitious without being ruthless. Polite – not something they saw a lot of in their game. They reckoned I still had that 'longevity' that people had talked about so long ago. But they were in fact inheriting a miserable situation. 'Day and Night' had come out and 'Something Deep Inside' was about to hit the shops. (I still can't believe I had a single with that title. What were we thinking?) I was working my socks off to keep up with Britney and Christina, and I had told them at Brilliant that I was happy to work. I wanted to compete. I thought that if I worked hard enough maybe I'd be better than them. But it was just a bittersweet fantasy. For all my fighting talk Nicki and Nick very soon realized how miserable I was. 'Something Deep Inside' went in at Number 4 – it was 'Honey to the Bee' all over again. I was gutted. They just had to scratch the surface to discover that I was finding life extremely difficult. The treadmill was going on at its furious pace, yet we were going backwards. Desperate and depressed, I called Rich. We started seeing each other again, though not officially. It was the worst kind of rekindling – the one where someone always gets burnt. No sex with the ex – it's textbook, for Christ sake. But I couldn't see the wood for the trees and thought I wanted someone on my side.

I had to go to Glasgow to do a TV show, but the dreaded cystitis returned and I was in agony. I was in tears (nothing unusual at this stage), it was an incredibly hot August day and I collapsed again (also not unusual). I was taken to hospital, and this time they checked me in as Minnie Mouse so that we wouldn't be discovered by the press. But there was another 'Minnie Mouse' already there – another pop star suffering from 'exhaustion'. Nicki called Mum and Dad because she thought they should be with me, but they couldn't just leave the kids and fly to Scotland and by now they were probably well and truly fed up with me. I know I was the cause of many arguments between them.

Mum and Dad told Nicki to send me down to them, but I couldn't because of the cystitis – a long journey would have been hell for me. I made it so hard on my parents. I told them about all the horrible things that had gone on between Rich and me, then got angry with them when they didn't welcome him back with open arms. Equally I told Rich about all the things that made me mad about Mum and Dad. I dug the rift between them myself, making it impossible for my boyfriend and my family to get along. I'm a little bit ashamed of the person I became at home and the person I became when I was with Rich. Our relationship was really breaking up, but what could my new management team do except paper over the cracks?

For a little while Nicki and Nick took over the job of parenting. They hired a cleaner for my flat and had food sent over so that I would eat properly – I didn't have the energy to shop, let alone cook. I was actually eating a little more at this stage because, with Rich around, I was getting the munchies again. What a pitifully unhealthy cycle I was in. No wonder my mother was at her wits' end. She had no idea what was going on – all she knew was that it was bad, and she didn't know how to stop it. My management knew I was in pieces but I was on the cusp of turning eighteen and in any case they weren't my guardians – I employed them. Hugh was being shielded from most of the worst stuff, and anyway I had a strong line going in denials and was adept at using the finger when it suited me.

My eighteenth birthday finally arrived. Boy, it had taken a while. Innocent threw another party for me. It was in the same place they had used for the 'Day and Night' party but the atmosphere was different. We had a Number 4, not a Number 1. I was jittery, as usual, from too much caffeine and nicotine. Rich was there, in a bad mood. I had to keep him away from my family. I threw myself into having a good time and getting lots of attention. My friends and family had a good time too, drinking loads of champagne and getting the full treatment because they were with me. Then a *Sun* reporter turned up with Charlie the sniffer dog. It was ridiculous. Would I let him in? No. This was a music industry party, not bloody Crufts.

Anyway, the straight-talking Justine Bell had given me a pep talk. It went something like this:

'Listen, Pipes, do yourself a favour. Don't do anything stupid tonight, just don't. Honest to God, it's more ag in your little world. Everybody who is in any position to do you damage will be at your party.'

As soon as I walked in, she took one look at me and pulled me to one side. 'You stupid cow! Don't do any more gear.'

'I haven't,' I told her.

'I know you haven't. Just don't do any more.'

My mum stepped up to us to ask what was going on. Quick as a cat Justine replied, 'Just telling Bill to take it easy on the drink.'

That was the closest we got to talking about drugs. She never saw me take them, and I never saw her. The same with my management – drugs were not discussed. It was a problem the press had created. Not us, not me. But it was beginning to make everyone nervous and we found ourselves back in the grey area between friendship and colleague. Yes, as part of my management team they all had carer duties, but they weren't responsible for my personal life. I was eighteen, so that was my job now. If I wanted to party until dawn, I was going to. And I did.

# Walk of Life

## The Highlands

The partying never got out of hand, thank God, because my schedule wouldn't allow it. For the rest of the autumn I was flying all over the world: We were due to tour Japan, New Zealand and Australia. We had a trip to Canada planned. Another visit to New York. I was asking too much of myself. Japan was excruciating. There, the same panic that had gripped me prior to going on *TFI Friday* threatened to suffocate me. I remember seeing my management team watching me through the glass of a radio station studio. I was attempting to sing live but it was going horribly wrong, and I couldn't meet their eye. We'd gone way beyond trying to visualize a note. I felt sick to my stomach. The frogs in my throat had moved in and set up a permanent home. Then the cystitis came back, so I came home from that tour early. I should have been thinking about getting healthy, but I had another video coming up. It was back on the 'old faithful' for me: I managed another five days without solid food.

To film the video for *Walk of Life* we went to the west coast of Scotland. Hugh came from the Highlands, and when he took us up there I was blown away. I'd never seen anything so beautiful and I fell completely in love with the area. Hugh remembers the shoot as great fun, and me as utterly delightful the whole way through. He'd heard some whispers about me not eating for the shoot, but that wasn't unusual in this business so he didn't think anything of it.

Strange. All I remember is tears. Constant tears. I was coming apart, inside out, living a half-life. Still obsessed with my weight. Still desperately trying to control one area of my life because everything else was out of control. I had kept the unravelling to myself, but now even the wind-up dolly was beginning to malfunction. I couldn't get it together. I couldn't even sing what I had once been able, if not to shine at, at least to get through.

Hugh would say that I'm not remembering it as it was, that I'm being unnaturally hard on myself. He can only recall the odd down moment, but then he wasn't with me every day. His memory of me is always with a smile on my face. I couldn't tell him what was going on because I admired him too much and I didn't want to lose his faith. And no one else was going to tell him either. He was shielded from a lot of things. No wonder he thought everything was going all right.

I'd spent so long convincing people I could handle everything that I'd forgotten how to ask for help. And I needed help because everything was out of control again. The video was beautiful, but it was all wrong for the time and totally missed the market. *Walk of Life* bombed.

# A Car Full of Roses

## A Street Scene

A few days before releasing *Walk of Life* with its ill-conceived video I went into the Virgin radio station to be interviewed by Chris Evans. Just like on *TFI Friday* the mood between us was easy, relaxed. I was relieved. We'd had such fun on *TFI* but I hadn't got to speak to Chris after the show, so I wasn't sure whether this vibe between us was only in my head. We'd gone to the pub but he was surrounded by people and I couldn't get anywhere near him. Anyway, at the time I'd had a boyfriend. Chris had waved goodbye to me and I'd left the pub feeling rather deflated. Since then I'd done a little research on him and I knew he too was now single again. And I hadn't imagined it – the buzz between us was just as it had been on *TFI*. We both giggled continually, then halfway through Chris popped the question. Not on bended knee with a ring, but like this.

'Why don't we get married and sell the photos to *Hello*, then give all the money to charity?'

I replied 'OK, let's.'

I didn't think he was being serious – but I wasn't absolutely sure he wasn't being serious either. It was December and the party season was in full swing. At the end of the show Chris asked me to his Christmas drinks. I was gutted because I had to be somewhere else that day, but I gave him my number.

A couple of days later, he called and asked me out. I had just done *Top of the Pops*, but we didn't finish until about 9.30 p.m. and by the time I got into London it was closing time. I went to meet him at his favourite pub, the Nag's Head in Belgravia. Nicki came with me. Chris and his friend Webbo were outside with their drinks, even though it was freezing. Suddenly Chris said, 'Right, let's go somewhere else!' And the four of us just left our beers on the ground and jumped into a cab. I don't know why that seemed so crazy to me, but it did. We went to a bar called Denim and had a few drinks, then went on to Stringfellow's. From the moment we met that evening we were inseparable. He had his hands down the back of my trousers all night playing with my thong, and I let him.

It was a bizarre night. Peter Stringfellow came over to talk to us, gave us champagne, then supplied the papers with a quote saying we couldn't keep our hands off one another. We watched a lot of horny ladies dance, then went on to the den of iniquity that is Brown's. Probably most of my worst behaviour took place there, but not with Chris. He is vehemently anti-drugs, which was pretty apparent from that first night. We were good and pissed, though. Chris was wearing brogues. Don't know why, but I love a man in brogues. I told him, so he gave them to me and I walked around Brown's in his brogues all night.

I remember him leaning towards me and saying, 'I just wish you were twenty-six at least.'

And as always I was saying, 'It doesn't matter how old I am. Let's not talk about how old I am because that's just going to hijack this evening and ruin everything.'

Once he'd mentioned my age I was conscious that I had to act really old, handle my drink and try to use big words. He was clearly a genius and thirty-four at that. I really wanted to impress him. Perhaps skipping about in his brogues hadn't been such a good idea. What was I going to impress him with – being a pop star? Suddenly that didn't feel very impressive – he'd seen them all, all the actors, all the divas, all the pop tarts. It turned out that what impressed him was me just being me skipping around in his brogues, laughing, looking at him and feeling it was OK to look. He let me be me. Now I had to remember who that was.

At the end of the evening he went off with Webbo and I with Nicki, who was absolutely plastered because I'd left her chatting and drinking with Webbo all night while Chris and I bonded. I'd just put Nicki to bed when my phone rang. It was Chris.

'What are you doing?'

'I've just made beans on toast.'

'Me too.'

It was a sign.

'I had a really great night,' I said.

'It was wonderful.'

I went to bed happy for the first time in a long time.

Next morning I woke up at about ten and had already missed four calls from him. He had left a message saying, 'Why are you not up, you lazy cow? It's a beautiful day – you have to see it. Wake up and call me, because I need your address.'

So I did. An hour later he arrived at my door with an envelope. He didn't kiss me, he just smiled and handed over the envelope. I was still in my sweat pants and had black mascara all over my face and looked like shit but I didn't care. I knew he didn't. I hadn't brushed my teeth and was wafting around in my own personal cloud of vodka fumes. It was all rather sexy. Turned out he hadn't done his radio show that morning. It was the first one he'd ever missed. But not the last.

Chris left after telling me to open the envelope. So I did. What was inside blew my mind. There were some car keys and a note. 'I know you don't care about any of this and nor do I, but I had to stop you in your tracks. If you don't want it sell it and give it to charity. I think you're wonderful. Will you marry me?' I held up the key. That unmistakable rearing yellow horse dangled from the ring. I don't think I screamed, but Nicki did. 'Oh my gawd a Ferrari!' We looked outside and there was nothing there, so we went out the front. The brilliant doorman, Abdul – a huge Nigerian guy – was clutching his stomach and laughing. There, parked outside the building, was a silver Ferrari absolutely covered in red roses. Inside and out. Chris was sitting across the road with Webbo on two Virgin bikes, laughing his head off. I didn't have clue what to do. What is the etiquette when presented with a Formula One racing car? Get in, I suppose. So I went over to the car and did just that. Believe it or not, I didn't give a shit about the car itself but I was loving the roses. I wanted Chris to see me in it. I wanted to show him that I liked it. And what I *really* wanted was to kiss him. I beckoned him over and he came to the gate and we had a quick peck between the bars. I said, 'Thank you', he said, 'You're welcome', and then he left on his bike. It was the most bizarre morning of my life.

I called my dad first because he's always been a huge car freak.

'Chris Evans, as in Chris Evans from *TFI Friday* and *Don't Forget Your Toothbrush*, has just bought me a Ferrari!'

He said, 'You mean the ginger guy?'

'Yes, Dad.'

'Why the fuck did he buy you a fucking Ferrari?'

'I don't know. I went out with him last night!'

'What were you doing, Bill? What did you do?'

Poor Dad, he sprouted a few more grey hairs that morning! The most ridiculous thing of all was that I couldn't even drive. I'd never bothered to learn. I hadn't had the time or the inclination, and anyway I was always picked up by drivers so there didn't seem to be any need. Bloody ridiculous. The engine was covered in glass. It petrified me. As beautiful as Ferraris are, they look quite aggressive. All I could think about was him. As I said, I really didn't give a fuck about the car, but I kept every single rose.

My next call was to Justine and Sara from Virgin. I rang and said, 'Oh, my God, there's a Ferrari outside my door.' They came over to join us and soon we were all loving it, jumping up and down, in a hysterical fashion. I read them the note and asked Justine what she reckoned.

She looked at me and said, 'He's the winner! He's the bloody winner!'

It was like being in a film – we were all feeding off the excitement.

Within a nano-second my managers were on the phone: 'Don't keep the car. It'll look terrible. Give the money to charity. Don't call him. You have to be careful.' Now, looking back, I think, 'You awful people – what were you thinking and why didn't you want me to call him?' But in their defence they were worried. They knew what sort of state I was in, and it was such a big gesture they feared my head would be turned. Well, it was. But by him. Not by the car. Even so, call me old-fashioned but it isn't every day you get given a Ferrari, so I decided to hell with it, I'd keep it. I wasn't going to drive it around, but I knew a man who would. Up to that point my car-loving dad hadn't seen a great deal of upside to my so-called 'fame and fortune'.

'Good girl yourself,' said Justine.

'Quite right,' said Sara.

'Don't be bought,' said Nicki Chapman.

Don't be bought? A bit late for that, wasn't it? I was up for sale, wasn't I? Wasn't that the whole point of the crazy business I was in? Wasn't I a manufactured product destined for the consumer market? Don't be bought. . . . She was quite right, but not for the reasons she thought. Slowly things started falling into place in my addled mind. Slowly I started to see sense.

The Ferrari had to be driven into the underground car park by Alistair, who worked at the management company, because he was the only one who could drive an H-shift. At first we couldn't even get it going – we had no idea how to get the immobilizer off. We were all sitting in the car laughing. I think Alistair rang a Ferrari garage to ask them what to do.

He said, 'We're trying to start this Modena.'

'That's funny,' replied the man in the garage. 'We just sold one of those to Chris Evans.'

I couldn't believe Chris had just walked into a dealership and bought me a bloody Ferrari! It was a head fry, a hysterical, wonderful head fry. I read the note again and again and again, trying to read between the lines. Not that I needed to. It was quite clear what he wanted. My hand in marriage. Woo-hoo!

Well, he'd certainly succeeded in stopping me in my tracks. The question now was what the hell was I going to do about Rich? We'd been together for two years, and if it had been an easy thing to walk away from then I would have done so. But it wasn't. It was as compulsive as the eating and the cleaning. I was confused, to say the least. That night I went to the Royal Albert Hall for a huge charity performance. I had a stinking hangover as usual. There were press everywhere. I thought I knew what it was like to be hounded by the press, but I knew nothing. This was major league. I suddenly realized that all I'd ever been was a minnow. It wasn't a depressing realization. It was refreshing. I could stop taking myself so goddamn seriously. Being bought? I don't think so. What was the poor man really getting in return? I'd gone from being a bubbly, fun person, always wanting to have a great time, to this withdrawn creature endlessly drawing on a Marlboro Light. My eyes had lost their shine. They didn't dance any more. I was a shell. Underweight, uninspired and boring. I had no energy to do anything. I had let the anorexia steal whatever fun I could have taken out of the experience and turned it into something to fear. Three days later *Walk of Life* went in at Number 25.

# Kissing a Prince

INT:

## A Cottage at Christmas

My second meeting with Chris was more or less a covert operation. I wanted to get cosy with this new species but I had another man whom I didn't want to hurt, who was still reeling from the Ferrari thing. I wasn't planning on marrying Chris when I arranged to meet him – I wanted a chance to find out for myself what was going on. So I lied to Rich – and then went and met one of Britain's most famous faces in secret.

Chris told me to meet him at the Grenadier, a beautiful old English pub tucked away down a cobbled street in London that you'd never know was there unless you'd been told. The Grenadier serves the best Bloody Marys in pub land, and they even have hot sausages on the bar. I arrived there at about two in the afternoon, wearing low-slung baggy jeans and a tight-fitting vintage brown biker jacket. I was also sporting a freshly cut bob.

I had requested that no one was even to get wind of our meeting, so Chris had secured a dark corner at the back of the pub. We greeted each other like old friends. It felt like we'd met many times before, and I felt certain we would meet again because I loved him the minute we started chatting. I quite simply loved this stranger who sat opposite me. People say love is blind, but my eyes and heart had never been so open. We didn't stop for long – you never do when you're with him – but quickly left through a convenient back door. Chris knew the bar staff and had set up this arrange-ment before I arrived. I asked him where we were going and he said, 'To meet an old friend of mine. His name's Fred and he's having a party. Let's go.'

Fred was blind and lived in an old people's home. He used to live next door to Chris before being moved into care, but Chris still looked after him. We had a very eccentric Christ-mas lunch with Fred and all his cronies, then drove to Chris's cottage in the village of Hascombe near Godalming in Surrey for one night. Nothing happened. I was trying to impress him, but I was nervous of him as well. His enthusiasm for life is engaging, inspiring, but in the beginning I was too knackered to take it all on. He started talking about stuff that was going on in the world from which I had switched off. By the end of that year I was jaded and cynical and fairly self-orientated – I felt so lived in and exhausted. Chris made it perfectly clear that doing nothing other than being a pop star was a pretty vacuous way to live. I knew it, but I just didn't know how to get off the treadmill. In the beginning I was a bit confused. I thought all I had to do was work, so why was he now telling me there was other stuff to do? Perhaps staying with Rich, staying in my 'pop stardom' world, was easier? Maybe this person was asking too much of me? There was something in my stomach saying this one's a keeper, but there were also so many other opinions and influences whizzing around – I had talked endlessly to the girls about him. The hysteria surrounding the whole thing made it hard to see things clearly.

Then Chris said, 'Life is happening and you aren't even aware of it. You have to grow up and stop being so spoilt.' Grow up? I thought I'd been convincing everyone that I had. But Chris saw through me in a flash. He was right: I had to grow up. But I wasn't sure how. He wanted to know what was going on with Rich. Was it on or off? I knew then that Rich and I had to end. Chris told me he was going to Madeira at Christmas. I said goodbye and headed home myself with this quiet thought going round and round in my head: maybe I could go with him?

I listened to his show every morning on Virgin, because that was the only time I could hear him and speak to him without feeling nervous and weird. I didn't call for a while because I was feeling so exhausted, and his radio show made this absent stranger feel more and more like a reality. I was just fucked, fried, miserable and angry with a failing music career that I didn't even want but was too scared to leave.

But for a few days at least I could try to put all that on one side.

I spent the beginning of the Christmas break in and out of pubs, meeting up with old friends for a bit of Swindon madness. It was a great opportunity to hang out with the folks and their friends. The conversation always went along these lines:

'So, a Ferrari, eh?'

'Yep.'

'What's he up to, that one? He's got ginger hair.'

'Yes, he has. He's got freckles, too, and I love it.'

'Oh no . . . anyway, my mate said that car would've cost him a hundred grand. Yeah, he went on the internet to check it out . . . yeah . . . he's a bit weird that Chris Evans . . . yeah . . . I'd be careful if I were you.'

On Christmas Eve I was out all day at a bar called Rudy's with Uncle Danny and all twelve of his builder mates. We had a riot. I drank six pints and a couple of bottles of Rudy's finest Shiraz. Then we went for a Chinese with Danny and his fiancée Claire. I'd finally broken up with Rich – it was easy this time, because we both knew it needed to happen. It was done over the phone. That sounds very Phil Collins, I know, but we were barely speaking then anyway. The phonecall was almost too much effort for us both. I suddenly had this overwhelming urge to see Chris. So I sat on the steps of the Chinese restaurant and rang him.

Out of the box, I said, 'Can I come on holiday with you?'

'Of course you can.'

'You said you were going on Boxing Day – when shall I come down?'

'Come down tomorrow.'

'Christmas Day?'

'Yeah – Christmas Day.'

I wondered what I was going to say to my family – I couldn't do that to them. But then some relatives came over in the morning, all bringing CDs for me to sign, and I suddenly felt so tired of it all. I wanted out. Just as Mum placed the prawn cocktails on the table mats, I announced that I was going to see Chris and then going on holiday with him. Mum didn't say anything, but I know she was gutted. In fact it broke her heart. She'd only just got me back and I was off again. We hadn't seen each other for such a long time. But equally I think she understood. Mum could tell I was knackered, so maybe a holiday wasn't such a bad idea. I was supposed to be going back to the Seychelles with Rich, but obviously that was no longer happening. I needed looking after – Mum knew that. It's just that *she* wanted to be given that job. Why, she would have been thinking, couldn't she put me to bed, cuddle me, wash my clothes, do all the things that mums are supposed to do? All the things she hadn't been able to do for years? Instead I was going off with someone I didn't even know. Again. But I was so bolshy and so headstrong, and so quick to fire, that she knew protest was futile. And anyway, as Mum says now, I was right to do it. Something in my heart was telling me to go. Something in hers didn't stop me.

I had my driver come and collect me. I know it sounds awful, but I knew I had to do it. At the time I didn't consider that it was out of order, I didn't consider the fact that I was taking him away from his family, and I didn't consider that I was leaving mine to deflect more questions about why their daughter didn't see fit to stay with them for the holidays. I was completely selfish, but I was so close to finding what was going to make me happy that all I had to do was get there.

I wanted to hug Chris and hold his hand. I kept thinking about all the freckles on his fingers that I'd seen the last time we'd met, and somehow it took away the big, scary TV persona bit and made him more like me. As I stared out of the window at the world rushing past me I wished I could get there faster. Finally we pulled up outside his little cottage, which stood on a beautiful estate in Surrey. I climbed out of the Mercedes, closed the door behind me with a thick, heavy clunk, gave my driver a bundle of cash, thanked him for his mercy mission and said goodbye. Then I turned to face this old wooden door, surrounded by climbing roses, and Chris opened it. He was wearing a red poloneck jumper with little white stars on it, Christmas personified – he beamed at me and held up a matching one for me. All the doubts and second thoughts that had plagued me in the car vanished. I looked at him and thought he was so great. He took my hand, led me into the kitchen and gave me an enormous kiss, a proper, full on, serious kiss – our first in fact. It was magic. My next adventure was about to begin. The following day we flew to Madeira, and just like that 'Billie' the pop princess disappeared. I'd finally kissed my prince and, in our own special version of the old fairytale, he let me turn back into a frog.

'Hey, Palm Springs! You know it's only moments from Las Vegas…'

Getting married Las Vegas-style.

Brits abroad.

On the lash with Webbo in Dungeness.

The best BBQ ever.

Off to see the Colosseum in, er, Athens.

Followed everywhere by the Pap (even when hammered).

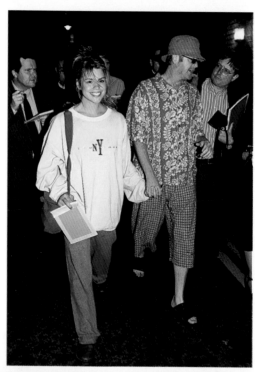

Chris leaves Virgin.
We leave London.

Big mate, little mate. In the kitchen at Hascombe.

Christmas at Hascombe.
The second set of
lights go on!

The proud
Mr Evans
admires
his pond.

David Coulthard eat your heart out!

# Act Four

*Being a Wife*

SCENE ONE:

# Petal

EXT:

## Madeira

When I was a little girl, my parents told me that when I grew up I'd get married and have a lovely life. I always imagined it would be with someone called Dave. His hair would be brown, with a short back and sides, and he'd look like one of those Next Directory Catalogue models. He'd be tall, well built, well hung. *Joke*. He'd cuddle you to death, making you feel small in his arms. He'd thank you for making him his tea and he wouldn't spend too much time necking lager. But then I grew up and realized that Dave didn't exist. And even if he did, he wouldn't be enough. I wouldn't want *him* – I wanted something impossible. And I started to dream. I dreamed about my impossible man, my impossible soulmate. I dreamed and dreamed and dreamed until one day he turned up on my doorstep and gave me an envelope with a letter inside asking me to marry him.

I gave Chris a Christmas present. In return for the Ferrari I gave him one petal from one of the red roses, in a box. I wanted to thank him but couldn't find the words. Nor could I match his gift. But what I could do was make him stop and look at the detail rather than at the big picture all the time. I needed saving, but in a way so did he. I never went back to my flat or to my parents' house. From that moment on we lived in each other's pockets. Or perhaps, if I am brutally honest with myself, I lived in his. But that was how I wanted it to be. How I needed it to be. In the beginning I think it freaked him out, which was not altogether surprising. The ballsy, skinny Number 1 singer who'd run around Brown's in his brogues and to whom he'd presented a Ferrari all but disappeared with that kiss.

It wasn't so much that I lived in his pocket as that I tried to burrow deep inside, curl up into a tiny ball and wait for all my responsibilities to go away. But that sort of behaviour doesn't wash with a man like Chris, and as early as that first holiday he started asking questions I couldn't answer. When was my next album due? How much money had I made? How long was I contractually obligated to Innocent? Why couldn't I drive? Why hadn't I taken any exams? Why was I ill? How had I become such a shell? Why, after all the work I'd put in, was I still living in a shitty flat in Kilburn? For the first time since my singing career had started I was embarrassed, not by my singing, but by myself, by who I'd become. I was embarrassed that I didn't know how to cook, embarrassed that I didn't know how to drive, embarrassed that I didn't have any control over the day-to-day running of my life. I could see it frustrated him, wound him up. I felt so stupid – this was my life, yet I didn't know the answers. I felt he was looking at me with disdain. How has this happened? Why are you in this position? Haven't you got a brain?

But he wasn't thinking that. He was thinking: You are this tiny little girl who should have been taken care of. Where was your support system? Who was in charge? He was angry. He blamed my management – though they were relatively new on the scene – the record company and, I suppose, my parents to a degree, and I probably let him think that because part of me agreed. Part of me still thinks that someone should have noticed what was going on and made it stop. Someone older should have realized that a girl as young as I was, despite all my protestations to the contrary, was never going to admit that she couldn't handle it. I grew up with a strong work ethic – it's ingrained in me, and is by and large a great foundation. But it also means that it's difficult to admit when you can't cope. It's difficult even to recognize that you're not coping. Someone with an overview should have seen that. But therein lies the difficulty: no one person did have an overview. I'd compartmentalized my life so much that it was impossible for any one person to know everything. Christ, even I didn't know. I had been purpose-fully and carefully unpicking my safety net since getting into the music business. But when someone says *they*'ve done this to you, you're more than willing to let everyone but yourself take the blame.

We hardly left the bedroom of our hotel in Madeira. Love's young dream? No, a burnt out eighteen-year-old with recurring cystitis. It was agony again. Poor Chris – he didn't know what to do so he called Mum for advice. I'm sure she was happy to be offered the chance to help, and I wanted them to like him as much as I did. But sadly that relationship didn't pan out as well as I'd hoped, and my parents and I didn't see or even speak to each other for quite a long time after I went off with Chris. Offered a large amount of money in return for a sweet story about their daughter and future son-in-law, they considered it long enough to call me and let me know. I got pissed off – I just wanted them to be my parents, not part of the publicity machinery. I'm sure others would consider such an offer but I didn't know how the relationship between Chris and me was going to end, so it was all a bit soon to be talking about our marriage and three red-headed children. Chris wasn't impressed. It created a rift between me and my parents. It was sad, but we couldn't even agree to disagree – we just argued, so I thought it was better just not to talk.

When we came back from Madeira I moved straight into Chris's flat in London and didn't leave his side except for when he went to work. After the argument with Mum and Dad I was terrified that I would lose everyone around me, terrified that this person who I knew could make me happy might leave me. For a while it was unstable, unbalanced and probably a little unhealthy. But Chris is uncompromising, too. Imagine the mix. So in the beginning there were a few incidents when Chris would go off to do his own thing, leaving me reeling. I was too needy. I was forcing him into a parent role, a role he didn't want. He wanted to be my equal, not my nurse; my lover, not my mother. Thankfully he cared for me enough to force the issue out into the open. Thankfully I loved him enough to stick around. But I pissed off a fair few people in the pursuit of love. Not just my parents but my friends, my managers and my boss.

I had effectively walked out of a singing career, but I still had outstanding commitments. There was a show in Ireland, a film I was up for, and I was due to release another single. On that Madeira holiday it was fairly evident fairly quickly what sort of mess I was in. I wasn't being a diva – I really needed a break. Chris understood the 'entertainment' industry and never let people fuck him over. He's very smart and very confident, and not remotely afraid of confrontation. I didn't think he was going to 'ruin' things for me, as was reported in the press; I knew he was only going to make my life better. For a start, I knew he wasn't interested in me because of what he could get out of me. There was no ulterior motive there – he certainly didn't need to date a 'pop star' to cement his celebrity status. And I wasn't using him to climb further up the ladder, because the last thing I wanted to do was scramble back up and show off my tush to the world again as part of a power couple. If anything, I was using him to climb *down*. He gave me something to hold on to – without him I would have fallen. I think he was quite angry with me for having lost control of my career. But in fairness I couldn't have lost it since I'd never had it in the first place. I was fourteen when I first had a manager, and from then on I had been micro-managed. The only thing my managers didn't do for me was brush my teeth. I still did that. But not always.

Chris told me to get control of my career, anyway. But at the time I was so tired that I didn't want control. I didn't know how to manage my life. People took care of everything for me; all I had to do was get up and dance or sing or whatever else was required to sell a record or two. It might have looked like I was taking ownership of things, but all I was doing was handing responsibility over to Chris. I didn't want it and I really, really didn't want to do the film in Ireland. I just wanted to be with Chris. But I couldn't face calling my managers, so Chris did it for me. He couldn't understand the problem. If I didn't want to do it, then I shouldn't have to. That's Chris to a tee. I remember him ringing Nick to tell him I wouldn't be doing the job. Nick was cross, of course, and kept asking Chris how he would feel if someone was booked on to his show and for no reason didn't turn up. But Chris was not to be swayed – he stood his ground. My ground. I didn't want to do it, and that was that. As far as he's concerned, no one should do anything against their will. So he and Nick had a row.

I remember Chris saying, 'You don't own her. She's the talent – you work for her, not the other way round. What do you mean she has to do something she doesn't want to do? She's a human being. . . .'

It went on and on. Nick was just gobsmacked that I was going to let everyone down. It's not something I'd done before. Not wilfully. I'd cancelled a few gigs because I was ill, but now I was just saying no. Or letting someone do it for me. Exasperated that Chris wouldn't put me on the phone – in fact because I refused to take the phone – Nick said something like 'It isn't your problem.'

To which Chris replied, 'Well, it is now.' Poor man, he'd just elevated his status from prince in shining armour to Saviour with a capital S. I put him on a pedestal that he had to force me to take down.

Shortly after that row I parted company with Nicki and Nick. But not before they had secured me a third record deal on which, as a goodwill gesture to me, they didn't take any commission. I saw an article which read as though Nicki had slagged Chris off for ruining my career, but I should know better than to believe what I read in the press. Isn't that what I'm forever telling my mother? It was the usual cut-and-paste job with things taken out of context and questions turned into answers. Nicki never went to the press about us, and although things didn't end nicely Brilliant did a good job managing me at the time and actually got me some money coming in for a change, so I would like to think any bad air is long behind us. There was so much I didn't understand. I was angry and lashing out. They just happened to be there at the time, but none of the mess was of their making. I think they knew I was in tatters by the end, fighting off depression, and they knew that although Chris was a scary adversary he was ultimately good for me. I put him in the position of 'bad guy' because I didn't have the tools to take responsibility for my actions. It's something I'm still learning to do.

I'd gone from a child–parent relationship at home to a child–manager relationship at work. And I'd stayed in that role of child. Always the child, but pretending to be an adult and being furious with anyone who told me otherwise. Chris stepped into that position by proxy, but more than anything he wanted me to think for myself. I thought a lot about his words to me: Grow up. It was not a process that happened overnight. I had to retrain myself. I had to re-educate my brain. I had to be broken up before I could bring myself together again. What I really needed was time to heal, breathe and be quiet, but I couldn't quite bring myself to admit my pop career was over. I needed something to bring to the table. I wanted to impress Chris. I wanted to be stronger. So I went back to Hugh to discuss my career.

# The Tide Is High

## A Record Company Meeting Room

Chris set me up with top-agent Michael Foster. Not a bad second. But at the time I had no respect for people in management or agents or any of them. I thought they were all parasites. I had got used to never picking up their calls, and always ringing back a few days later, if at all. When Michael called me I didn't get back to him for three days. So he called again and left me in no doubt that he expected a response from people he was actually trying to help.

He's like Chris: he isn't scared. All I'd ever had was yes men. 'It's fine that you haven't bothered to call me back . . .' (which of course it wasn't), all smiles out front and back-stabbing behind. We were all fucking up. But this was something different. He instantly raised my game. We went to Innocent together to talk to Hugh about 'The Tide Is

High' and decide what the next step should be. At that time I was still thinking about releasing the single. I knew I needed time off, but I was still clinging on to it. I hadn't completely washed my hands of it. I still wanted to be wanted by the record company – the words 'You've been dropped' still terrified me. I wanted time off *and* I still wanted to have a record deal. I was scared about the thought of having nothing, and part of me wanted to fulfil my end of the bargain and give them something for that 'longevity' they'd always talked about. I guess I was operating on auto-pilot and doing what I'd always done, keeping the show on the road. I must have been convincing, because after Michael and I left the meeting we were going through Westbourne Grove in a cab when he told me he was quite impressed and was excited to be working with me. And trust me, Michael Foster doesn't suffer fools gladly.

Why, then, did I decide not to release 'The Tide Is High'? Maybe because within days of that meeting I had realized that I couldn't pull it off. I couldn't go back to that schedule. Chris and I were working out our differences. I asked him to explain to me what was going on in his head rather than disappearing, and I in turn made a conscious effort not to pull him under. We'd started off with such a bang that inevitably there needed to be some adjustment. Chris wasn't used to compromise, but you can't have an equal relationship without it. You also can't have an equal relationship if you give over your entire being. Luckily we met in the middle, and in doing so really did become inseparable. But maybe it was something else. Someone else.

Her name was Juliet Peters, and according to her many phone messages she wanted to kill me. Not just me, but my brother too. She was very open about what she wanted to do to me, and to be honest she wasn't very clever about it. She never hid her identity, for one. I think Justine would agree that it was all blown out of proportion. No doubt about it, she left some well moody messages at Innocent and once spoke to someone and told them she was going to kill me, but since she also left her name and address perhaps it didn't need the response it got. It had all started on the *Pepsi Chart Show* on Channel Five the previous year. She was in the audience and thought I had given her a dirty look, but what I was actually trying to do was move into position to do a link in the show with Foxy and she was in the way. The first message that came in was: 'Billie Piper is a fucking cow and a fucking whore that needs cutting up into little pieces. She can sing and dance but she's a bitch and she's going to die.' Then they progressed to my family: 'I'm going to kill her parents. I see them out shopping all the time. They are going to get their heads cut off very soon. The silly cow is a skinny bitch and she's going to be dead.' I probably quite liked the skinny bit. Or would have, had anyone actually told me about any of the messages when they came in. But they didn't. I wasn't privy to any of it. I didn't hear them until I arrived at court, so I didn't have much to say to the police when they interviewed me.

By the time the court case came around I didn't care about it any more. I was so much in love with Chris that I wanted to stay with him in his world, not go back to mine. I forgot why we were going to court: she hadn't actually done anything to me apart from making threats, but everybody had got very busy and convinced me that it was the right thing to do. I told Mum I wanted to drop the charges, but she was having none of it. The whole thing had been tough on her. It wasn't just the Peters threats but the hundreds of letters that started with 'Bitch!' Or the multitude of others: 'I hate you! Watch your back! You're dead!' Or my personal favourite, which was a photo of me with the words, 'I'm a stupid slag and my mum shagged Mr Ed' (as in the talking horse). Peters was the straw that broke the camel's back. I don't think she was dangerous, but I'd been getting so much hate mail because of my relationship with Rich that her last one tipped everyone over the edge: 'Next time she appears on stage she's going to be shot dead.' At the time that message was picked up I was due in from Canada to do a big live performance in London, and poor Mum was in the crowd searching madly for the one person out of the hundreds who was going to hold up a gun and kill me. (Rich got it from her too: 'A gormless f****** four-eyed c*** who wears too much make-up, silly f****** tosser, I hope he has a rotten birthday on Wednesday.' Though I'm told her bedroom was covered in pictures of him, which may explain her fixation.) But honestly, 'rotten birthday'! Those words feel too childish to be those of a murderer.

At the time it all felt very dramatic and completely unnecessary. I in turn felt stupid for letting it happen. Here I was, doing what everyone else told me to do and not what I wanted to do. My head was elsewhere – I was trying to move on. I had nearly escaped, but now here I was about to appear in court in a tired old suit from my sixteenth birthday party that I'd had to go back to my horrible flat in Kilburn to get and then do up with a safety pin because the button had fallen off – it epitomized everything I was trying to leave behind. All the time I was thinking, 'I just want to get home to Chris.' Everyone around me was getting a lot more worked up about the situation than I was, and because of that I had to face someone who wanted to kill me. I kept thinking, 'Why am I here? Why am I doing this? Who is this for? It's not for me, and I don't think it's for her. She doesn't need to serve time, she needs help.'

And so, on 17 February 2001, I found myself in Blackfriars Crown Court facing Juliet Peters. Only then did I get scared. Listening to her threats, catching her eye, feeling afraid again. I hated being back in the world where my life was being managed and I was this stupid frightened pop star. We had to listen to the tapes detailing how she wanted to chop my head off and burn my body, and at one point it threatened to overwhelm me. One message to the 'fan club' said, 'She needs her body to be set on fire and burnt to cinders where she's banished from our screens so we don't have to suffer her any more.' If I hadn't been having a panic attack myself I would have told her I was working on that

245

very thing, perhaps without the funeral pyre. She said in court that the messages were only jokes, but no one was in a joking mood, least of all me. She said she never intended the phone calls to be taken seriously. Her statement sums up how nothing the whole thing was. 'I was bored, I haven't worked for a long time, so I used to sleep throughout the day and be up throughout the night. I started to get depressed. I don't even know where to get a gun from, and if I did, I couldn't afford to buy one.' She was found guilty, and the jury indicated that she should receive psychiatric help. I have no idea what happened after that. I left the circus.

Mum now worried endlessly about me being kidnapped and held to ransom for Chris's money. But I didn't want that negativity, I didn't want to hear her paranoid thoughts. So once again a little distance was put between us, because once again I didn't want to be told I was doing the wrong thing. Because this time I knew I wasn't, and that's why I didn't release 'The Tide Is High'. The court case succeeded in doing what I alone could not: cutting the ties. Without it I might have been tempted back. To quote a line from the epic *Sopranos*: 'Just when you think you've got out . . . they drag you back in.'

And what is the end of this little chapter? Well, Hugh gave 'The Tide Is High' to Atomic Kitten, who were also on the Innocent label, and guess what, it was at Number 1 for weeks. But that was OK. I knew by then that I wanted out, but more importantly than that I was happy because it had been my idea in the first place. I had taken it to Hugh. I knew it was going to be a huge hit, and it was. Did I think it should have been me? Not once. Have I wondered since? No way. That one thing might have changed everything and I wouldn't be doing what I do now, which is a far, far better thing. So no, there was no bad feeling whatsoever. Not only was I having the time of my life with Chris by this point, I allowed myself to feel a little validated. Maybe I wasn't such a muppet after all. Maybe I could start believing in myself again. With the help of my friends.

# The End of Loneliness

## A Field

I know it sounds like a heavily lop-sided relationship, but this is my book, not Chris's. However, I think it's fair to say that he started to enjoy everything because I was doing so, and because he was happy I was even happier. I was so excited about what he had to offer me. He always held my hand. I loved that particularly. We'd go out drinking, then stop off in a pie shop in Soho on the way home and eat a pie. He'd take me out into the country and we'd roll down hills, laughing all the way. Sometimes we'd just sit quietly in his garden, reading. Or plant herbs. Taste different cheeses. Drink wonderful wine. It was a long way from stuffing myself with tissues. What had happened to the laxatives and starvation? Out the window. I knew Chris wouldn't tolerate that sort of thing. And drugs? No more. I left it all behind.

And it was easy. He's never taken drugs in his life, yet he's been offered them countless times. Frankly, he doesn't need them. I was so happy that I didn't need anything like that either, and as far as eating was concerned I couldn't be bothered with forcing myself to be something I wasn't any more. Namely a size 0. There were too many things to try, to do, to see, to taste. I had been infected by Chris's appetite for life, and sipping a diet Coke and sucking on a Marlboro Light just wasn't going to cut it. When he said, 'Let's get on a plane and go . . . wherever', I was like, 'Yeaaaaah, let's get on a plane!' When he said, 'Let's find some sun', I was the first to pack.

There was a pivotal moment in our relationship. We hadn't been going out very long and we were lying in the long grass in the field at his cottage after one of our mighty walks. I stared up at the sky and felt secure enough to admit to him something that I had barely admitted to myself: that a lot of the things I had done, 'achieved', seen and experienced I didn't feel. I couldn't feel. My Number Ones. The appearance on *Top of the Pops*. Fame.

I asked him, 'Do you ever think, "Why can't I feel this?" Do you worry that you should be able to feel and enjoy these things more than you do?'

He sat bolt upright and said he completely understood what I was saying. He said he often felt that way too.

We lay in the field and slowly worked out why all the things that had happened to us meant so little. This is our theory. The trouble with ambition is that you are competing with your peers. So you need some incredibly strong friend-ships from the time before you become famous, because chances are you won't make many on the way. And even if you do, they are often left behind as you strive ever forwards. You leave people in your wake. Not maliciously – it just happens. Once you gain a certain celebrity status, though you still feel the same, those around you behave differently. It's hard to know what people's motives are. Chris and I needed to find each other in order to feel again. We needed to bounce things off each other, experience them reflected in each other. On our own, there was nothing to deflect any of it off, and therefore we hadn't been able to feel it. And it's not just about being with *anyone*, it's about being with someone who really loves you. Who you mean the world to. To quote the woman who inspired me in the first place, the fabulous Mrs Ritchie: 'I've attained all things anyone wants to attain. And it doesn't mean s\*\*t.'

After that day in the field, Chris and I became equals. The jostling for position was over. I knew what he was doing for me and I knew what I was doing for him. I didn't need a record career to bring to the table. All we were asking of the other was to receive the love that was being offered and treat it with the care it deserved. And we did that. Our timing was impeccable, because shortly afterwards everything he'd worked towards was pulled from under his feet and he walked off his radio show after reaching an impasse with the management.

While he was still doing his radio show I would sometimes

go to work with him, or meet him after work and spend the rest of the day with him. We might go to Champneys, the park, a great restaurant, a gallery, a museum – all these things that London had to offer that I had never bothered to sample. I was rediscovering the city, enjoying going to the theatre, the pictures. We'd spend hours on Hampstead Heath flying kites and sharing stories about our childhoods and the places we came from. It was a romantic, desperate love and it was beautiful. We walked and talked, holding hands everywhere we went, getting to know everything there was to know about one another.

We did a bit of travelling because he had loads of holiday entitlement he'd never got round to taking, so we'd choose somewhere in Europe and travel around the region for a couple of days. Just the two of us. Our first trip started in the Loire Valley in France. We'd seen it advertised on some holiday show a few weeks before. So off we went in the Jag to catch a ferry, with one outfit between us and a few blankets. We'd buy the basics wherever we went – cheap slacks and tops. I usually ended up wearing his clothes. I even wore his flip-flops. I'd never been on a ferry before, and I remember being unsure whether or not we were actually on it. When we were queuing for our ticket and our *petit déjeuner* I was sure I could feel it moving, I told Chris.

'Feel what moving?'

'The boat.'

'We're not on the boat, you lulu!'

Lulu became my name when I had my blonde moments.

Which were many. Especially in the early days. We arrived in France and spent the next ten days wine tasting, eating goose fat on bread in *caves* and learning about Joan of Arc. We visited the place where she was born and explored the Wednesday flea markets. I was eating like a horse and I knew it, but I didn't care. We loved sharing food – it was one of our biggest passions – and I was so relieved that I could enjoy eating again. The only trouble was I liked it so much that I couldn't stop. But I didn't mind – the pounds piled on and I felt sexy. Chris made me feel sexy and was the first to celebrate my new-found curves. And that made me feel great. Good enough to dress even more casually. . . .

I hadn't washed my underwear for four days, so I took to going commando. No knickers. No bra. Very French. I loved it, and felt as free as a daisy. I hadn't brushed my hair for a week, either, so it was starting to dread but it didn't faze me. We were having so much fun that we decided it wasn't time to go home yet. We left the Jag in France and decided we were going to visit the Colosseum. So after a very nice lunch we hopped on a plane to Athens.

Too much Chablis at lunch, methinks. We knew the minute we arrived that we'd made a terrible mistake. We decided to mull it over in the hotel bar. The first beer was silent as we stared into the glass, willing it to magic us to Rome where the Colosseum had sat for over two thousand years. Finally Chris spoke.

'Well, at least we can see the Parthenon.'

'Sure.' (Not knowing what the hell that was.)

We laughed at our ignorance or drunkenness, and off we went to see the Parthenon. And it was marvellous. But although we were living life, work for him was getting harder and harder. Things were changing at the station and Chris didn't like the direction those changes were going in. I didn't throw myself into the details – I just wanted to be there for him when he had a bad day. And when he said, 'Let's get out of here', I didn't question it, and we'd pick another city and explore for a few more days. I think he got into trouble for taking time out but it was, after all, time he had owing to him and was allowed to take.

There was also a fair amount of drinking going on. As with any new couple discovering each other, the wine and beer flowed. Despite the photos – I looked like shit and was wasted a lot of the time – I was having a great time. Even though I was weak when we met, I was getting rapidly stronger and if I didn't want to go out I wouldn't go. Chris wouldn't judge me, or force me to go – it wasn't like that. If I was feeling out of control then I'd say so, because for the first time in a long time I felt I was in a place where I could. Anyway, it wasn't the endless drinking that people thought it was. Yes, for a little while we rebelled. We are two big partiers, so naturally we went on the lash and nowhere more regularly than our London local – the Nag's Head. But it wasn't us sitting in the pub comparing phone-rings. There were people at Chris's local who were war veterans, poets, alcoholics, people who'd worked in the movies, travelled the world. Just a chat with Kevin, the maddest landlord known to mankind, was an eye-opener. I remember an American came in once and asked for a half of bitter. Kevin poured a pint. The American said, 'I asked for half', so Kevin promptly drank half of the pint in one gulp and returned the glass to the man. He would let us climb in through the pub window and eat a sausage sandwich before opening time.

It was a lot of fun. I was constantly learning things about life and people, and things that I didn't know existed. I had left ordinary school at twelve to go to drama school. We had academic lessons at Sylvia Young's, true, but to all intents and purposes my education stopped then. I knew nothing. I could do a dance routine, I could open my mouth wide and hold crazy poses for the cameras and be a 'mad' pop princess, but the Second World War? Barely anything at all. Life outside the record industry didn't exist. I had stopped developing. My brain, as a muscle, was less exercised than my calves. So yes, I sat back in the pub, drank a few beers and listened to stories that reignited my lust for life. I hung off their words. It got me thinking again. The horrible misconception voiced in some quarters that Chris was ruining my life, that I was throwing it all away, could not have been further from the truth.

It's true I did drop a lot of people when I met him. I stopped calling my friends because I was too busy being head over heels in love. But I also didn't want to talk about him. He wasn't just any bloke. He was Chris Evans, with a bit of a reputation (he'd had some interesting girlfriends) and twice my age. Most people had quite a bit to say about that. Everyone I talked to had preconceived ideas about him and very quickly I realized that I didn't want to discuss our relationship any more, let alone defend it. I got tired of trying to change people's minds and bored of listening to 'But he's thirty-four. . . .' And I was hurt when people said, 'It's never going to last.' And they said it a lot. It was the same old thing – everybody loved telling me what to do, they all had an opinion, they all knew better, so I stopped listening. I felt I had no choice. This was a matter of survival.

Back at Virgin, Chris was becoming increasingly frustrated with how the station he loved was being run. Since I wasn't working and he was having such a shit time, we decided to escape to the sun. We flew to LA but there was a thick fog hanging over the city. It was the beginning of May, but the June Gloom had come early. We decided to move on, and drive until we found blue skies and sunshine. So we hired a Mustang – granted it wasn't classic, but it was still a Mustang – and drove with the roof down from LA to Palm Springs listening to Howerd Stern all the way. I donned the red lipstick, tied a scarf around my head and bought a packet of Marlboro Reds. We were living in dream sequences. I'm the same in Europe – when I go to Paris I want to buy flat shoes and drive about in a 2CV. And in Italy eat pasta, marry into the Mafia and sing 'That's Amore . . .'. (I'm generalizing, of course.)

When we arrived in Palm Springs Chris looked at me in the way that only he can, and I knew he had mischief on his mind.

## Billie

'Hey, Palm Springs! You know it's only moments from Las Vegas?'

'What do you mean?' I asked.

'Well, shall we go and get married?'

# May the 6th Be with You

## The Little Chapel of the West

As soon as I said yes, which I did immediately, there wasn't a moment to waste. We got hold of a marriage pad (a pad with all the arrangements in it) and started to write down who we were inviting, where we were going to stay, what we wanted to eat at our reception and so on. Then we hopped on to a private jet and flew to Las Vegas, teary-eyed all the way. As I looked out of the window at the clouds I genuinely felt so happy, so excited and finally so alive. We had talked about getting married from very early on – Chris had even spoken to my dad about it – and of course I had thought about getting married since I was small. But not in my wildest dreams did I think I'd be cruising over the desert in a private jet heading to Las Vegas with Chris Evans.

We spent a few nights in Las Vegas getting ready for the

wedding. After finding the chapel we went to Banana Republic to choose what we were going to wear on the day. I opted for a white shirt and sarong and flip-flops. Chris bought a blue shirt and some fab stripy trousers. You can't actually walk off the street and get married, even in Las Vegas – you have to get a licence first. So Chris and I went to the office to get one. It was the happiest queue I'd ever been in – very long, but everyone was smiling. Usually queues are miserable and people are bored and complaining to anyone who'll listen that it's all taking too long, but in this one all you could hear were these really high-pitched voices as women (some already in their wedding dresses) were getting more and more excited. Chris and I were fascinated, watching everybody watching everybody else. Occasionally you'd see a look of panic flit across someone's face, but mostly it was just laughter all the way. After we'd done the paperwork we went and bought a video camera. Then we took it and our marriage licence back to our lovely room, lay on the bed and talked about getting married.

Chris was brilliant and paid for our chosen friends to come over and join us. Danny Baker, who was our witness, Webbo, Gillsy (Chris Gillet) and his girlfriend Zanna all came out. Of course I was thinking all the time about the people who weren't there. We'd decided not to invite family because we felt our wedding day was about *us*. It wasn't for our parents, it wasn't for the world press – it didn't belong to anyone else, it was for Chris and me. And that, in my head, didn't seem unreasonable. I was doing something for myself, which I hadn't done for a long time. That was all I cared about. I was aware that it would hurt people but I knew I would be given the chance to explain things later, after we were married. I thought, 'If they love me, they'll understand why I'm doing this.' I couldn't call my mum and say, 'We're getting married but you can't come – and by the way I'm still really pissed off because of what you asked me to do.' I didn't want to go there. I just wanted to have a nice time. I didn't want to justify and fight for what I was doing. I didn't want to be told it was a bad idea, and I knew there was a chance that they would say that and I didn't want to hear it. To be honest, I didn't give a fuck what anyone thought – I just didn't want them to spoil it.

I'd never done anything with such conviction since starting my music career. There was no doubt in my mind. I had left my cynical head at the door when I met Chris. Anything was possible. Anything was achievable. We were as solid as a rock. I never even flirted with the idea of failure – it didn't enter my thoughts in any way. I'm glad of that, because I wouldn't have married him if it had. I thought we were going to be together for ever, but I knew that not everyone had my faith. By keeping our wedding small-scale I was protecting myself, my marriage and our day. The people who were there were perfect and have stayed friends ever since.

The night before our wedding day Chris and I went to a casino and watched a magic show. When I woke on the morning of 6 May it was another glorious, sunny day, and like any bride I had butterflies in my stomach – not from nerves but from excitement. I'd been trying to slim down a tiny bit for my wedding day, but then we ended up having a huge steak lunch just before it. After lunch we stood in the pool, had a daiquiri each and talked about becoming husband and wife. Finally the moment arrived and we drove to the Little Chapel of the West where Elvis had married his child bride. Just as on our French trip, I don't think I was wearing any underwear on my wedding day. I know I didn't wear a bra because one of the benefits of pigging out was that my breasts were looking quite perky and lovely. I don't think I was wearing any knickers either. It was all quite sexy.

We got to the chapel, chose the 'basic package' wedding ceremony, picked our pink carnation bouquet out of the fridge and took our vows. We didn't do rings – we didn't want to, and because this was Vegas we didn't have to. It didn't matter to us. We just wanted to call each other husband and wife. You couldn't wipe the smiles from our faces. It was a perfect happy day.

After the ceremony we all piled into a limo, drove to the airstrip and flew straight back to Palm Springs.

When we arrived we had our 'reception' at the amazing hotel we'd been staying in before: it was called the Kurokai, which means 'crow'. We all sat around this big table and ate *the* most amazing food I've ever had in my whole life: mouth-watering tuna and fabulous wine. It was probably the most civilized evening any of us had had together. I think we were all expecting a bit of a mad one, but somehow the occasion didn't call for that. After dinner we sat in the pool for a while, then went to our room to be alone on our wedding night. Not that interesting, but true – and real, and I was happy.

I woke up the next day and realized I was a wife. Chris Evans's wife. We lay in bed, looking at each other, smiling because we were so happy. The first thing I did was point at him and say, 'You're my husband. . . .' It was weird hearing myself say it. He found it a lot easier than me in the beginning. But when you get used to it, you can't stop and you find a way to get 'my husband' into every conversation. And of course people would look at me quizzically because I looked like a child. I didn't care – I was immune to it. We spent two glorious weeks in Palm Springs. Chris played golf. We ate, we went to the water park, we read books. And we had no idea about the furore we were causing back at home.

After meeting Chris, I never picked up a tabloid or a copy of *Heat* or any of those magazines. And I was wise not to do so, because a lot of people were writing a lot of horrible things. Old teachers whom I hadn't spoken to for ten years were coming out of the woodwork to comment on my marriage. Apparently they were worried about me. It seemed odd to me that people were worried when I was so happy and so healthy. It was reported that our wedding night was spent swanning about Las Vegas, quaffing vintage champagne and gambling thousands of pounds away on slot machines. We weren't even in Las Vegas! They made it sound shoddy and unromantic, as if all we were doing was getting pissed and numbing ourselves to what was going on, but that couldn't have been further from the truth.

None of my friends called me to congratulate me, yet they all knew I was married. I've spoken to Justine and I realize that it was weird for them too, this elevated position I was in. If I'd been a normal mate who'd eloped with the man of her dreams, then they'd have called. But I wasn't a normal mate, and I wasn't marrying a normal man, so the whole thing got whipped up into this frenzy of everyone being pissed off that they hadn't been let into the 'inner circle'. It wasn't like that in reality, though. We were just keeping it small. For us. Eventually I called my friends and said, 'Why haven't you called me? Why aren't you happy for me?' And then it was OK and things settled down. Those were relatively easy calls – I still couldn't face ringing my parents. Of course, they were reading all the horrid stuff too. I know Mum and Dad weren't mad about our relationship in the beginning, but they could see from the photos that I was happy and they couldn't take that away from Chris. They were pleased I was putting on weight, they were pleased I wasn't that preened, made-up creature any more. I was going out dressed in whatever I wanted because I could – it wouldn't impact my sales if I didn't look the part, because I had no 'part' to play. But Mum and Dad were hurt, too. They didn't understand what they'd done wrong. They knew we were thinking about getting married because Chris had spoken to Dad and asked his permission to marry me.

But they only knew him from the television and I think they thought we were probably just mucking around. Then Mum came home and saw that the street was packed with press. The neighbours were out in the garden.

'Why are this lot here?' Mum asked.

'Billie and Chris got married today.'

Mum's heart leaped into her throat. 'Oh, yeah?' she said, bluffing it. 'Course she did!'

She went into the house, shut the door, tuned into Virgin Radio and heard it for herself. Chris Evans and Billie Piper have had a gunshot wedding in Las Vegas – rumours about a pregnancy bounced about and there was much debate about my 'bulging stomach'. It just broke Mum's heart that I hadn't told her. She couldn't understand it. Why didn't I just call her and let her know? She says now she wouldn't have told me not to do it, but at the time I couldn't take that risk. Our relationship was at an all-time low, and I didn't trust either of us not to end up rowing. I'd been so miserable up until that point. I knew Chris would make me happy and I knew that one day they'd see that, but not soon enough for me. I didn't want them to pollute my head and tell me things I didn't think were true. I knew why I was with him and I didn't need them to understand it – and I didn't care whether they did or not. It was very selfish, but I thought I had no choice. So I didn't ring them for a long time after I got back. But they didn't ring me either.

We came home to the UK, to Ginger Towers – the building in London's smart Belgravia district that Chris had bought and filled up with his mates. It was called Ginger Towers because all the girls were dyeing their hair red at the time, not as in Trump – I've got loads of dosh. It was never that with Chris. It was always funny, always tongue-in-cheek, always a laugh. He and I were on the bottom floor, Zanna and Gillsy were on the top floor and three or four would come and go on the middle floor. We'd leave our doors open and pop in and out of each other's flats – it was quite bohemian and I'd never experienced that before.

While we went on celebrating married life things at the station were getting progressively worse for Chris, and he started skipping shows. Communication between him and the 'suits' totally disintegrated and he wanted out. I don't think anyone expected him to walk away from his job because so much money was at stake, but for Chris it was a question of principle. So on 27 June he walked off the show and didn't go back. So now neither of us had to go to work. And that was OK. If we wanted to have a ten-hour lunch we could – and we did. In fact the Belgravia Lunching Society was born. We'd go out to lunch with friends and one of us would take minutes. Someone did this. . . . We played this game. . . . This dare was performed. . . . Silly nonsense really, but fun. Of course there were paparazzi everywhere we went: we were married, out on the lash, and he'd left Virgin. Chris told me to ignore it. So I did. But it didn't go away, and in the end it all got too much for everybody.

# The Good Life

## A Vegetable Patch

Mum and Dad decided to take the kids out of school, sell their house and move to Spain. They got themselves a nice house with a pool, and the kids went to a great new school. Everyone out there was a bit shady and kept their personal details to themselves. No one had any idea who Mum and Dad were, and that suited them just fine. Anonymity was what they were after. We escaped too. To Surrey. We moved into Chris's cottage. It was originally called the Pump House but we re-named it Christmas Cottage because it meant so much to us. We kept our Christmas lights on it all year around – in fact we kept our Christmas tree up until the middle of March. Unlucky for some, but not us. We decided that we were going to create the 'good life' for ourselves down there while the big house was finished. We promptly set about creating vegetable patches and planting everything we could think of. Chris dug a pond. I've got so many pictures of him digging that pond, each one hilarious.

I was learning to be a wife, learning to look after a man and dogs. This time for real. Chris had three dogs – Percy, Epstein and Enzo. I'm now a really good cook because of our time squirrelled away in Christmas Cottage. Not the greatest, I've still got a bit of work to do on my flavours, but I can make a damn fine curry and a pretty impressive stew. I taught myself how to bake. We went to meetings about the local fête, we got involved in bonfire night and befriended all the fifty-year-olds in the village. Chris encouraged me to take driving lessons and pass my test. Most young pop stars can't drive – they don't have to because they are driven everywhere. Every day, bit by bit, we were learning to get our world back together.

Chris had never intended to live in the cottage. It was just part of the estate he'd bought. The main house was up the road. It was a stunningly beautiful listed building but it was really dark inside and needed modernizing. Chris wanted to knock some of the rooms through to make the place seem bigger and lighter. He had great ideas, some of them really spectacular, but it took a long time to achieve anything because the planning officers were really tough on him. Eventually, however, the approval came through and the rebuilding began in earnest. It was a huge operation. There were trailers full of builders, and a project manager called Mike who was great. It was very handy having people like that around all the time, because they could knock me up a shelf here and there, mend a loose tile, open a stuck window. We visited the site nearly every day. I loved it, and slowly the house and my life started to take shape.

The funny thing was, the more time we spent in the cottage the more we wanted to stay. Eventually we thought that after we'd done up the big house we'd sell it. At Christmas Cottage we didn't need someone to do the garden – we could do it ourselves. I learnt about plants, and to name flowers and trees. Now I'm an urban dweller again my tree knowledge is down a bit, but I'm still good at shrubs. We'd harvest our own food, then cook it and eat it while the sun went down. We didn't need help cleaning the house – my passion for a good cleaning product hadn't dimmed, and I was happy to do my own housework. More than that, I loved it. Chris got me into reading – I'd never read a thing before because I was so lazy. I'd thought it was boring and a bit crap, and I really didn't understand the appeal. I'd certainly never allocated time to sit down, just me and a book, and not feel scared. I'd always felt I had to be doing something, so I'd feel guilty if I wasn't. It's weird.

These were our halcyon days. Sometimes we'd just curl up on the sofa and spend the afternoon watching a film. We were very happy baking, cooking, making jam – it was domestic bliss. We did silly things like buy a teapot from Oxfam in Godalming, then go to Waitrose and buy all the different types of tea we could find and experiment to see which one we liked best. We had the luxury of time. We didn't have to work, so we didn't. I grew up a lot that year. I became a nicer person. I learnt to care less about the things that weren't important in life and more about the things that were. My life as Mrs Evans shaped me in so many ways, and his life as Mr Piper was teaching him things too: how to be sensitive, that it's OK to cry, OK to let it all go sometimes. He'd survived on his own for so long. Nobody understood what he was going through – or very few, certainly, and even fewer who understood his kind of mind. I didn't understand it either at first, but I embraced it. It didn't scare me: I watched and learned.

Since our life had calmed down, and I felt safe and secure and had been proved right in my decision to marry Chris, I called Mum and Dad. She very sweetly pretended to be happy for me and claimed to understand my decisions, but I knew she was cut up inside. In her place, I would have been. I didn't try to explain myself on the phone – I just wanted her to come and see for herself that I was happy now. So Mum and Dad came down to visit. It was a little icky at first, but we got over that and went to the pub for lunch and ate ham, eggs and chips. It was nice. Being with Chris didn't make me feel more removed from Mum and Dad. If anything, after that initial period of not talking I wanted to show them that I had acquired new skills, that I'd achieved something. When I went to visit them in Spain I would offer to cook for them, to show them what I was now capable of. I could pickle beetroot, harvest corn, make jam, reverse the car – stupid little things that meant so much to me. I wanted to show them I was healthy and happy and our marriage wasn't as bad as the stuff they were reading. Slowly, it seemed to work. They realized that I was happy, that I had been right to marry him and that I had been right to run away to fix myself.

Chris and I never really talked about what was going on with Virgin and the court case, though obviously I knew it was bad. He was being sued for breach of contract. Lawyers came down to the cottage and I made them all tea and tuna sandwiches, but then I just left them to it. I had very little interest in it all. Perhaps I should have paid more attention, but at the time I felt I was intruding. I wanted Chris to be able to leave the meeting and come to me for a hug, then go back again if he had to. I wanted to be there for him if it didn't work out. When it didn't, we sat in the woods and only then did we talk it all though. As usual he intellectualized the whole thing and worked out what he was going to do. How he was going to cope with losing all that money. He had worked for every penny and, though it doesn't guarantee happiness, he still didn't deserve to have it taken away like that.

I got angrier about the court case than Chris did; he was managing to deal with it. I'd seen how good he'd been to all those people – we'd been out to dinner with them. As far as I was concerned it was Chris who'd got them all to where they were, and now they wanted to be the people who brought down Chris. His luck ends now! Except it wasn't anything to do with luck. I think people had started to resent him and there was quite a lot of jealousy and middle-class envy. Sometimes it felt like the playground all over again, and I should know – I hadn't left it all that long ago. They had dressed it up as something else, but I saw it for what it was: good old-fashioned spite. Chris managed to make sense of it all, thank God, otherwise it would have eaten him from the inside out. They say what doesn't kill you makes you stronger and that's very commendable – but hell, it's hard! Chris made peace with it. He washed his hands of the whole sorry business. As the Dalai Lama says, why do we ever worry about things that are outside our control? It's hard to do, but if you try and live like that things do get easier. They are powerful thoughts, and they made sense to Chris. And if you try you can apply this philosophy to every problem in your life. I try, but sometimes, when I'm tired, I let the black thoughts in. Like I did as a child, I almost indulge them, let them take over and then enjoy it. But you have to fight those moments, because otherwise they can and will swallow you up. I think a lot of other men who'd lost that sort of money would have gone mad. Not Chris. He just moved on.

In Hascombe there are only two things – a pub and a church. Luckily the White Horse is one of the finest pubs I have ever known. It's ridiculously expensive, because it's Surrey and everyone has stupid amounts of money. Old and new. But we didn't socialize with the lip-liner brigade. Our friends were in the village, and the only time we left the gates of our property was when we went down there to hang out with the locals. I'm not joking, my friends were fifty-year-olds. Characters like Al the Egg, who – you guessed it – sold eggs, and the mole man, and Roy the Fridge who had an air-con company. But we were rarely pulled out of our idyll. I wanted to be at home, in the cottage. Chris didn't have a mobile phone and I switched mine off. London turned back into a big dark scary place where we would lose control (and when we were there we often did, because there was so much temptation). At Christmas I secretly got the guys to build a hut in the woods for Chris so he could go there and think and work. The hut was on stilts, overlooking the woods and the valley beyond. I had it painted white with a red trim, for obvious reasons and took him to see it on Christmas Day. In return Chris gave me two calves that I named Mary and Josephine. We were Christmas crazy.

I even worked in the kitchens of the pub for a week when Sue, the landlady, needed extra help. Being a perfectionist, I wanted every plate to look like something Gordon Ramsay would approve of. I drizzled and tweaked and wiped and fussed until Sue shouted at me to get a move on. Nothing felt quite so good in my hand as the pay packet she gave me at the end of the week. Sue was only a little younger than my nan, but she became my best friend down there. She was legendary, the talk of the village. And my God was there a lot of talk! I thought London was bad, but it's nothing compared to rural life. I felt green compared to all these naughty farmers. The stuff that went on had my eyes out on stalks: wife-swapping, affairs, everyone having sex with everyone else – you name it, it goes on. You walk into each other's houses and know about everybody's rows because life there is so open. It was great at first, like living in a Jilly Cooper novel, but at times it became quite incestuous.

I used to have these decadent 'ladies' lunches' when I'd cook for all of them. In the early stages, before I became a dab hand in the kitchen, I'd have to ring up Justine and get her to tell me what a rack of lamb was and how to cook it. I still had my mates in London, of course, but they wouldn't come down very often. True Londoners, through-and-through Londoners, don't leave the city very often. It's too much hassle and they think it's weird wanting to be away from the hustle and bustle. My friends would come, but there was no mobile phone coverage in the village and they were always pushing to get back. I in turn would urge them, 'Come on, stay, it's beautiful.' I don't think the villagers liked all these townies strutting around very much – too arrogant for their taste. But I did miss London a bit. I'd talk to Justine and she'd be off having a whale of a time with Blue, and I'd think, 'God, I used to do that!' I didn't want it back, but there's only so much gardening you can do in your twenties and thirties. We had rested long enough, and now we needed to change gear.

# La La Land

## Lionel Ritchie's house

Why LA? Because we'd spent some time in LA before and really liked it. We liked the lifestyle. At first we thought we'd get away for a while and rent somewhere while the house was being finished. We'd been talking about moving forward, about what we were both going to do next. My intention was to study, his was to write. We were two impetuous kids living out our childhood romantic fantasies together. I'm glad we went to America. It got my juices flowing again.

One of the first people we met was Gordon MacGeachy. What a name! What a guy! He was a realtor and we were looking for a house. He walked in fresh from a spinning class and an hour of yoga, shining with good health and toned like no other. He used to be a motivational speaker, so you can imagine the sales pitch. He looks a bit like Simon Cowell, though he doesn't like me to say that. Chris and I walked in looking like a pair of pikeys and you could see the mistrust pass across his eyes. We wanted to buy a house in the hills? With what? A couple of coppers? But since Helen Fielding the author of *Bridget Jones*, had vouched for us, he didn't throw us out of his office. We had made no effort to look nice for three years, and I loved it. I'd spent most of my life trimmed and tucked in – years of being uncomfortable and holding it all in. The current look was part of the rebellion, doing the extreme opposite to what I'd done before. Work-horse to domestic bliss. Dolly bird to something the cat dragged in. I let it all hang out. Literally.

Gordon took us to see this beautiful place in the Holly-wood Hills which turned out to be Lionel Ritchie's old house. Outside in the driveway a Jag was parked, and in the window was a woman's face with a very prominent jawline. I was sure I recognized her. I'm obsessed with jawlines – since I look more and more like David Coulthard as the years go by, I feel a strong kinship to anyone else who resembles Desperate Dan. Then this girl with long dark hair walked up to the car and I realized who the two of them were. Courtney Cox and Jennifer Aniston. I was frozen to the spot, abso-lutely riveted – I loved *Friends*. They were viewing the house at the same time as us. Then Brad Pitt walked in with Patricia Arquette. Brad didn't really do it for me because he was too buffed for my liking – as I said, I like men who like pies, like my dad. My pie-man was of course cracking jokes with them, which I found too excruciating for words: I kept having to move into a different room to get away. We ended up beating Courtney Cox in a bidding war. We moved in and furnished the house in days. LA is hilarious: with the right money you can get someone to 'stage' your house in five hours, complete with mature wisteria and olive trees, right down to lit scented candles around the bathtub. They'd probably run your bath for you too if you asked. It's a different life out there. Fun to dabble in. But it's not real.

LA is the best and the worst place to be. It's all about the entertainment business, and every conversation is based around it. We were going out to see bands, great films, and we were getting back into the arts, which we hadn't been doing for a while because we'd been living in the country. Everyone is producing, directing, starring in, writing or in some other capacity working on something that might some day become something. It fired me up. I became strong again, happier than I'd ever been; the misery I'd felt had gone, and even the memory of it had faded away. Chris and I had a conversation about what I was going to do with my life. I felt rested and fit enough to consider entering the business again. I liked what I'd been listening to in America and it had put fire in my belly again. But I was clearly deluded. I think it was probably a bit like childbirth. You forget all the pain and go and do it again, but on the first contraction you think, 'Oh my God, why am I doing this?' Well, that was how it felt when I stepped into Hugh Goldsmith's office. Oh yes,

I arranged a meeting with him and flew back on Virgin to discuss my career.

There are some things that you never tire of, and one of those is Virgin Upper Class. I can't understand how people get on those flights and fall asleep. No way. There are eighteen movies to watch, video games to play, free champagne to drink – I mean, come on. I flew to London, had the meeting and flew back. I guess I wanted to give the meeting some gravitas, to let Hugh know I was serious, and I thought I was. I was ready to go – or at least ready to find out if they wanted me back. Shortly after meeting me, Chris had gone to see Hugh to discover what my position was. I knew from what Chris told me of that discussion that if I did go back and make another record it was going to cost me money. Being the businessman he is, Chris had asked Hugh if we could wipe the unrecouped slate clean. I couldn't make any money out of a new record if I had this millstone around my neck, because I would have had to sell an enormous number before breaking even. Unfortunately it wasn't in Hugh's gift, and if it had been every artist would be knocking on the door trying to lose unrecouped balance. So I knew that if I went back I would have to go back big time. I really don't know what I was thinking.

I adore Hugh and always have – maybe I wanted to make him proud of me and reassure him that he hadn't backed the wrong horse. I was completely fired up in the meeting, but as soon as I walked out I had this strange sensation. It was like having sex with the ex. I couldn't believe I was putting myself back there – that I was even thinking about it after everything I'd done to claw my way out. I felt bad for wasting his time. I got straight back on the plane, which gave me fourteen hours to have a long hard think about what I wanted to do. The answer had always been there in my heart, but for the first time I was asking myself the right question. Acting. It had always been acting.

# Billie Evans

## An Acting Class

I knew it was going to be hard. I knew that people would dismiss me before I'd even started. But I didn't care – just the thought of having a script in my hand excited me. I went back to LA and told Chris I wanted to start acting classes again. He didn't baulk. Anything is possible in Chris's world, if you know what you want. I found a class in the Santa Monica area at the Stella Adler Academy, which taught audition techniques and Stanislavsky Method acting. At the beginning of the first class, you had to stand up and introduce yourself. I didn't want anyone to give me any kind of special treatment, so on the spot I made up this character called Billie Evans. Well, the character may have been made up but the name was mine. Billie Evans was on my passport and my credit card, and I loved it. I told them my husband

Sharing a kiss with Orlando.

Jimmy Nesbitt tells another one of his fascinating stories on the set of *The Miller's Tale*.

Playing the mistrustful Bella in *Bella and the Boys*.

'Today the weather will be mostly sunny.' On the set of the BBC adaptation of *Much Ado About Nothing*.

On the arm of the ninth Doctor.

Backstage on *Doctor Who*, Series 2.

The family.

With the
lovely David
Ten-inch.

Celebrating my
National Television
Award.

The geniuses behind *Doctor Who* – Phil Collinson, Russell T. Davies
and Julie Gardner.

First night nerves.
On stage with the
lovely Kris Marshall
and Laurence Fox
in *Treats*.

was a writer and I'd come over to learn how to act. Frankly people like that were ten a penny out there and nobody paid me the slightest notice. I lied about where we lived, because an address in the Hollywood Hills tells them too much. Americans are so inquisitive that they just ask outright. You can't rely of their sense of discretion if they get a whiff that something's up.

I also enrolled with a private tutor called Sabin Epstein, who concentrated on Method acting. He was fucking great – a mad, eccentric thesp who lived on Sunset and Franklin high on a hill in a Spanish villa with his dog Murphey. We'd talk, read plays, act out scenes and discuss the arts, then I'd go home or to the gym and afterwards out to dinner. It was a wonderful life and I couldn't believe I was living it. I was studying again, which made me feel good about myself. My confidence and self-esteem kept on gaining ground.

I got the acting bug, the big bad bug, and it happened fast. I enrolled in as many classes as I could and was soon doing something every day. I was loving the Adler school, although sometimes those classes bordered on therapy and you'd leave the class crying for the girl who'd lost her cat the night before. It was quite heartbreaking watching people going though all this shit just to hone a skill. Married couples would do it together, which was all a bit too LA for me: 'OK, darling, I'm off out now to do a bit of acting.' Like they were going bowling. 'I've got my acting bag, darling. . . . See you later.'

The Stanislavsky practice makes you really put yourself

through the mill in order to get real emotions out of yourself. It teaches you how to tap into your unhappy memories when you need to be sad, and your happy ones when you need to laugh. Not only tap into them, but be able to do it for take after take after take. It wasn't the same as at Sylvia Young's. Most of us there were too young and too protected to have had experiences strong enough or vivid enough to unlock those sorts of emotions over and over again. Things were different now. My palette was pretty full and I discovered I could get at them, mix them up and make more. I knew exactly where I had to go to cry, and where I had to come back to in order to laugh.

Santa Monica is a little pocket of LA where the Brit celebs congregate, so naturally there was a market for the paps. They were always hovering around trying to catch Geri Halliwell getting a Starbucks. Once they followed me from the house to my acting class, and when we came out they were still there. By then I'd befriended a few classmates and they were saying, 'Who are they taking photos of?' I just ducked the question, said I had no idea, jumped into my jeep and left. I didn't want people to start looking at me differently.

A few mad old things happened in LA, but mostly it was just Chris and me doing our own thing. One evening when we were in the Sunset Marquee we met an old plugger whom Chris used to know called Adrian. He used to plug for Ozzy Osbourne and was a good mate. We were invited to Ozzy's house in Bel Air to watch the debut showing of the *Ozzy*

*Osbourne Show* with the family in their house. I had no idea who the Osbournes were and no idea how big that show was to become. We were met by Sharon at the door with her little dog, and then Kelly took me up to show me her room. It was a bit odd, but they were absolutely lovely. Afterwards we went and had ice cream with Sharon on Sunset Plaza. She was fabulous – really special. I do think she has the X-factor, whatever that is.

Our best mates were Gordon the realtor and the two stunning lipstick lesbians who lived upstairs from him. We'd play volleyball on the beach every Saturday morning. Chris was writing endlessly and reading. I read lots of what he wrote: observations, ideas for shows and poetry – he had a massive A4 pad of poems with illustrations.

America was great for us and to us. We really enjoyed the anonymity it gave us, and the good manners. People telling you to have a nice day is not a bad thing, whether they mean it or not. We were living the healthy California life, going to the gym every day for hours, eating well and going to bed early. We were just Mr and Mrs Evans, and we thought we'd stay like that. But then Mike, our project manager, called from home and told us the work on the house was finished. We only returned to England to sign the papers on it and planned to go straight back to LA afterwards. We promised ourselves we wouldn't be suckered in by the lure of the big fancy house, that we would stick to our plan of selling it, keeping the cottage and going back to LA. But that didn't happen.

# We're Going a Different Way

## The Phone Rings . . .

What Chris did to Hascombe was phenomenal. The kitchen was indescribably beautiful: he'd designed the island, for instance, out of wonderful old railway sleepers and stone. Our bath was egg-shaped and sat in the corner of a room with panoramic views of rolling hills and woodland through glazed arches. But I was nervous of it. I wanted to stay in Christmas Cottage. I didn't want anything to change and was desperately hanging on to things. I felt like I'd just found my feet. But after all that work and all the time he'd put into making the house his it would have been churlish not to give it a go. Hascombe was simply too stunning to leave.

We were moving towards summer again in England and the countryside looked spectacular; our gardens too were really something to behold. There was a swimming pool, but because the house had been empty for so long the water had turned a sludgy green. It looked like a beautiful pond from a forgotten time, so we left it as a pond. We stayed, shipped over all our furniture from America and set to work 'dressing' the house. That was my job and it was great, but it took a wee bit longer than five hours. We gave the rooms themes. I spent hours in antique shops, finding the right pieces for the right rooms. I loved doing it and thought it was the best project in the world.

When we moved in I got my hands dirty making it a home. I was delegating, which I found quite hard to do. Especially when I thought the big burly builders must have been standing there thinking, 'What a joker', 'We know your game', 'Gold digger.' Maybe they weren't thinking that. Maybe that was my hang-up. But I've grown up with builders and if there's one thing I know about them, they love having a good gossip about their employers. Men with trowels are no different from a knitting circle, just slightly broader. And just to prove me wrong these builders were actually very courteous!

I wanted the house to feel full and finished as soon as possible. It was very shabby chic with heavy floral curtains. I was quite into damask print. I wanted to close the space in and make it feel smaller, so I'd put damask on one wall and then paint the rest. We put big low heavy sofas everywhere, so you could just plonk yourself down in every room. We bought big low coffee tables and covered them in Chris's books; he filled the library with the rest of them. I was trying to keep the place feeling relaxed and easy – not like a museum, and not too grown-up and stiff like some of the houses we'd been in where everything matched and was too perfect and neat. I spent a lot of time on making Chris's mum's room homely. She used to come and stay a lot. We gave her a big sleigh bed, a trunk coffee table, big chairs and a big chest – lots of wood. I was into wood and soft furnishings. Having said that, we never put curtains into our room because we loved the light.

For every upside there's a downside. Hugh is right: life is one long balancing act. We had the house of our dreams, beyond our wildest dreams actually, but we lost our privacy again. Like so many others we were seduced by the idea of the big house with the library, the pantry and all those things, but there were always people around maintaining the house and that was a bit annoying. Don't get me wrong – I really liked the couple who worked for us and got on exceedingly well with them. Trouble was, I wanted to scrub my own skirting boards. Bob was the groundsman and Jacky helped in the house, and they lived in a cottage on the estate a bit like Christmas Cottage.

There were other compelling reasons to stay in England other than a big house. We had both got a taste for work in America but it was here that I had an agent – not that Michael had been earning a great deal off me – and it was here that I had more weight and more opportunities. So off I went once more to get those treasured 10 by 8s and Michael started sniffing out the best projects. If there was anyone rooting for me it was Chris. Just to demonstrate how encouraging he was, how keen to broaden my horizons and scope, he went to the secondhand movie shop in Notting Hill Gate and bought me the top hundred films ever made. I think I studied them as intensely as someone at film school. It was so exciting to be learning once again how to do something I loved.

I was in London doing an audition for a Working Title project. Chris had gone sailing with his great friend James Ward, the landlord of the village pub, on James's boat to Cowes in the Isle of Wight. Webbo and Gordy went too. I would have gone with them, but then the audition came up. They'd had lunch in this really lovely restaurant on the island, then Chris rang to tell me they were just about to set sail and come home. I thought they were going to be ages, so I took myself off to see Ivan's XTC in the Trocadero. On the way back the boom came loose, swung round and hit James in the back of the head. He was knocked overboard. Webbo jumped in immediately to save him, but the current was so strong he was nearly pulled under himself. He got to James but he was already dead – the boom had knocked him out and the tide had pulled him under. Webbo was nearly killed just trying to hold on to his friend's body. It was awful.

When I got home the house was empty. I kept calling Chris from home because he should have been back by seven and it was already nine. I thought they'd stopped at the pub, but then he called me in tears to tell me that James had just died. I couldn't believe it and I said, 'Stop fucking around!

He's not dead.' But it was true. Webbo was in hospital being kept under surveillance. Eventually the boys came back, and we sat up all night in the kitchen in total shock. The next day the villagers got together just to be together, to cry, to try and understand the impossible.

Now every year we have a big party in Hascombe, and the guys who got James and Webbo out of the water come down with their lifeboat to remember. It got us all thinking. Why wasn't Webbo taken down too? Was it that his name simply wasn't on the bullet, that it wasn't his turn? It makes you realize that you have to live every day, find something to appreciate every day, do something with your life. James's death silenced the village for days. He was the life and soul of the place, always humming with activity, and we were lost without him. It was a desperately sad time. The old salty sea dog had lived well, and it made no sense that he was gone.

I didn't get the Working Title job. We got the usual response: the director was 'going a different way'. Which might have been true, but I would rather have had them tell me *why* they didn't give me the part so I knew what to improve. I didn't enjoy auditions. It isn't an enjoyable process walking into a room when everyone knows exactly who you are, or thinks they do, and you can feel them thinking, 'Come on – show us what you've got.' I felt like shit. I started to think, 'All you've done is look at my name and thought, "Let's get her in for a laugh and go and tell all our mates about how shit she is."' That's what was going on in my paranoid mind. Then I thought, 'You've got to

sharpen up, girl, sort it out. Be more headstrong and believe
in yourself more. Because if *you* don't, why should anyone
else?' I had studied hard and was constantly going to the
theatre and seeing films. I watched all the movies that Chris
had given me – the greats, like *Betty Blue*, *My Beautiful
Launderette*, *Being There*, and ones I didn't even know
existed. You go to an audition, get close, then miss out.
Go to another, get closer, and still miss out. Then, finally,
the break – even if it was only a small one to start with.

# Lights, Camera, Action

## A Movie Set

The door opened a tiny crack for me with a cameo role in *The Calcium Kid*, a film about a boxer with Orlando Bloom. He was lovely. He was off to do the first *Pirates of the Caribbean* and we spent most of our time talking about swordfighting. It was exciting to work on a film, but although I got to play Orlando's girlfriend it was really a very small part in a fairly nondescript movie.

The year marched on and no more jobs came in. It was frustrating for both of us. Chris was trying to relaunch his career, while I was trying to cement mine. It was during that time that we decided Hascombe was no longer right for us. We had started to be jealous of anyone who lived in a smaller, manageable house, one with hardly any mainte-nance or upkeep, and eventually we realized that we didn't

288

want our house because it was simply too big. Neither of us is from that sort of background; it felt alien and we didn't know what to do in this huge space. We felt like kids rattling around. And we didn't want the necessity of employing staff to look after the place. I'd always preferred to clean my own kitchen and rearrange my own spice rack anyway. Listening to the radio and spuddling around my kitchen was bliss. I was there because I wanted to be there, not because I had to be there. We didn't have kids to deal with – it was just Chris and me. In the end the most interesting thing about moving into the big house was learning that we were happier in the smaller one. And in the end we moved back into Christmas Cottage and sold Hascombe.

But before we left we had one last Christmas there. I made Chris buy this twenty-foot Christmas tree for the middle of the hall. It took about ten men to get it in and (I'm not joking) it took me three weeks to decorate it. I had decided to make all the decorations. Nice in theory, a right teeth-grinder by the end because I was sewing the bloody things. Chris was selling Christmas trees at the pub all day, chatting to excited children while sinking a fair few pints of Guinness. I sat under our own enormous tree at home pricking my fingers every five seconds while trying to make the ultimate Christmas stockings. Ambitious, yes. Frustrating, incredibly. But I asked for it and come Christmas Day the tree looked magical. I was very teary (for a change) from too many sleepless nights worrying that I'd forgotten to turn off the four sets of fairy lights that sat happily on the tree. One accident and Hascombe Court would have been the brightest star ever to blaze at Christmas – you'd have been able to see it all the way from London.

Then I got another role, this time in a small scale dramatization of life inside a care home. I was playing the lead, the mistrustful, defensive, abused Bella in *Bella and the Boys*. I went in green – eager to impress. It had a social conscience and it moved me. It was harrowing, but I enjoyed the challenge. Chris had gone to Portugal, and I stayed in our flat in London throughout the intensive rehearsal period. His going away was great, actually, because I could put into practice what the character was going though. I was living alone, which enabled me to remember what it was like to feel lonely and abandoned. Chris and I had barely spent a night apart since getting married, so although it was strange to be away from him it let me tap into the feelings of my past. I think I began to realize then that all the shit I'd been through during my singing days was stored up waiting for me to use to my advantage. That maybe all that had happened for a reason, to take me forward to this place. Although I'd forgotten what it was like to feel lonely I could go back and feel it again. It was an amazing process and I loved feeling that sense of accomplishment when I'd delivered each testing scene. It was an extraordinary story, a million miles from my own, but I could do it. And I was keen to do more like it, but the parts dried up.

Then in April, Michael, my agent, called me and said,

'They're doing a remake of Chaucer's *Canterbury Tales* with Pete Bowker and he's really great.'

'Who – Chaucer or Pete Bowker?'

'Pete.'

I was only pretending to know about Chaucer – I probably went home to Chris for a crash course in Ye Olde English Literature. I had no idea what it was going to be like, but I was anxious to prove myself in something different. So I went to the audition, held in one of the big studios like Shepperton, which was exciting to see for the first time and gave me impetus to go on. I met the director, John McKay, a shy but intense man who clearly had a lot going on upstairs. We discussed what we both felt about the character. The first person I saw coming out was the actress Lucy Amy, who played Chardonnay in *Footballers' Wives*. As soon as I saw her, before even walking into the audition, I reckoned it was all over. I thought she was perfect for the part and I didn't stand a chance. Luckily for me, they thought differently.

I was wearing denim jeans and a denim shirt, and went quite brassy and teenage and a bit stroppy. I coated myself with lots of lip gloss and spice lip-liner and decided to go for it. It went well – I could tell they were pleasantly surprised – and I was over the moon when I got a recall. They were concerned that because of my limited experience I might not be able to deliver the goods. When you work in British television you are fighting the clock constantly, so the last thing they wanted was someone who couldn't hit the mark or take direction. Then I had a 'test' with John to see whether I could listen to what he was asking me to do, digest it and react accordingly. We had a nice long chat about what *I* wanted to give the character, how I wanted her to walk and run and skip and so on. Poor man! But I listened to what he said, and reworked the character in my head to suit his vision. I used every trick I'd learnt in my audition technique classes to show him I could do it. I was desperate to pass the test.

I hadn't done much with Michael and he was frightening, so even though I wanted to call him I didn't dare. The audition was on my mind constantly. Then I heard Jimmy Nesbitt was going to be Nick and Dennis Waterman my husband, and now I wanted it even more. I have to admit that I had no idea who Dennis Waterman was. In fact I thought they were talking about Pete Waterman from Stock Aitken and Waterman. I was thinking, 'OK, that's interesting', but I didn't say anything because I was in no position to question their casting and had no clout. I think Michael finally responded to the blank expression on my face and said, 'Think *Minder*, think *The Sweeney*', and then luckily I realized who they were talking about before I started mentioning Kylie and Jason.

There was a lot of to-ing and fro-ing, but finally they gave me the part. I was with my nan having afternoon tea in the Berkeley Hotel when Michael phoned me. The first person I called was Chris. He was so pleased for me because he just wanted me to realize my potential. It can be so hard going up for jobs, so horrible, and even tougher for the people around you because you get so worked up for the ones you love. I do it for my friends now: I know when they're going in and check my phone, and then you can tell by how they say hello whether it went well or not. You get another no, then throw yourself back into the lions' den. But that's the nature of the beast and you can't bitch about it – you just have to be incredibly thick-skinned. Girls have to be a certain size, and we are judged as much on our looks as on our ability. I was of course painfully aware of that, but I couldn't be bothered with trying to make myself a certain size again. All that was over. I considered myself a completely different person now – I had put all that to bed. Anorexia wasn't going to rear its ugly head again because I had changed beyond all recognition. Sitting there with my nan in the Berkeley I tucked into a whole load of scones, knowing that it was the last time I would be eating with impunity. I had three weeks to get into shape.

However hard auditions are, I had dreamed about doing them way back when I was a kid in Swindon. Now that I *was* an actress it was a matter of convincing everybody else. I knew it wasn't going to happen overnight and I didn't expect it. But now at least I had my chance.

Who I was – an ex-pop star and wife of Chris Evans – probably closed as many doors as it opened. It had its advantages – it might have got me into the audition room in the first place because people were curious – but it had its disadvantages too, because people didn't want that sort of baggage on their projects. But John McKay saw something in me and was prepared to hire me for *Canterbury Tales*. I didn't realize how full circle I'd come until I went to the set. It was Jacobs, the studio where I had recorded 'Because We Want To'. As the car turned into the pea shingle driveway I realized that what had been a stately home to my fifteen-year-old's eye was just a large country house with a recording studio in the barns. I got out of the car and looked around me. I couldn't believe that this was the place where my singing career had started. Talk about parallel universe. Yet here I was, six years later, standing in the same recording studio, some cans on my head, a mic in my hand. But this time I didn't have to mime, because this time I knew I could do it.

# Act Five

*An Actor's Life*

# Rompy-Pompy

## A Closed Set

My role in John McKay's modern-dress update of *The Miller's Tale* was that of an upstart young woman married to a much older, rather grisly, possessive man. She liked to think of herself as a singer, loved karaoke, but was never going to do anything with it or with her life. It wasn't a singing part as such – the whole point about her jealous, doting husband was that he was pushing her to make something of herself. Which is how she met her lover, the record producer. I loved the script when it came through, and practised my lines every day. It was all very slapstick and raucous, with a lot of sex scenes. I'd never done a sex scene before and had no idea what to expect. What I did know was that I had to show my arse off, and there were no bottom doppelgangers for me. Just me and my big arse.

However, I'd been working out hard once I'd discovered that my kit was coming off on national TV. This time I tried to do it sensibly. By the time it got to the shoot I wanted to be alive and aware of what was going on, not physically drained and running on empty. We had a treadmill in the TV room at the top of our house, and I could watch MTV and run. My motivation was beautiful women and loud music. Or *Sex and the City*. Just Carrie's calves kept me running for forty-five minutes without noticing. I never understand people who watch the news when they're in the gym. How can that be at all physically motivating? It makes me want to slit my wrists. I also did a bit of Atkins – frankly because it works every time if you need to shift some weight really quickly. It lets me eat all my favourite things, like meat, and I don't get hungry. I can't stay hungry any more – I don't have the willpower. I was eating two whole chickens a day, and steak with a fried egg and Boursin cheese on the side. But I couldn't do it indefinitely, because if you go on eating only protein your breath starts to stink. That obviously wouldn't go down very well for my kissing scenes. So I didn't go stupid about it. This time I was very, very aware of not going mad.

On the day of the first read-through I didn't think I'd ever been so scared in my life. I hadn't slept the night before. But I met Jimmy Nesbitt, who was so at ease with everyone and everything that it was intoxicating. He's a friend of Chris's and we'd spoken on the phone, which was a nice ice-breaker and not only for the read-through. Within hours of meeting him, or so it felt, we were doing *Carry On*-style sex scenes. He made it easy for me – oh, the charm of the Irish! Jimmy's super-smart – he doesn't push it in your face, but you know that he is. He possesses that ability to make you feel like the only person in the room. After the read-through he said, 'I'm going to the pub. Do you want to come?' Kenny Doughty, who played the obsessive, hopeless romantic Danny, said yes and I had this moment of huge dilemma: I don't want to drink because we've got a rehearsal, but equally I don't want to go and not have a drink and look like a proper square. In the end I went and had a vodka lime and soda, my drink at the time to keep myself trim, and luckily the afternoon went brilliantly.

They brought in a voice coach to untie my vocal cords, which had bunched up at the thought of breaking into song. It was the wonderful redhead Carrie Grant from *Pop Idol*. She was so encouraging, and had the gift of making you feel confident about the good bits you'd got. I had to sing Gabrielle's 'Rise', another reminder of my past, and Elton John's 'Don't Go Breaking My Heart'. And thanks to Carrie, I did it. It didn't matter that I wasn't pitch-perfect. In fact it was good that I wasn't. It's what the part required. With that job I was completely blessed.

The day I had to do the sex scene was our second wedding anniversary, and I was feeling very odd about it. But again Jimmy made it easy and soon I was laughing out loud. I couldn't actually believe what we were about to do. I had a thong on that was split at the sides and was stuck to me with tit-tape. Jimmy wore something like a cricket box. Sorry Jimmy. It was sex on the mixing desk, sex on the sofa, sex up against the wall, sex on the floor. It was *Carry On Canterbury Tales*. What a mad job, eh? And what do you do about kissing? What's the etiquette? I still don't know. When you kiss, can you use tongues? People say it's not allowed, but I've always gone for the full on pash. You want it to look as real as possible, right? I don't know what if anything Jimmy and I decided – I don't think we even had the conversation.

I think the weirdest part of doing that sex scene was *where* I was doing it, not what and with whom. We had pretend sex on the mixing desk of the recording studio where I had recorded 'Girlfriend' and 'Because We Want To' almost six years earlier to the day. If I felt any doubt that I was doing the right thing now it vanished the day I had to put the cans on and sing. As I belted out 'Rise' I remember thinking, 'This is where I want to be. I'm in this studio again, but it's so different from the last time and I'm so happy that this time round I stand here knowing I can do the job.' Because the first time I stood there thinking, 'I can't do this. I can't do this. I'm a charlatan and they all know it.' All I wanted to do from that moment on was make a career for myself in the acting profession.

When the job finished I got quite teary because I thought I might never get the chance to do it again. And now I'd tasted how good it was I wanted more. Ten days of filming wasn't enough. I was so sad. I'd met all these lovely actors who were so funny to be around: it reminded me of drama class again and that family feeling that I'd always gravitated towards. And of course you think you're going to stay in touch with everyone for ever, and you get everyone's number, and have lengthy goodbyes. When we wrapped I bought everyone a red rose to say thank you for making me feel so happy. There were sixty people in all. But I bought the director a cactus, which he told me later he'd been quite offended by – he didn't understand why everyone else got a rose and he got a cactus. I had to explain to him that the cactus would last for ages whereas the roses would only last a day. I was so grateful to him for giving me that job that I wanted him to have something more permanent.

Desperate for more, and buoyed up by critical acclaim for *The Miller's Tale*, I started another round of auditions. I thought the film world would throw its doors open to me, but I was seriously deluded. The jobs just weren't coming in. It was a frustrating time. All the more frustrating, in fact, because I now knew how good it was out there. I went up for a few big films like *Freaky Friday*, which went to Lindsay Lohan, and *Alfie*, which went to Sienna Miller. Nothing came to fruition. Chris was wholly supportive of me and this new chapter of my life, and I couldn't have done it without him. His devotion made it easier to go back out into the lions' den and try again. And I was prepared to do so, for as long as it took. But then I hadn't thought it would take quite so long. It was a bit of shock that after every job I was back to the drawing board.

For bonfire night in the village that year I'd been put in charge of the cake stall. I went to the cash and carry to get the ingredients and came back with enough flour to keep Pâtisserie Valerie in business for a year. Chris came home to find me furiously kneading dough and cracking eggs. The kitchen and I were covered in a fine layer of flour dust. He must have thought he'd married a mad, bad Nigella, more imp than goddess. I got completely carried away and made hundreds of cakes. There weren't enough children in the local village or the surrounding ones to eat my cakes, so I did. It was really time I got another job. I went up for the part of Nancy in Roman Polanski's *Oliver*. Got to the last four, then turned down.

Finally, after what felt like a year of rejections, I got a role in *Things to Do Before You're Thirty*. The village shared a communal sigh of relief. I was going to be working with actors I really liked and admired and had watched for years: Dougray Scott, Millie Fox and an old friend of mine, Shaun Parkes. After such a long break since my previous jobs I was nervous. I felt I was going in as a wife, as Mrs Evans, not as a jobbing actor. I still didn't have enough experience under my belt and I felt totally green – quite rightly, because it was my first big feature. It was also my first time away from home.

Once again I was blessed with the people I was working with. In fact I made two of my best friends on that film: Al Southey, a superb actor, and his girlfriend at the time, Jess, the associate producer of the movie. As usual, I fell hard and fast in love with them both. It was instant – we got on so well it was one of those 'I can't believe you're real' moments and I knew I'd found best friends for life. We went out one night on the Isle of Man, where we were filming, and I said we shouldn't leave each other's sides that night. And we didn't – we were inseparable from then on.

*Things to Do Before You're Thirty* is, of course, a film about young people. The cast was therefore young, which was to have a huge impact on me. I hadn't been hanging out with people of my own age group for a long time. My best mate in the village at home was the fifty-year-old landlady of the pub, Sue. She was wonderful and I love her, but something was missing from my life. Jess and Al were slightly older than me, but we were at least the same generation. On the Isle of Man I started to get a taste for people my own age and I suppose, if I'm honest, a taste for independence. We had a honeymoon period, Al, Jess and I, when we were experiencing the same things together. We'd have endless conversations about films, for we shared a love of them. We would study aspects of a film rather than dossing on the sofa and watching it. Actually that's a lie – we did a bit of both. For the first time since being at Sylvia Young's I could talk obsessively about acting.

Jess's nickname is Jessica Rabbit. She was the first woman I met who celebrated her curves, and she made me realize that it was OK to be curvy and that it was good to eat properly. All the men fancied her – she was the sexiest woman on the shoot by far. And I started to think, 'You know what? I *will* have the Mars bar ice cream for pudding. Let's go crazy and have two!' Naturally she became my heroine. People gravitate towards her because of her bountiful energy. She had energy because she ate well – I don't think I realized until that moment why I'd spent so long curled up on a sofa at the end of a day doing promotion or shooting a video. It all made sense. I had no energy left. No wonder I got to the point where I felt I couldn't go on – the battery had run out. Food is fuel, and without it you come to a grinding halt. I loved being around Jess: I fed off her positivity and vowed to myself I would never wither up and dry out again. Life was too short.

When I was making that film I was going back and forth by plane to see Chris at Hascombe. In the beginning he loved it. He was really enthused and encouraging me to do more, to aim higher. He was so happy for me and loved hearing all the stories about the crew, all the gossip. He's a complete film buff himself and appreciates good actors, good directors and the art of film. We hadn't previously had the type of conversations I was having with Jess and Al, but we started to now. It was nice. I liked having something to contribute.

When filming finished I missed my two new best friends horribly. Determined to stay in touch with them, I didn't want *Thirty* to end like the other projects I'd worked on, where after the wrap party everyone says goodbye until you bump into each other again on some other set. I think I had finally grown into my own age – it had taken some twenty years. So through the spring I started to go up to London to see them. On my own. It was a bit strange, I thought. Why was I choosing to go there rather than spend the weekend in Hascombe? Why was I choosing these people over Chris? It was a bit scary, actually, and I felt the ground shift beneath my feet. But I still did it.

# Not Just Any Old Companion

## An Auditioning Room at BBC House

Isn't it typical? You stand around for hours waiting for the bus, then three come at once. My professional life suddenly picked up speed just as my personal life expanded. As *Thirty* wrapped I was called to London to do an audition for a horror film called *Spirit Trap*. It was an ensemble piece and they wanted about six actors for it. It was about a group of university students sharing a house in Camden in north London, where strange things start to happen. Supernatural forces take hold and manipulate the group, and they start to turn on each other. The situation creates anarchy and people become obsessed. It was very dark, but it seemed like a good idea at the time. I met the director and liked him – it was a very positive experience. They'd cast most of the other parts but hadn't found anyone yet to play a girl called Jenny. I went in at the last minute and fortunately was given the part. I had one audition, then one recall to read opposite Luc Mabley. It was all quite rushed. I found out that I'd got the part and that the cast were due to leave for Bucharest in Romania not long afterwards. I was going to be away from Chris, with no visit home, for six weeks. So we decided to go on holiday before I went, just to hang out together and have a quiet time.

While we were planning our trip to LA I was told that the *Dr Who* scripts were doing the rounds. Michael called me and said that it was being revived, with a brilliant writer called Russell T. Davies, and I should consider looking at the role of Rose, the Doctor's sidekick. They had just announced Chris Ecclestone was going to be the new Doctor, and I thought that combination sounded good to me. I knew it was going to be big budget, and I knew there would be special effects, so from the off I was fairly sure there weren't going to be any shaky sets and makeshift Daleks. Michael sent me the script, and right off the page I fell instantly in love with the character of Rose. She's an insignificant, ordinary nineteen-year-old who lives on a council estate, eats loads of chips and has a boyfriend she's been with since she was eight. She lives with her mother – her dad died in a car accident when she was very young. She leaped off the page at me – partly because she spoke to me, but mostly because Russell writes women so damn well. Suddenly I just had to play this part, and the more I read the more I wanted it.

307

The fact that Russell and Chris were involved made it even more desirable. I know I'd just got the part of Jenny, but I still felt quite anxious about my *Who* audition. However, I loved this character and I wanted it so much I thought, 'Get over your audition fear and go in there and fight for it.' So I practised my lines endlessly, but by the time I got to the audition I had no idea if I was playing it right or pitching it right. As far as I could work out it was essentially this mad, big old romp and Chris and I were the tour guides. I had no idea if the people auditioning me felt the same.

I was actually quite ill with a fluey cold on the day of the audition. I was wearing a green Fruit of the Loom sweat-shirt and baggy jeans – I needed comfort clothes and I needed to feel young and as uninspired as the person I understood Rose to be at the beginning of the series. When I arrived at Radio Two I was half an hour early so I went to Caffe Nero. I never eat before an audition because I'm normally so nervous that my appetite vanishes (a rare thing), but today I needed a sugar kick. So I sank a big milky coffee and two really sugary fudge brownies – and then of course felt guilty and full and fluey, and the doubt crept in. I thought, 'What am I doing here? Why am I putting myself through this? It's making me neurotic again, and I don't want to be that neurotic person any more.' Those thoughts enter my head at most auditions. The fear never lessens, annoyingly so.

I was met by Andy Pryor, the casting director, and Phil

Collinson, the producer, who showed me into a nice light room. Some audition rooms can be really oppressive with lots of downlighting and you know you look like shit. The feeling I got when I walked into this one was that it was going to be OK. It was a warm open space and I was surrounded by talented, beautiful souls who were welcoming and down to earth and all spoke in wonderful round Welsh accents – there were seemingly no egomaniacs in there. I liked them all instantly. It was the first time I had met the inspirational Julie Gardner, head of Drama at BBC Wales. She is one of a kind. With her big hair and glasses and huge boobs she's very sexy, very lovely and incredibly intelligent. There's never a wasted word when she speaks: it's always considered, but never laboured. Some women can be so intimidating in those situations, especially when they are surrounded by men – it can make them feel empowered and mean. But not Julie – she was a star player. Then there was this six foot seven giant sitting in the corner – the genius writer, Russell T. Davies. If my memory serves me correctly, Russell was wearing a collarless shirt of the type that Take That wear in the video for 'Pray'. But I may have got it wrong and he may be horrified to read this! Whatever, he was all smiles with a big open face, big eyes and big mouth – almost a Disney character.

So I relaxed and thought that even if nothing came of it, it would be a nice audition, a good experience. As I sat down to read I said to them, 'Look, I've got a really bad cold, so if anything comes flying out of my nose or my mouth I apologize in advance.' They said, 'Hurrah!', and started clapping before I'd even begun. It was like being with your mum and dad, not because they were like them or even old enough to be them (wink, wink), but because they were so encouraging. It was lovely: I started reading, and every time I finished they applauded. Russell wanted me to be more cockney, but there are different levels of cockney and I didn't want to go too full on because I think it can hijack a performance – and in truth I wasn't that confident with it. However, it seemed to go well and I left happy. But in those circumstances you can never really tell. It's like taking an exam – you don't really know whether it went OK.

On the way to the lift Andy Pryor said, 'That was really lovely – you should be very pleased.' I thought what a sweet guy he was to say that, but I was none the wiser – I assumed he said that to everyone. I asked my agent to call them and find out how it had gone, and to my delight Michael said they were apparently very pleased and excited. They had other people to see, of course, but they'd get back to me. I did another reading after that, and then just before going on holiday with my Chris I got a call to come back and do a third reading, this time with Chris Ecclestone. I was down to the last three. I knew that was good news, but I was terrified and thought I wouldn't be able to do it. At such moments this awful panic takes over and I think the same stupid thoughts as I always used to. Why am I doing this to myself? *Can* I do it? I'm such a charlatan – they're going to find me out and it's all going to be a catastrophe! And I have to sit very still for a moment and just breathe and remember that it isn't the same old thing. I'm just responding in the same way to a different thing.

When I arrived, one of the other girls was walking out. I recognized her as Keira Malik – we'd worked together on a film. Keira is physically very different from me – darker and more petite. At that point I was pushing eleven stone, which is frankly beyond the 'curvy' stage. Still, I felt it was OK for the part of Rose, though I would have lost the weight if they'd asked me to, or at least given it a go; but they didn't ask. Keira walked out as chirpy as anything and I thought, 'She's got it.' I reckoned I could tell by the way her ponytail was bouncing so high. Again, *slam dunk*, what's the point of even going in? The whole process is like being on a roller coaster.

Anyway, I did walk in and there were Julie, Russell and Phil sitting in a panel behind Chris. We shook hands. Chris was reading off the page even though he'd obviously learnt some of it. I on the other hand had wanted to be word-perfect. I don't think I was on the day, however, because I didn't trust myself to close the script. Again they tried to push the cockney accent, so I did it a bit more than before. Chris seemed very quiet, respectful, tolerant and patient, and didn't have an opinion or suggest things. He made it clear that that sort of input was very much up to those who were casting, and that he was just a cog in the wheel. But in fact he was absolutely critical to the process – we had to gel. The longer the read-through went on, the more and more I wanted the part. But I also thought my accent was shit and I could have done better. Did Chris Ecclestone think I was crap? Who was I kidding? I'd never get this part. I left the read-through, and two days later we went to LA on holiday.

What was it like for the other people sitting across the desk, with their impenetrable smiles? I spoke to Julie Gardner and she was really sweet about it. She said I had been in the frame ever since they'd seen me in *Canterbury Tales*, which they loved. There was a quality about me that they were interested in. I fitted the image they were looking for, which was a young girl between nineteen and twenty-two who could not only connect with a new generation of *Dr Who* viewers but appeal to a younger audience as well. Russell's story arc, his whole reason for Rose, was to take an ordinary girl and make her extraordinary. I think they had met ten actresses, and had come close to casting the part, when I walked through the door. Julie says that every time I read I got better, that my reading was 'extraordinary' – though I find that hard to believe. But thank you Julie for saying so. You're so damn lovely.

Russell, on the other hand, was more wary about me than Julie was. He was worried that I was going to come in pissed all the time. All he knew about me was what he'd read in the papers about me being out on the lash all the time. He thought I might be a loose cannon on set. He didn't go as far as sniffing my breath on the day of the audition, but he might have wanted to. I was a complete country bumpkin by then, but whenever Chris's and my names were mentioned in the press they always harped back to those boozy first few months of our relationship.

Some actors come to auditions dressed for the part, others come dressed normally. Julie's impression was that I'd come dressed for myself. Which I had. Jeans, sweatshirt and carrying a soya latte from Starbucks – my signature couture. They saw in me the epitome of a young modern girl, very real, very Rose, and they took a gamble that the audience would connect with me as her in the way they did. Julie was very kind to me, very reassuring, and again I thank everyone at BBC Wales for the platform they gave me. Julie says I exuded a natural charm and intelligence – if I did, it's thanks to everyone I worked with who gave me the tools to keep my demons at bay and get me through the reading.

Chris (Evans, that is) and I stayed with Gordon when we were in LA, just chilling at his flat with his dog. It was all very Melrose Place. We sat in the garden with a huge fire roaring in a pit, we ate at our favourite restaurant and spent a lot of time watching the waves and the surfers on Malibu Beach. But in the back of my mind, like Musak in a lift, I was wondering, wondering, wondering – would I be the one to bring Rose to life? I know the reason why Rose spoke to me is that Russell has this rare ability to make women three-dimensional, he gives them complexity. He makes them sensual and sexy, and at the same time raw and silly. It's a gift. He celebrates every female quality and trait, our madness and over-analytical minds, our insecurities and torrid emotions. The character was full of untapped potential. That was something I detected straightaway, and what I really wanted to do with the part of Rose, and what was already on the paper, was to make her as real as the script suggested. Obviously the world of the Doctor is surreal, and fantastical when you're meeting aliens and flying through wormholes with a nine hundred-year-old guy in a blue box, but even so Russell was making the scripts a lot more domestic than they had been before. I wanted to make her real as Russell had. I prayed and wished and hoped and waited for The Call.

Finally it came. They wanted me. Did I leap about to loud music and scream with joy? Yes. At first. Then new worries started to creep in. Did I really want to do this? It would mean nine months in Wales, away from my husband whom I loved so much. How would we manage? Where was I going to live? How often would I be able to see Chris? It really concerned me. Chris is all-consuming. He lives by his lore, and his lore alone. That suited us just fine when I had nothing else to fit in around him, but I was worried that such a dramatic shift of my attention was going to put pressure on our relationship. Apart from times at the very beginning, we hadn't had an argument in three years. What was there to argue about? The man had saved my life. And there would be other difficulties, too. The thought of living in a hotel scared the shit out of me – I knew where that kind of space could take my head. And I didn't like what it did to me. I was so adamant that I was now a completely different person, but I was fearful all the same: fearful of the association.

So Chris and I talked it over. I voiced my fears aloud and they became smaller for the telling. Chris, as ever, was so supportive and enthusiastic and encouraging that I thought, 'Yes, I can do this.' That was what Chris did for me – with someone loving you like that you can take on the world. And he was right. I was mentally and emotionally fitter than I'd ever been. So I said yes, I would be Rose Tyler. And despite what subsequently happened between Chris and me, it is a decision I have never regretted.

# A Horror Film

## Bucharest

The last thing in the world I wanted to do was get on a flight and leave home for six weeks. I wanted to get my teeth into Rose and *Dr Who*, and when you discover a new enthusiasm like that it's hard to go back to the less riveting stuff. But that's what I had to do. I had to change hats and head for Romania to film *Spirit Trap*. I had a goodbye barbecue and made the most disastrous chocolate fudge brownies I've ever made in my life. I was supposed to be doing the Atkins diet because I felt so huge at the time, but I didn't really care enough to do it properly and the willpower I once had for self-starvation had, thankfully, deserted me. Chris, Jess, Al and I had a great feast at Table No. 1 (our favourite spot in the garden) and watched the sun go down. The next day Chris took me to the airport and kissed me goodbye. I didn't know whether he was going to come out to see me – all I knew was that I wasn't coming home for ages.

The first person I met was Sam Troughton, who is ironically the grandson of Patrick Troughton, the second Dr Who. He was on the same flight as me, two rows behind. He introduced himself and I thought he looked quite cool – he had a beard and specs and was carrying a *Guardian*. He looked like the kind of guy I wanted to hang out with; also he was my love interest in the movie, so I wanted to get on with him. When we arrived we shared a cab, and by the time we got to our hotel we had bonded. It was a modern, quite clinical hotel with a great Benihana Japanese restaurant in the basement – the kind of place where they do 'sushi acts', cracking eggs mid-air with a spatula and throwing raw fish around the place. A yellow fin circus. It was a bit pricey, so we didn't want to do it every night, but it was nice to go and treat ourselves occasionally. As soon as I was in my room I tried to make it as homely as possible – despite the political changes it was still a bit Eastern Bloc. So I went around propping up a few pictures and lit some candles. But I missed Chris so much – it was the first time I'd been away from him, and I worried about our relationship. I hoped that a couple as stable and inseparable as we were would be able to cope with such a big change.

On one of the first few days Sam, two of the other actors and I went to see the set. It was in Castle Studios, where they had shot *Cold Mountain*, and there were lots of other amazing sets there too. The work that goes into designing and constructing them is phenomenal, and they work hard out there for very little money. But sets are one thing, one's colleagues quite another. I wasn't sure how I was going to get on with one of the other girls in the ensemble, who wasn't really my cup of Rose Lee – I found her quite intimidating. Maybe I brought that on myself because I was feeling self-conscious, but even so we didn't gel. I spent a lot of time trying to work out a way to make it work. Up to that point I'd been blessed with actors like Jimmy, Dennis and Rafe Spall – lovely, sweet, humble people. I'd only worked with one young actress before, and she was a breeze. This one was a little different. Anyway, we had ten days of intensive rehearsals in a vast empty warehouse, which enabled me to feel more confident about the part of Jenny. But really I just wanted to get on with the filming and go home.

This was the first film in which I'd played a lead. The days were tough. The director was a very lovely man who was very compassionate about his artists and worried if we didn't see eye to eye, and because the dynamic on the set was sometimes interesting – to say the least – he would worry and ask me how I thought we could improve it. I was trying, but nothing I did was working. I know my strengths and I know my weaknesses, and getting on with people isn't one of my weaknesses. There was more time available to take on a scene than I'd experienced before and I think that can often lead to overshoot, overkill, which makes it hard to keep the scene fresh and new. I worked out a way to do that which stands me in good stead now, but it was a challenge in Bucharest.

After a typical day of acting scared for ten hours, it wasn't very surprising that I wasn't in a mood to socialize after work. I would spend my free time on my own in my room, eating cheese. Having done the Atkins diet I became obsessed with this selection of cheeses that I was supposedly allowed to eat: mozzarella, ricotta, Boursin. But it wasn't working. I think the mini-bar selection of chocolate may also have had a lot to answer for. I was comfort eating on cheese and chocolate, so, with my face doubling in size and my Shirley Temple curls becoming tighter and tighter, I really was a sight for sore eyes. Outside the hotel wasn't that much better. Bucharest is quite grey because so many of the buildings are. The People's Palace dominates the city and stares down at the mortals on the street, a constant reminder of what they don't have. Lots of the children I came across were street urchins who lived in the sewers or on the side of the road. I'd never before seen children with missing limbs begging me for coins. It was hard work. The locals would tell us not to give our money to the kids because we'd never get away from them, but sod all that. I gave them food, fags – to sell, not smoke – and money. It made me sad. I wished my husband was there. I could have handled it all rather better if he'd been there. But he wasn't.

Left to my own devices, I spent most of my downtime walking round the city. There were a few wild nights out in Bucharest, which normally meant that Sam and me, some of the crew, the camera operator, the grips and a sparkie called Russell who was great, would go to a huge outdoor club in the middle of nowhere. It was the sort of place that pumps out loud trance music, and there are hundreds of dancers on the table tops. Sam and I would pour a load of vodka down our throats and have a go. I think it was surrounded by a lake, or a river, but I couldn't work it out because I was too trashed on vodka. We were trying to have a mad night out. Apart from that I was in my room, trying to concentrate on the work and not get too depressed. Since I had had to give up my cheese hobby, I started another. I was desperate to buy a 1989 Porsche 911, white with a black leather interior with white piping. There was a lot of faxing between Chris and me as we tried to find the perfect one.

My other hobby was Rose. I wanted to get my head around *Dr Who*. I called Russell and asked him to recommend his best episodes, because I hadn't watched them as a kid. In the beginning I panicked a bit because I didn't get it. I hadn't understood the beauty of sci-fi before *Dr Who* came into my world. At this stage all I did know was that I didn't want the companion I was going to play to be anything like the Doctor's previous companions. Women had changed, I was aware of that. When I went back to the text, however, I quickly realized that that wasn't going to happen: Russell was forging into new territories with this new companion. One day Chris Ecclestone gave me a call. My heart leaped into my throat and I became hysterical, so out of breath that I could hardly talk. Chris was talking about us sticking together and making sure there were clear lines of communication between us. I was doing all I could just to stay upright. He wanted to find out where I was going to live once we were filming in Wales – he told me he'd found a flat, and suggested I speak to his woman. She could help me. He was being all matter-of-fact, and there was I being all gushing and sycophantic. Eventually he made some comment about me sounding a bit over-excited and wondered whether he should call back at a better time. I was so embarrassed. When I put the phone down I thought, 'God, I wasn't funny.' I had nothing smart to say about the Doctor or Rose, or anything about this project that we were both about to embark on for the next nine months of our lives. I wanted it to start straightaway. I stared out of my hotel window and wished the time away.

One night I had gone out after work to watch a big football match – crews and football are close travelling companions. We were in this bar and then suddenly Chris walked in. My Chris. Out of the blue. No call, no warning, nothing. Typical Evans behaviour. Utterly impetuous. Over the moon to see him despite the shock, I just leaped out of my seat and threw my arms around him. It was so nice to be able to finally embrace the city; hold hands, have a laugh. I think I was about half a stone heavier when he got out there, because my cheese theory had had the opposite effect. He took me out to dinner to eat some real food and drink some wine, and on my days off we went to see all the churches and all the rest of the touristy things. But it was a bit weird between us. I'd been away from home for over a month by then, and I'd had to persuade myself to enjoy this opportunity because I knew I was fortunate to get the part. I'd had to stop myself from missing him so much, because if I did I knew I wouldn't be able to get anything done. Now that he was back in my space again it was odd. We were out of synch. And we didn't have enough time to get back into synch. Chris had come out for a fleeting visit because he'd missed me. I'd never doubted that he loved me but this was a strange reversal, with him needing me. I always thought he could do fine without me.

Finally the last week dragged to a close. I was really glad to leave, glad to get home to the cottage, Chris, the dogs and our little domestic life. The whole project left a strange taste in my mouth. I still can't work out whether the problem was the dynamics among the cast or the material. It was a dark, intense film; the sets, though impressive, were oppressive, and the days were long. I thought, 'I hope not every job is going to be like this.' And, of course, there hasn't been another one like it. I bought the DVD of *The Second Coming*, which Russell wrote and Chris (Ecclestone) starred in, and it was quite something. It gave me impetus to push through to the end of the *Spirit Trap* job and get to Wales.

I spent the rest of the summer walking around the garden in the sunshine, learning lines. I would try new things out, see where I could take the character, work on new techniques. I wrote up my back story, considered it and let it roll around on the tongue. I was desperate to talk to Chris

Ecclestone and Russell about all these thoughts that were whizzing around my head, wanting to be in the thick of it right away, but equally I didn't want them to think I was some mad stalker. As soon as I was back with a script in my hand, the character took hold of me again. I just loved the part and couldn't wait to get started.

Meanwhile, in September 2003 I turned twenty-one. My coming of age wasn't such a milestone for me since I was a married woman who'd been earning her own money for six years. If anything, there were times when I thought, 'Jesus Christ, I'm married and I'm only twenty-one!' But very quickly, and not because I forced the thoughts but because they were genuine, I'd add in my mind, 'Yes, I am only twenty-one, but why does it matter?' My party was epic and lasted for three days. We hired a room in the Groucho Club and decked it out like the set of *Moulin Rouge*. The walls were draped in heavy red velvet, and by the end of the night people were wearing it. Like my sixteenth and eighteenth I looked around to see who was there, but this time I thought, 'Oh my God, you came!' which was followed by lots of shrieking and kissing. We had a DJ from Swindon. I'd been there recently and met this guy who I thought was amazing, so I brought him up to London. I knew he wouldn't be as precious as the London DJs and would play requests. I don't care how cool you are, I want to play 'Come On Eileen' at my birthday and leap about doing the Robo dance. And I don't care how many times you've heard it, either – it's my night. Jimmy Nesbitt and Chris sang a few Beatles classics. It was gold. Life had stabilized, we were sitting comfortably. We weren't going out very much, we had our home and our dogs and a future which looked very promising. There was nothing boring about Chris, nothing ordinary. He was always the life and soul of the party – just like my dad. Always striving to make the most of himself and of me.

# Sonic Screw Driver

## Welsh Wales

Chris drove me to Cardiff for my first day at work. We spent the night in the Hilton and across the road, all lit up, was Cardiff Castle. Tom Jones was playing that night and I thought how wonderfully Welsh it all was. Chris and I had a nice dinner, but I was terrified about the read-through the next day – it felt like the entire BBC was coming down to the Millennium Stadium to listen. The following morning, Chris kissed me goodbye and I was collected by the second Assistant Director, a lovely guy with a beard called Steffan Morris. He was so delightful and sweet and warm and exactly the type of person I needed to be handed over to that first morning of what again felt like one of the most terrifying experiences of my life. Steff was an angel, and became my best mate on the crew. I owe a lot to that man. *Dr Who* owes a lot to him.

We drove to the stadium and then I disappeared into this absolutely massive conference room overlooking the empty ground. I felt very small, but safe. Talk about a cast of thousands. Everyone was there, from Julie Gardner down to the last line editor. And the brilliant cast and Chris Ecclestone. I felt like I'd been shot with a stun gun. I couldn't move for nerves, so I found the Welsh cakes and sank a few to bring me down from the ceiling. Complete comfort eating. Chris looked tanned from his jollies, but he too looked a bit overwhelmed. He pulled out a card with the wrapping still on it. There was a picture of a monkey on it, covering his eyes and ears, and we stuck it in front of us before we started reading. It was kind of like the monkey was saying, 'Fucking hell, here we go!' We really didn't know what to make of it at that point. No idea which way it was going to go. Camille Coduri, who played my mum, turned up with her hair in bunches, a tiny skirt, schoolgirl socks and an incredible rack on display. In a tasteful way mind. I had no idea how old she was – I just knew she looked fabulous. She came over and gave me a huge hug even though I didn't know her. I loved that – I like tactile people, people who hug and comfort. Camille's definitely a cuddler. She was panicking about how she was going to have to scream about three times before the break because we'd been told to go for it from the off.

It's a weird experience, a read-through. You can't hide behind a character because you're sitting there in your own clothes with your own make-up, your own hair, around a huge boardroom table, so you're quite exposed. You watch every actor, and they are watching you, trying to gauge the level, trying to make sense of it, trying not to be too confident, too eager to please, too keen – but also not to be a mouse. They always start by saying, 'Please tell us your name and who you're playing.' It embarrasses me, and I dread it.

Chris went first: 'My name is Chris, and I'm playing the Doctor.' That's all he had to say . . . then there was this huge great ice-breaking applause. After that I could feel the blood coming back into my legs, so we got on with it. Chris and I were sparring off each other, acting to each other – we didn't have our heads in the scripts and it felt fun and light. All the work I'd put into learning lines and practising endlessly in the garden had paid off. I felt great, my adrenaline went through the roof. I felt a need to nip out for a fag, but luckily Camille loves a ciggie too so I could ponce one off her. I'm a bit of a scav when it comes to fags. I'm crap at buying them, especially on set, because I start every day thinking I'm not going to smoke today and then proceed to nick everybody else's. Poor Camille – I must owe her hundreds!

During that first phase of rehearsal the hours were pretty normal. The brilliance of Russell's writing was coming to the fore. All his characters, even the baddies, were three-dimensional. It was all becoming more and more real, and I started to think we were on to something here. It was a sacrifice, but it was worth being away from home for. I spent a lot of time turning the flat I'd rented into a show-home. I'd wash and iron, dust and hoover, to my heart's content, then pop over to the local Spar to buy half a roast chicken. It wasn't as sad as it sounds – I liked the routine and the order. I needed to be domesticated, because I enjoyed it. It wasn't me being neurotic – well, maybe just a touch. Out came the photos, the candles and a few soft furnishings. Mostly it was me missing home and trying to create a world that felt as close as possible to it minus three huge dogs and a six foot two husband.

Every day I would be driven to a big warehouse on the outskirts of Newport. From the outside it looked like a big grey box sitting in an industrial park – the kind you used to snog behind as a kid. But inside that box there was something else: a whole world of sci-fi. Surrounding the Tylers' flat and the Tardis were various other interior sets, such as the viewing room in Act 2, Satellite 5 and Captain Jack's two small rockets. I loved the prop store. You could get lost in there for hours looking at photo frames, gas masks, a sonic screwdriver, laser guns – it went on and on. In front of the studio was a second floor where the geniuses of the Art Dept created their iconic sets. Everyone in there was amazing. Their creativity blew my mind: they humbled me and left me feeling inspired about the whole project.

The hours eventually became quite taxing. In the first year we worked six-day fortnights. In other words one week we'd work six days and the next week we'd work five, with three days off every two weeks. The hours would change depending on what the episode required. Normal days, like rehearsal periods, were seven till seven. Split days were 11 a.m. to 10 p.m., and night shoots were 5 p.m. to 5 a.m. We started with the night shoots, which played havoc with your sleeping patterns. Except for the odd music video I'd never worked through the night, and never for consecutive nights. Videos were easy in comparison, because I was on autopilot. I knew the steps off by heart and could do them in my sleep. I *was* doing them in my sleep. Night shoots were different because you had to be on the job constantly. But I was so keen that actually I found the prospect of filming at night exciting – especially since it was in London, which meant I could go home at the end of the shoot. I remember driving to the set on the Thames Embankment, and the first thing I saw was the floodlights illuminating the place like a football stadium. There were cameras going up and the crew prepping for the evening shoot. It was magic. TV magic. It was all I'd ever wanted and here I was, in character, in costume, ready to walk into the middle of it all and make the scene come to life.

After that first night of filming I flopped into the back of a car and was driven the hour's journey home to Surrey. I wanted to get back to Chris, but he was getting up as I was getting into bed. I probably should have just gone home to the flat, but I was so near the cottage I couldn't bear not going back there. I was a sleeping wife by day, and then got collected again to be an actress by night. You have no social life when you're doing night shoots because you have to try to sleep during those hours that you have off. But it's hard to lie in bed when your body clock is telling you to get up. I barely saw my husband – we were the proverbial passing ships. The hours were pretty tough. I was trying to feel emotion at three in the morning, trying to make it real, when all I wanted to do was curl up in a ball and go to sleep. By the end of two weeks you feel like you've lost your soul and yet you're still having to react to the scene around you, to respond to what people are saying, to take direction. You can't do it by rote – you have to concentrate all the time. Everyone, not just me, was stretched to the limit in those first two weeks; we were all exhausted. I wonder if Julie wouldn't admit that, in hindsight, it was a bad idea.

Then again, *Dr Who* was a series drama like no other. The stakes were high. There was a lot of pressure on everyone because so much money had been poured into the production. Time was in short supply, so it had to be shot quickly. We started filming in July. Night scenes needed to be done, but the summer nights were short, so they had no choice but to work us hard. It was an enormous undertaking, and I think we were probably all learning, not just me. It's an extraordinary series, unlike anything anyone had worked on before. It's not like a police drama, where you have days and days filming on one set such as the station, or in some long-term character's flat. In *Dr Who* you're travelling to a new world in every episode. And that world has to be created: the builds they were erecting were highly complex. Then you have to add to that all the action, the stunts, the special effects, the CGI, the prosthetic work, the make-up jobs – the make-up alone could take hours and hours. I look back at my call sheets and realize that every day we'd have at least two, and usually all, of the above. Obviously everyone had a certain level of experience of their own field, but to combine them all, was a major undertaking, a tremendous collaboration.

So although it was a bit hellish, it was also quite bonding. We were all in it together – there was a whiff of the Blitz about it. That was the good thing that came out of it. We were leaning on each other, quite literally, to prop each other up, especially Chris Ecclestone and I. We'd talk about music, and he introduced me to Sam Cooke and Donny Hathaway. He's a serious, intense actor, but he can do absolutely brilliant impersonations and every accent known to man. He has a great sense of humour and was always extremely self-deprecating. We'd collapse in the trailer during breaks and chat about our pasts, our families, our romances. (I was a wife; other men didn't come into it. But it wasn't doing my marriage very much good.) There was a lot of jokey banter, and I got on well with Chris's driver, Robin. We'd gossip about who was in the papers, who was shagging whom on set – not literally on set, obviously, but back in the choice rented accommodation.

I didn't find the part of Rose easy, but I wasn't struggling with her either. I was very sure of who she was. I'd done more work on that character than I've ever had time to do since. And in many ways I'm quite like her – which is possibly why they picked me, though Russell says he wrote the part long before I was involved in the project. It shows how well Russell writes women and how universal our situations are. She's a girl who's been living what she considers a dull, miserable, ordinary life. He refers to it in most of my speeches: her life was all about getting up, going to work, working all day, getting back on the bus, buying chips and going to bed. But she has so much more to offer. All she needs is someone to shake her out of her stupor and make her realize her potential. That was how the Doctor found Rose, and it was how my Chris found me. I thought the world was a quite a scary place when I was eighteen, and then I met someone who completely changed it around for me. I could totally relate to both of Russell's main characters. The Doctor was someone who could show Rose what else was out there, what else was going on. Chris reminded me that life should be celebrated. Both put the onus on other people and not on themselves, but in the process are all-consuming.

I think that was why I could inhabit the character. I liked Rose a lot. I knew how she felt. Russell doesn't just show women as sweet, emotional, happy-go-lucky. He shows them as needy and manipulative and conniving. Rose was all of those things and also insecure. She was more than just a cheeky cockney lass. I love the fact that the first time you see her she's wearing these frumpy jeans and a baggy hoody top. It mirrors her life. She hasn't decided who she is yet. She's awkward and uncomfortable. Towards the end, as she gets stronger and bolder, the clothes change. Everything on that show was done for a reason. I wasn't wearing a red top at the end of the series simply because that was all we had in the cupboard. I'm wearing a red top because Rose could carry a red top. She was brave, she knew what was right and what was wrong, she knew that you had to act for the greater good. That red top was a sign that Rose could do things on her own now. She was empowered. She was in love. She could face difficult moral dilemmas and do the right thing. She could love unconditionally but could also stand on her own two feet. The colour red suggests all of those things. However painful the separation from the Doctor was going to be, she would survive and be better for her time with him.

One of the most interesting parts of the character for me was getting to grips with an ordinary, bolshy, annoying teenager. Being a teenager was very fresh in my mind, but Rose was different from me in one major way. I wanted to play her as a young nineteen-year-old, not as the old, lived in one that I'd been. I knew other nineteen-year-olds didn't feel like I had, so I went back to the drawing board and started to study my sisters. It was a revelation to me. The things that are important to them – their secret societies, for instance, and the closed world of the teenage girl – I had missed out on totally. I slightly envied their teenage tantrums, their constant texting and emailing of friends, their shared boyfriend dramas. I could easily inhabit the extraordinary world of the Tardis, but I have to thank my sisters Ellie and Harley for showing me the ordinary world at home, and what an exciting world that is.

# Fly Away

## A Heart

At exactly the same time that parallels in my work and home lives appeared so clearly to me, my home life changed. Chris and I had been locked away in a little world of our own making, but I had stepped out of the safety zone of Christmas Cottage and embarked on an adventure of my own. I was so happy to be given this chance to build a sustainable career that I gave it my all. Chris, meantime, was doing his own thing and projects were beginning to take off. We got busy again, and we rapidly grew apart. I knew something had changed but I couldn't work out what it was, or how to change it back. We weren't arguing, but it just wasn't like it used to be. I never saw him; when I came home he'd be busy, and he was hopeless on the phone.

Perhaps the bar had been set so high that in the end it was

unsustainable. Neither of us wanted it to stay up there because we both knew it wasn't real. I don't know what exactly happened, and perhaps I'll never know – and perhaps that's a good thing. Obviously those six weeks in Bucharest had tipped the scales but, rather than get things back as they were, shortly after coming home I was gone again. We were people who worked brilliantly when we were together all the time. We were each other's best friends and we very rarely left each other's sides. Then suddenly we were the complete opposite, and as a couple we couldn't cope. It wasn't that one or the other fucked up, it was just a weird vibe between us that we were too honest to ignore. On the surface of it, it seemed like we had stopped seeing each other and therefore stopped trying to make it work. But our relationship went to the core and so obviously something else was going on. Something that both of us found it increasingly hard to admit to. I feared that Chris felt he would be slowing me down, or stopping me, and though I used to think that wouldn't have been true, I couldn't give everything to him *and* to work. The part required me to be physically else-where. I think we started to guard our hearts a bit to protect ourselves from the long physical absences that were lying ahead. He didn't want to hold me back, but maybe he didn't like me being that far away. And perhaps I for once couldn't put him absolutely first. It's hard to be objective about it because I know what he did for me, what we did for each other and what we did together.

During the filming of the second block of *Dr Who*, Chris

336

came to Wales and began the dialogue that was to result in us splitting up. The conversation about breaking up was never final; it was about separating with a view to sorting it out. We both knew it wasn't working, but we weren't able to fix it. The relationship had suffered because of absence, so I don't know why we thought a separation would make it better. Me being away had taken a greater toll on us than either of us had imagined. Things were different now. He slowly – maybe to protect himself, maybe not – started to let go of me and in the process let me fly away. He drove straight back to Hascombe, and I went to work. I was in shock.

Mum was in Spain, Dad at the time was in England. I had spoken to Mum a few times, so she knew something was up but not exactly what. She had a journalist friend out there who had seen our split announced on Reuter's, and he called Mum immediately to tell her. She kicked the car in fury. Dad rang as soon as he heard and told Mum to get out of the house immediately, but she already knew why he was calling. He was fairly staggered that Mum knew, but good gossip travels faster than the speed of sound. By the time I got hold of her she was furious with me that yet again I hadn't told her about an event that was bound to generate publicity, and gave me what for. As she says, she didn't give a shit about my feelings, but was just furious that she'd had to hear it from someone else. After she calmed down, she rang me back and apologized. She felt really bad because I was in pieces. My parents' friend offered his house to them, but they too had had enough of running and just stayed at home and didn't open the door.

As soon as I could, I ran to my friends – the friends I'd made since meeting Chris, who remain my friends now and who I believe will be friends for life. Zanna is my oldest London friend. She's my saint. I've never met another like her – smart-dressing, fast-living, real-talking. What a beauty. Paula, her sister, is our mother hen, more loyal than a labrador, with the finest set of pins in London. I love her and her make-sense ways. Ellie is a newish addition to the fold, but what a find! She's deep, emotional, funny to a fault and makes you feel great about being alive, being female, being you. And then there's Gracie, our little blonde angel, all sweetness and light but with a wicked tongue. She's the perfect listener, an even better talker, a beautiful soul. And, of course, there's my friend Jessica. You know her.

I couldn't have been in better company. They're real women, my friends, the ones who truly know me. They forgive me and my idiosyncrasies, and encourage me to cry and rage and sing – *loud*. They're the bestest friends I could ever wish for. Thank you, angels. Late that Friday night, when I finally arrived in London, they congregated around me and held me up when I thought I would once again fall. They squeezed my hand as I talked them through splitting up with Chris, just once that first night. Then we changed the subject. I didn't want to rehash it and be given hundreds of opinions. Perhaps I was as guarded and protective about our separation as I was about our wedding, because, though I was in pieces, deep down I knew it was the right thing to do and I didn't want to be talked out of it. In a way I think it worked. The split was absolutely awful but it wasn't polluted by others, so it never became poisonous. I hurt and I was right to hurt, but I was right to take the positives with me. If Chris had taught me anything, he'd taught me that.

Zanna had just met a hot young New Yorker, so after talking about Chris we threw ourselves into that chat and talked into the early hours. I started to fantasize about moving to the States and finding myself a hot Italian American and maybe even doing a Broadway play. At three in the morning we were all gassed out, so we stayed at Jess's flat and I was grateful for the safety they provided me. Al, Jess and I slept three in a bed, with Jess in the middle. Zanna, Paula and Gracie were on the sofas, Ellie on the inflatable. And when I wasn't working that's where I stayed, with Jess and Al, for the next three months. And I was OK. Well, I was OK when I was there – I wasn't so good when I went back to Cardiff.

The biggest single shock to me when I broke up with Chris was how quickly I fell back into the same terrible pattern of starvation and wild nights out that I'd experienced before. I'd go mad on the weekends, get completely wrecked and just see where I ended up. Fun for a while, sort of fun . . . well, I'd tell myself it was fun. I was dividing my time between my friends Jess and Al in north London and my flat and the crew in Wales. Thank God I had *Dr Who*. It kept me focused and my head almost screwed on. They were wrong when they said that *Dr Who* had been the cause of my marriage breakdown. In fact the truth was quite the opposite: it kept me sane, and the crew and actors kept me going. It was a positive experience throughout. Life carried on. *Dr Who* helped me prove to myself that I could do it regardless, that I was capable of doing it without Chris. And I had something to do every day, and full days at that. As long as I could work, I had something else to think about than obsessing about being on my own again.

About a month after we split up I stopped eating. It was never as severe – and I hope never will be as severe – as the first time around. This time it only lasted about four months, not two years. I don't know if I was starving myself because suddenly I was single again, or whether it was a control thing. It was like I was saying, 'I'm in control of my life even though my marriage is breaking up.' It started so slowly, so surreptitiously that I almost didn't realize it was happening. Almost, but not quite. I'd start by missing one meal, then two, and it was hard when I started. I couldn't do it, so I'd slip up and consume a couple of chicken wings or a 'cold plate' at work. But I'd get better at it, better at working through the hunger. I needed to get to the end of the day and feel that I hadn't eaten anything. Eventually I stopped eating at work and quite quickly lost a lot of weight. I'd hardly eat during the week. I'd drink soya lattes in the day and eat a bit of chicken and salad at night. But when I went home to my friends I'd go crazy – pulled pork, bender in a bun, mash sandwiches. Maybe it was about community, or maybe it was about not being caught. My friends wouldn't have turned a blind eye – they weren't my parents, but they wouldn't have let me get away with it. So it was different from what I'd been doing before. My safety net was intact because I hadn't dismantled it.

I'm thankful for the security *Dr Who* gave me. I'm grateful for the camaraderie it provided. I remember working with Simon Callow on *The Unquiet Dead*, the third episode of the first block where the Doctor and Rose find themselves in Dickensian Britain, with Callow playing Dickens in his own inimitable fashion. He told me, 'When I was younger I used to do what you're doing now, standing around having a laugh with the crew. You should contain it, preserve your energy, because otherwise you'll get to your take and the monkey will be all performed out.' He's right, but when you're with a crew it's all about bantering, having a crack between takes – you're constantly putting on a show, trying to be funny back. Or they're putting on a show for you. There are very few wilting flowers in the television industry. I'd watch Simon – he'd have moments of downtime between takes, go away on his own and be quiet. I'm not ready to do that yet, because I just love that camaraderie. The crew were a talented bunch of people, and always funny. It's all you can do to keep up, but keep up I try. I mean, you have to have a laugh, don't you? But I do benefit from quiet moments. Those moments when I'm alone. It's just the thought of them that I hate: I practise 'alone time'. I take advantage of the silence when I'm working on an emotional scene – that's an absolute must for me. If I have a crying scene I never put myself back in the banter zone; I don't go near anyone with a sense of humour. Some people can just turn it on and off. I don't have that skill. My tears take a bit of time.

The show must go on, and it did for seven more months. I met the Daleks for the first time, and saved the world a few times. The Daleks were brought out at the end of the second block, in episode 6. It was a huge deal for everybody else, but not for me because I'd never seen *Dr Who*. I know the wonderful Eddie Izzard always teased people who'd been afraid of Daleks, since they were such immobile things. All you had to do was run upstairs or throw down a shag-pile carpet and you'd get away. But the new audience was in for a shock. The Dalek had had a make-over, an upgrade. The voice was the same, and they looked the same, but they could elevate. All the shag-pile in the world wasn't going to help you any more.

With the help of my friends and colleagues I gradually got over the worst of the split. I was sad because both me and Chris had thought our marriage would be for ever. And it wasn't. But Chris helped – his ethos stood us proud. Always find something to be positive about.

And for me that positive thing was the four incredible years we had together and the friendship that came out of it. I absolutely know we were right to get married, and now I think we were right to break up. We were right to get out before we started doing horrid things to each other. It meant our friendship was preserved. Neither of us wanted to accuse the other of anything just to get the divorce through, so we opted for two years of separation. It's gone so quickly that I can't actually believe it's happened. So much has changed. The Doctor for one.

Chris Ecclestone left the show for reasons I'm not privy to. His dad was quite poorly towards the end, and I knew he wanted to spend more time with him. Nine months in Cardiff filming twelve-hour days is not really conducive to family life. I'm sure he wanted to try new and different things, and he did what was right for him. *Dr Who* has a history of change: the Doctor changes his appearance and the companions move on. I was lucky to have worked with Chris, who is a brilliant actor. And then I got lucky again with David Tennant – 'Get down on your knees, people!' I'm joking. He's not like that – I just want to do that when I see him because he's so bloody special. Russell and Julie knew him from *Casanova*, and I suspect they knew straightaway that he would fill the hole perfectly. We met in secret at Julie's house one night because it was all hush-hush while the identity of the new Doctor was being kept under wraps. She cooked lamb shanks for us and sat back to watch and see whether we'd bond. We did. It was immediate. He says you'd have to be a particular kind of cretin not to like me – well, ditto, Mr, you're a big shiny star. I was really pleased when they told me he'd been hired for the job. His timing couldn't have been better. Just when I needed a right old laugh he appeared, licked his teeth, said, 'New teeth, weird!'

smiled at me, and the series ended as it had begun, on night shoots. We were all knackered and we needed a break, but we'd pulled it off. *Dr Who* was back on the screen and people seemed to be liking it.

Just as we were finishing filming the series, a new opportunity came my way. The BBC were doing a Shakespearean season, rather like with *The Canterbury Tales*, giving the plays a modern overhaul. I finished filming at 4 a.m., drove home and was at my audition by 10. Michael, my agent, had recommended me for the part of Hero in *Much Ado about Nothing*, but they didn't want to see me because they didn't think I could do a well-spoken boarding school girl convincingly. What a red rag to a bull that was! I was more determined than ever to prove I could be more than a cheeky cockney bird. I went in a short black dress, black tights and black boots – which was about as far as I was prepared to take the look. I stopped off at Bar Italia for a shot of espresso to wake me up, then went into my audition. Brian Percival, the director, Diederick Santa, the producer, and Di Carling, the assistant director, were all waiting for me. I don't know whether it was the challenge of proving them wrong, but it was the best audition I'd ever done. It just worked.

David Nicholls, (of *Starter for Ten* and *The Understudy*) had adapted the play brilliantly. Hero was a posh chav weather girl with some money but not an ounce of taste. I was so happy when I heard I'd got the part. The job fitted perfectly into the gap between the two *Dr Who* series and it was so different from Rose that I was looking forward to it. I got on brilliantly with the rest of the cast when we started filming. Damian Lewis is one of those annoying ex-public schoolboys who can do absolutely everything from playing the piano, Jools Holland-style, to winning man of the match at some big golf charity event. And Sarah Parish, whom I adored, is wonderful. Because the play was set in a regional newsroom it often got quite 'Alan Partridge' on set and we'd all fall about in hysterics. I was dressed in the sort of icecream-coloured suits that Ulrika Jonsson wore in her early days, but without the shoulder pads – I didn't need them. It was a short job compared to what I was used to, but what a corker.

Back in Cardiff, the second series of *Dr Who* started shooting. I didn't think it was possible, but actually I loved the second series more. The relationship between Rose and the Doctor becomes more interesting. You see her selfishly wanting the Doctor all to herself, getting jealous, having to put up with his ridiculous crushes. It got a bit does-he-doesn't-he, will-they-won't-they, and it was fun. In amongst all the alien invasions and Daleks, Russell made our two characters more and more human. I don't know how he does it. But he does. And really well.

Going back to work on the second series was like going back to school after the long summer holidays. I wasn't the new girl any more. I knew my way around Cardiff, I knew the crew, who'd stayed on, and I had the pleasure of getting to know David. Actors came and went in the series and we were the only constants. But we didn't get on just because we were thrown together – we got on and became proper mates. Neither of us can remember what it was we found so funny for nine months, but for nine months we giggled. We are similar in many ways. We know how fortunate we are to be in this position, we don't take it for granted, we know we can do the job but we both have moments of self-doubt. We could chat for England, Scotland and Wales. Once a reporter asked whether we had nicknames for each other. I don't know where it came from, but the words 'David Ten-inch' popped out of my mouth. I think he was secretly pleased.

I was so sorry to leave him. So sorry. But I started to feel that it was time to go. I thought long and hard over leaving *Dr Who*, leaving my beloved Rose, but she was fixed now and it was time for her to stand on her own two feet without the Doctor. When I told them I wanted to go they were so supportive and gave me words of encouragement that I will take with me on my next adventure. Russell put pen to paper and gave me a spectacular exit. Rose died in one world but lived again in another as a stronger, better, more fulfilled person than before. We had all become such good friends, so when we went to Scotland to promote our Scottish episode, *Tooth and Claw*, they decided that, as a leaving prezzie to me, we would be put up in a luxurious hotel for a bit of a jolly. I brought my wonderful new boyfriend Amadu along – he'd become part of the *Dr Who* family, and they were more than happy to have him join in the festivities. We met Julie at Gatwick and flew together up to Scotland. Of all my travelling to date this trip was one of the best. Julie may say otherwise, since her trip was a long, itchy tearfest. The poor woman had hives. We sat in the airport discussing remedies while we waited for Amadu to return from his shoe-shining session. Brogues. He'd brought them especially for the trip. I love a man in brogues.

When we arrived in Scotland we drove through eye-watering countryside to this amazing hotel, where Amadu and I explored our room like two children.

'Check out the bathroom!'

'Woah, look at this cross-trainer!'

'I'm gonna have a sauna, followed by a steam, followed by a bath, followed by another sauna!'

Our room was ridiculously fabulous. We left it massively damp from all the steaming and bathroom antics and went down to meet David, Russell, Julie, Phil and Euros (our wonderful director) in the restaurant for dinner. Julie's itching had subsided but David had gastric flu so he wasn't on the wine – however, the rest of us were very much on the sauce. We tucked into three big courses and the wine and chat flowed. Most of it was about Noel Edmunds's much-enjoyed revival. There was a lot of love being expressed for Noel that night – he should have been there to listen to it. After the brandies and cigars we retired to my amazing room to drink tea and exchange gifts and say our goodbyes. I did exceedingly well on the prezzie front. Bose headphones, chocolates, books and cards came my way. My smile was stretched from ear to ear. Then the *pièce de résistance*: my own personal farewell DVD. They'd made it for me specially. It was everyone in the production team and crew saying goodbye, with clips of Rose's finest moments and some hilarious out-takes. It instantly became one of my most treasured possessions. We all cried while we watched it, and I cry and laugh every time I rewatch it, which is quite often. It was desperately sad, but I'm glad we had that moment. I'm glad we managed to find a space in the midst of the madness to say thank you, I love you and farewell. When my last episode of *Dr Who* was finally screened, I asked Amadu to leave the room. Then I clutched a pillow and sobbed my heart out. I miss them all and thank them from the bottom of my heart for the springboard they gave me. The experience was out of this world.

# A Happier Me

## Inside and Out

I am happy now. So happy. Working hard. I know that it was working too hard for too long that got me into trouble the first time, and sometimes I feel stretched, and panic, and I have to pull myself back and take time out. But it's not the same as before. I never felt comfortable singing. I loathed being in a recording studio or, worst of all, singing live. I felt like a complete phoney, but I didn't dare tell anyone. I knew there was a place I wanted to get to, and I thought that if I put my head down and worked hard enough I'd get to where I wanted to be. And in the end I did, but I got very lost on the way. I wonder if my longest-running and most convincing performance to date was the one that started on 19 December 1997 and ended when I met Chris. Me performing live(ish) as a 'pop star'.

I don't feel any of those things any more. I'm not quite the person I was before the singing either. I no longer possess the unadulterated bravery, the absolute self-belief or the un-flinching confidence I had when I was a child. But that's probably a good thing. The pendulum is resting somewhere in the middle. There are good days and better days, and I try hard to keep the demons at bay. I feel the same way about my appearance. I was overdressed during my singing career, absurdly underdressed when I was married, and now my job is to find a happy medium. Happy to slob out, but, like any girl, equally happy to scrub up.

I know why I got into trouble. Success didn't make me feel the way I'd thought it would. But how could I admit that I was disappointed? What kind of person was I that even *Top of the Pops* wasn't enough? I used to think, 'God, if this isn't enough, then what is?' So I pushed those thoughts away, pretended to myself that I didn't feel like that, that I was just tired, and kidded myself that I was having the time of my life. But back in a hotel room, alone, drinking tea in bed, I would wonder why, given that I'd dreamt about this mo-ment almost since I was born, I couldn't feel anything. What was it going to take? What was wrong with me?

So you aim higher still. Until your ambition renders you completely unreachable. The more successful you become, the easier it is to give way to bad behaviour. You become selfish and self-orientated and lose all sense of perspective. It drives away everyone who really loves you. So you go on again, thinking that the next thing – the car, the boat, the plane or whatever – will make you happy. But still you feel nothing, because ultimately you can't love an inanimate object. More than that, it can't love you back. I don't care what anyone says, as fabulous as a Porsche is it's only as much fun as the person sitting next to you, and dolly birds don't count boys because they are inanimate objects too. And you've burned so many bridges on the way up that you've got no one to share them with when you get there anyway. Worse, you are surrounded by people who like the glare of fame, but will vanish as soon as the light starts to fade. The sort of people who realize you are in trouble, but turn a blind eye. I know how absolutely terrifying it is to have every success you've ever wanted, and feel empty inside. No wonder that along the way you start looking around for something that you *can* feel. Pain. Pleasure. A high. Hunger. A win. A loss. Obliteration.

The trappings of success aren't the only things that you can't feel – fame itself is intangible. Like an inanimate object, it can't be felt. In fact the only tangible thing fame does is affect everyone else around you. It's the weirdest bloody thing. Why didn't I confide in my parents? Why, if I was so miserable, didn't I want out? I don't know if I will ever fully understand the draw. But I have my theories. I was so afraid of going back that it was better to go on, no matter what it was doing to me. I mean, if having the time of my life felt that empty, what the hell would happen if things started to go downhill? I had spent so much energy getting to a place I thought I wanted to be that I hadn't dared question why I was doing it. Why open the trap door when you know dark monsters dwell inside? I would rather have my coping mechanism kick in and take over than face those demons – and my coping mechanism was denying myself food, fuel for life. Anorexics are accomplished liars. They lie to everyone, but the person they lie most to is themselves. I honestly thought I was in control of my eating. I knew I had no control over any other part of my life, including my relationship, my career and my timetable, but I had control over the calories that entered my body. I could control my silhouette but at the cost of so many wonderful things. And, stupidly, I was willing to start the proceedings and say goodbye to any zest for life – because that's what it does to you ladies and gentlemen, those of you who are dealing with it as I write. It breaks you. It breaks your family. You become a vapid soul, with nothing to live for except this one focus, hobby, vocation, that in the end will kill you.

I'm talking about this for the first time because I feel ready to and because it is so rife and yet it's one of those addictions that seems to get glossed over, or worse, celebrated. I find this frustrating and desperately sad. People need help and advice and love, not websites telling you how to loose your last remaining pound, or scantily clad, deeply anorexic celebrities parading round flaunting their golden bones. I did that, and I feel bad that I did it. I had a problem. I should have got help not gone out there when I was approaching starvation. Anyway, enough with the rant. Just get help. I say just – it's not just, I wish it were as simple, but it's vital because it never truly leaves you. It's always lurking in the shadows ready to pounce when you are weak.

I'm working on it myself. I'll probably be working on it forever, which is a boring realization but it's better than nil by mouth, because nil by mouth sucks.

Would I point the finger at Hugh and say, you ruined my life? Never. Ever. I adore him now as I did back then. Could it have been different? Yes. Did we both get hurt? Yes. Would we do it again? Yes. Actually – he wouldn't. In fact he's fallen out with friends who have wanted him to listen to their young child, desperate for them to go into the music business. He refuses to even listen to a CD, let alone take a meeting, with anyone younger that eighteen. What he said to his friend is this: If you love your child – don't.

When I met Chris I'd lost all sense of perspective. For four years I'd thought of no one but myself. I thought my problems were worse than anyone else's, which of course was bullshit. It made me selfish. Selfishness isolates you, and isolation is lonely, and loneliness is destructive. Then you start doing stupid things that make it all worse. Chris saved me from all of that – he was my Dr Who. But I was fixed now, and it was time for me to stand on my own two feet. I returned to my world a stronger, better and more fulfilled person than I'd been before. I was a bit rocky at first, but I got better and braver. It took a while to get over the routine of starving and bingeing, but even that is OK now. I've passed some big tests. When I do photo shoots they say, 'Smile with your eyes', and it's taken me a few years to work out what that means. More than that – how it feels. But I do now. I have wonderful friends and a pretty spectacular ex. I love and trust them all, and I didn't have that before.

Chris and I speak to each other all the time – we meet for catch-ups, we live opposite each other which is handy. Some people probably think that's bizarre, that's okay, it is a bit bizarre I suppose, but I couldn't have let him go completely. We couldn't have lost our friendship. That really would've been a waste. Chris and I met when we needed fixing. And now we're fixed. We can go back to our own separate worlds, and luckily we don't have to cause a rupture in the universe every time we fancy a quick chat. Chris even owns a mobile phone now.

## Chris V/O

'She is special, very, very special. She is naughty, funny, sexy, grumpy, good at cooking, a brilliant dancer, an excellent writer, a talented mimic (she can do anyone, almost perfectly), she can sleep for days, row with the best of 'em, has a massive sense of humour. She's loving, she's kind and she's gentle.

Now, that's all good but there is something else. Billie has no bad in her, none at all. Bad has passed her by. It took one look at her and decided to move on.

I'm not saying she's the only person in the world who has this quality: Thankfully millions of people do, but not many in her position.

That's why, in her hands, viewers of television, film and anything else she may care to do are safe. They are not being dealt their drama by a fake. What Billie does is take the writer's words and interpret them in a way which best serves the piece, and not the way which best portrays her. It's honesty that has made her so successful.'

Writing this book has made me see why my relationship with my family suffered most. At the time I needed parental guidance I didn't want to be told I was messing up. I pulled away from them at exactly the moment I needed them more than ever. I had gone from being a girl who told her mum everything to a young woman who didn't even let her mother into her room at night. I was being managed by a dozen but parented by none, and I didn't want any of them to know I was unravelling at the seams. But because I didn't confide in her she believed my life was one long party. That's all she ever saw in the press, and that's all she ever knew. No wonder she didn't understand why I ran away with Chris – she had no real idea of what I was running from. When the record people first came down to my parents' house in Swindon to ask questions about our past, Mum and Dad felt nervous that they had to cover up for some things. It turned out that they did. Not about what they knew, but, as I became more successful and more distant from them, about what they *didn't* know. When the hundredth 'How's Billie, then?' of the day came their way, their only honest answer would have been, 'I don't fucking know! She never tells us anything!' But they couldn't. They were peddling the myth just as much as I was.

The whole thing has been hard on them – the poor sods have had people going through their bins on several occasions looking for dirt or dodgy finances. One journalist rang my mum up and said he had her bank statements in front of him. 'Great,' she said. 'You couldn't do anything about my overdraft, could you?' You can imagine what she really wanted to say. Covering up and trying to keep their dignity – that's what my record deal did for them. I brought this into their lives. It was my fault. I was off having a ball and they had no upside. No wonder so much resentment set in. But we're putting it behind us and I feel I have my family back. It's not completely plain sailing, because I put my parents through a lot. But I think for the first time they realize that I went through quite a lot too.

When I first heard there was a book deal on offer, I was pretty reluctant about it. I've learnt a lot about the value of privacy. But some arse was putting adverts in the local Swindon paper asking for stories about me and my family. He was writing a book about a person he'd never met. It pissed me off. Even though it's my story to tell, my thoughts, my feelings, I felt quite odd about doing it. But actually it's been an amazing experience. It's made me remember where I was, what I've done and how far I've come. But also how much I've yet to learn. It's brought my mum and me closer again, and that makes me really happy. It's given me tools for work. I'm a fatalist at heart. I believe that everything happens for a reason and, as Hugh Goldsmith says, life is one long balancing act. I am only where I am today because of where I've been. There were some bad moments along the way, but I can see them all now for what they were: growing pains.

# A New Challenge

## The Garrick Theatre, March 2007

I'm sitting backstage at the Garrick Theatre on Charing Cross Road. It's Press Night for *Treats* – my West End debut – at the end of the most stressful fortnight of my life. Everyone's telling me not to worry because tonight is just like any other night at the theatre. But my dressing room is stuffed with bouquets of flowers and good luck cards saying 'You'll be great . . .', 'this is amazing . . .', and I'm thinking, 'I thought you said this didn't matter!'

My mind keeps going back to what David Tennant told me. He said that on Press Night your body experiences as much adrenaline as it does in a car crash. Thanks, David! He's a serious thesp. He must've done at least a dozen massive press nights, so he should know what he's talking about.

It was David who convinced me to try some theatre. I haven't been on stage for ten years – not since I was thirteen. But David loves it, absolutely loves it, and he kept telling me these stories and it just sounded so good, like being back in drama school again. I've been leaning on him a lot, asking him all sorts of questions about how I'm going to deal with tonight, and he said, 'You can't really talk someone down from the ledge if they're there. It's just something they've got to go through.'

And he's right, there's only so much you can say. I've just come back from the Garrick Arms pub next door. I went there for a glass of wine with Laurence (Fox) and Kris (Marshall) – the other actors in our little play. We get on so well – I'm in good company with those boys – but tonight we sat in silence, sighing and yawning and chain smoking and not looking at each other in the eye. But at least the wine took the edge off.

We toured the play for six weeks before we arrived in London. It was a huge success – really receptive audiences, full houses, and lots of fun – so tonight should've been straightforward. But touring the play in places like Malvern, for example, is so different to playing in London. People are more blasé in London. They go to the theatre all the time and there's a much wider choice. There's *The History Boys* playing next door and *Wicked!* is on just down the road. The competition is that much tougher.

So when we arrived in London we decided to do a week of previews. It was supposed to give us a little extra time to work on the play, and get used to being in town. But it backfired. We were playing to half-full houses and losing confidence fast. We panicked and pushed press night back another week and ploughed on with our warm-up shows. And then the stories started . . .

'Billie On The Edge'

'Piper to Marry Again'

It was already an incredibly stressful time, but now every time I stepped outside my whole life was being documented. And everything was being misinterpreted. *Everything!* The pregnancy rumours, the engagement rumours, the split-up rumours: it was just the biggest load of rubbish I ever heard in my life. And then there was the day I met up with Chris. I was staying in my north London flat and I went to see him because I was stressing out about the play and I needed to talk to someone who was used to live audiences. I'd just crawled out of bed, and I hadn't even showered or brushed my hair, and I had two days' worth of mascara on, and it was sunny and I was squinting, and suddenly – CLICK! – this turned into my breakdown moment.

It was hysterical. I try to avoid the gossip magazines, but I walk to and from the theatre every day and it's impossible not to see all the free newspapers. And there's my face on the front page all puffy and squinting and I'm thinking, 'Oh God, what's happened? I'm never going to leave my house again.' And then I arrive at the theatre and there's thirty photographers and a bunch of journalists going, 'So when's the baby due?'

The whole week was as mad as my early days with Chris. It's a level of attention I could've really done without. It planted a seed of doubt in my head. I've been lying awake at four in the morning convincing myself that people are waiting for me to fall.

Theatre is so different to anything I've ever done in my professional life. It's the level of concentration that just amazes me. Filming *Dr Who* was a completely different experience. We'd do a take and then the lighting wouldn't be right so we'd go and have a coffee and a fag and then come back and concentrate for another two minutes and then break again and go and piss around with the crew. It was built around these tiny moments of control. But in the theatre you have to pace yourself and concentrate like hell because your brain keeps telling you that you're about to skip a line. You have this inner critic going, 'You're going to screw it up . . . screw it up . . . screw it up . . . everyone's laughing at you . . . your buttons are undone . . . they can see your breasts' and you just have shout 'SHUT UP!' and trust your instincts.

I've had to teach myself a new routine too. I'm actually a morning person so starting my working day at 6.30pm is quite tricky. I've become quite anal about the whole experience. I eat the same thing, in the same restaurant, at the same time. It's not so much superstition as knowing that something works for me. It's all about preserving energy and being peaceful throughout the day. I just want to sit there simmering all day and then come to the boil in the evening. Winding down after the show is less of a problem. I've worked out how to deal with that amount of energy and I spend the second half of the show in tears so I'm pretty exhausted anyway. When you've been crying in real life you just want to go to pull the covers up and go to sleep, so it's pretty easy.

People always ask me how tough it is to cry on stage like this every night, but by that point in the play my character, Anne, has taken so much grief from the two boys and she can't stick to a single decision she makes, so that you kind of do want to cry, naturally, because you feel so bad for her. And I'm a big crier anyway. I cry quite easily at most things. I went into Marks & Spencers the other day and they do these tiny miniature loaves and that got me going – I started crying over a stupid loaf of bread in Marks & Spencers!

But it's quite difficult to shake the character. I used to find it so annoying when other actors would say, 'Yeah, I'm finding it really tough at the moment because I'm playing this arsehole and I feel like it's really filtering through in to my real life.' And I'm like, 'Get over it! You're an actor. It's called acting!' And now suddenly I'm going through it. I'm playing this really beaten-down woman every night and I end up feeling constantly argumentative and I want to fight and I'm on the verge of tears. So I'm definitely the most neurotic I've ever been right now!

I hope I shake Anne off before my next job. I'm doing a TV drama called *Belle de Jour*. The series is based on a real blog written by a high-class call girl working in London. There's something really interesting about it. We're not talking the sex-trafficking kind of prostitution here, this is about a girl who gets paid a lot of cash and selects her men very carefully and they treat her well. So she's selling her body for sex, but she doesn't feel bad about it. I've been meeting with some of these women and it's strange because I keep expecting there to be some tragedy in their lives – like maybe they were abused as a child, or maybe they just weren't loved enough – but what it actually boils down to is that they just really like sex, and they like having a lot of money, and they're very in control.

It's another completely different role for me. I always think you've got to try something different if you can. But it's going to be weird. There's quite a few sex scenes in it. I've been watching people being sexy on telly recently and thinking, 'What do I do when I want to become sexy?' I also get to wear lots of cute little outfits. I can't wait.

It will be great to be back on TV. My last job before *Treats* was filming *Mansfield Park* for ITV last autumn. It was one of my favourite jobs. Sometimes you're just on a really good gig and you're in great company. This time we were sort of forced together because we were filming away from home, but there were a lot of like-minded people in the cast and crew so it was a right laugh. We filmed in one place – Newby Hall, near Ripon – solidly for four weeks so it became our home and we became the children of the house. So I was really sad when it was time to leave.

But I rolled out of *Mansfield Park* and straight in to my book tour, which was amazing in its own particular way. It was a surreal experience more than anything, because I was just quite amazed that anyone cared. But it was life-affirming too. I had been really worried about writing about my battle with anorexia, but the book tour made me realise that it had been the right decision. There were so many sweet people and it was good to meet some girls who had struggled with anorexia too. It was a tiring week too, in the way that I didn't think it could be. How hard can it be to say hello to everyone and scribble your autograph? But I was conscious that they'd been stood there for two hours and I just wanted people to have a good time and get to know them a little. People are quite nervous and that always surprises me and makes me nervous too. I don't want them to shake and stuff because I'm really no different from them.

It was a crazy autumn at the end of a crazy year, and I really couldn't wait for Christmas. I had been married to my career for so long that my personal life had definitely suffered. I had been working fourteen-hour days and travelling all over the country and I just couldn't give my boyfriend the attention that he deserved. We split just before Christmas.

I've made a decision not to talk about Amadu and not to talk about future relationships. I think that's the best way. I've talked endlessly about my marriage and I've talked quite a lot about Amadu, and all this talk probably isn't the brightest idea. Relationships are hard enough anyway without it being public knowledge so I think it's probably best. But I'm such a blabbermouth! I just love sharing stories, that's my problem. I find it really hard to go, 'No, I don't want to talk about that because I'm very serious now and my life is far too superior . . .' When I read interviews of people going 'Next question!' I think 'Come on! You're a human, show us what's going on, what you do with your evenings – we want to know!' But the boring thing is, it probably is the only way, so everyone can get on with their lives without being hounded by journalists and paparazzi. So I'm going to try and put that in practice – learning to keep quiet. But I can't promise anything!

\*\*\*

*May 2007*

I survived the first night. I didn't read the reviews. The boys said they were great but by the time they came out I didn't really care. I wasn't expecting people to say, 'That's the best thing I've ever seen!' All I wanted was for them to say, 'That's not bad'. I just wanted people to come along and have a good time and think, 'That's an interesting little show. I laughed a bit. It touched me in certain ways . . .'

The play has definitely made me stronger and more confident as an actor. And I hope I'll really see the difference when I start my next job. It's been an amazing experience and I'm grateful to David for making me do it.

David and I still speak quite a lot. I can't say I've been watching the new series of *Dr Who*. But that's not a deliberate decision, it's just that I'm on stage every Saturday night at the same time, and I haven't figured out how to use my Sky+ yet! I thought I'd feel really jealous towards Freema, but it's been fine. I've been replaced. Life goes on. I've been busy with the play, and I've barely thought about it. So when David and I talk we end up talking about our lives, not obsessing about *Dr Who*.

I'd like to have a crack at a film after *Belle de Jour*. But first things first, I need to take some time off. I'm going to move out to the country for a bit. It's too much in town. I think it's time to take a bit of heat out of my life. I feel like for the four months I've been doing the play I've been holding my breath. When the play is over I'm going to slip into a really big sleep. I can't wait. And when I wake up I'll be ready to breathe again.

# Thanks

I'd like to thank Gay Longworth – the woman who helped me to write this book. I'd be lying, terribly, if I said that I penned every word myself. These are all my thoughts, experiences and conclusions, but I've had help. I couldn't have collected so much information or structured it on my own, but I'd like to try one day. I've really enjoyed this venture and I'm so thankful to you, Gay, for being so brilliant and so patient and such a good listener and also such great company. Thank you, thank you.

I'd also like to thank the following people for holding my hand, spurring me on and just generally being brilliant, beautiful individuals. In no particular order:

Martin Beaumont, Laura Evans, Pat & David, Tracey, Sylvia Young, Hugh Goldsmith, Cheryl Robson, Justine Cavanagh, Sara Friedman, Nikki Trevelan, Zoë Marchel, Paul & Phil, Mark Anderson, Karin Darnelle, Wendy &

Jim, Tim, the BBC, Lorrit, Hiten, Hodder & Stoughton, Gordon MacGeachy, Gillsie, Webbo, Mrs Webbo, the Barbers, Sabin Epstein, Bob & Jack, all at the White Horse, Kev & Jen, Jimmy Nesbitt, Brian Hill, Chris Ecclestone, Wayne Humphries, Sally Price, Rob Collins, David Price, The Rockley Babes, Tressa, Gary, Grandma, Nanny, the Greens, Danny Kent, Michael Foster, Oriana, Sue Latimer, Russell T. Davies, Julie Gardner, Phil Collinson, Steff Morris, Bob Falls, Tim Hodges, all at Dr Who, David Tennant, Jessica Rabbit, Gracie, Ash, Paula, Ellie, Zanna, Al Southey, Lucy Duran, Syra Sowe, Mr E, Gareth & Sarah, Maddy, Aunty Lean, Charlie Piper, Rachel Harley Piper, Ellie Piper.

Mum and Dad.

# Picture Credits